Touched By The Hand Of Bob

Epiphanal Bob Dylan experiences from a Buick Six

by
Dave Henderson

First published 1999 by The Black Book Company Ltd, Box 2030, Pewsey SN9 5QZ, United Kingdom

ISBN 1-902799-00-3

Copyright The Black Book Company 1999

A CIP catalogue for this book is available from the British Library.

Designed by Keith Drummond
Reprographics by Rival Colour
Cover by David Black

Black Book Company Ltd
"Also trading in red, white and blue shoestrings."

"I wrote this..."

Dave Henderson works across the music magazine portfolio of EMAP Metro in London, England, concentrating his efforts on Q, Mojo, Select, Kerrang!, Mixmag and Smash Hits.

He is directly involved in producing The Q Awards, The Kerrang! Awards and The Smash Hits Poll Winner's Party. He co-ordinates the Glastonbury Festival programme and daily paper for Select magazine and occassionally writes on music, film and television for a variety of publications.

During his 20 years in the music business, he has played in several dodgy groups, promoted film and music all-nighters, designed record sleeves, run a variety of small record labels and written for Sounds, Music Week and Q about acts as diverse as Wilco, Slayer, Duane Eddy, Throbbing Gristle, The Dillards, Holger Czukay and Jimmy The Hoover.

In his spare time, he writes, designs, spellchecks and enthuses over Happenstance magazine - a bi-yearly chronicle of music that covers the extremeties of his record collection, from Mickey Newbury, The Sun Sawed In Half, Nicodemus, Son Volt, Davy Graham, Sparklehorse, Gene Clark and The Orange Humble Band to Dino Valente, Miles Davis, Dennis Wilson and Danzig. He is a fervent, quasi-religious follower of Giant Sand, from where the magazine took its name.

He is currently working on a proposed five-part series of this book for BBC Radio 2, delving yet further into the psyche of Bob's faithfull. He is married with two children who recognise Bob Dylan as a man with curly hair or, indeed, a cowboy with a guitar. His wife is not a Bob Dylan fan.

Forward

Touched By The Hand Of Bob

Let's take a moment before we begin...

Before I wrote this book, I was uncommitted about Bob. Certainly, I'd witnessed the effect his strident harmonica could have on fellow tube travellers as I listened to him on my Walkman. I'd seen their grimaces. But, I could take him or leave him. No problem.

But, after being enticed into his world first of all by my job, I was then completely knocked for six by the release last year of 'Live 1966'. However good anyone ever said that album might be, however big the rumours of its gargantuan proportions might have suggested, nothing could have prepared me for actually hearing it. I was reeling. I just had to find out more.

I read the books. I heard the music. I talked to anyone who would listen. Inevitably, a succession of stories followed. Revelations were close behind. Some were recounted in hushed whispers, some like true confessionals. I was instantly fascinated by the power of the man.

There was an almost-religious zeal to people's enthusiasm. His disciples were many, their love of his lyrical couplets, their joy in his musical arrangements or just their besotted intrigue at the cut of his winkle-pickers was amazing.

What quickly became apparent was the simple fact that Bob Dylan had changed people's lives. His music moved mountains and as a record collector, I fast became aware that my vinyl hillock was riddled with Bob influences, Bob songs, Bob interpretations and, well, Bob himself.

And within Bob's music, there was an intrinsic roots flavour which permeated his every song. In the same way as he had dug back to discover his own history, Bob's descendents had dug into him to find theirs.

Fully grasping the theory of relative separation, it was obvious that everyone was just one other person away from Bob Dylan and everyone else had a Bob story to unload.

JOE CLIBURN, *Dylan fan, via the internet*
"How about the image of sitting at a dinette table in the kitchen of a (non-air conditioned) house 'way up a dirt road in Mississippi, hearing 'Like A Rolling Stone' for the first time on the AM station from New Orleans?"

I was fascinated by people's Bob panorama. By the huge emotional bond that his fans had developed with him and his music. Especially when it seemed to sometimes border on radical fanatacism, brooding self-analysis and, on occassion a psycopathic devotion.

DORU DAROCZI,
Dylan fan, via the internet

"I first heard Dylan live on a local FM radio station. It was a concert with Joan Baez - I don't remember which one. I was amazed about how they let him play along with Joan. So, I guess, I was one of those giving away shit about how his voice sounded.

"The turning point was a few month later when I listened to 'Blood On The Tracks'. I got

Interviewer: "Do you think that among your audience there are a number of people who are going to be changed by listening to the material that you've done?"

Bob: "No. No. I don't think that anybody's gonna actually be changed from something to something else. They might get a weird reaction or something but it will only last until the concert's over, if it's ten minutes after and they're on the way home when they talk about it or something, but it certainly can't change everybody's way of thinking."

Sutcliffe recalled...

"The only connection I've ever discovered between my two wives (That's consecutive m'lud) is that they both walked out on Dylan on the controversial tour when he went electric - one at the Royal Albert Hall and one in Manchester, if memory serves. I've never been able to attach a meaning to this coincidence, though conceivably Mr Freud might diagnose something along the lines of it demonstrating a certain Puritanism in them which appealed to the ever vigilant puritan in me."

Bob works in mysterious ways. And these ways make for intriguing apochryphal tales. Anecdotes

Before Bob there was a wild traditionalism in folk music, typified by Alan Lomax and Pete Seeger and the only Dylan in town was Welsh...

it from a friend somehow. It was instant love. After that was 'Desire'. From there, it started. I began colecting stuff, reading, listening... And that was it.. I am in his church now..."

Of course, I puzzled at what Bob might make of such devotion. But he's a careful fish, unforthcoming. Non-commital. But, as I traversed through his back pages, I stumbled across a brief muse about the idea of his majesty in a Detroit interview from back in 1965. It adds some perspective, well almost.
It went like this...

In 1965 Dylan had already moved away from his proverbial finger-wagging songs of old. He was already preparing the way for an electric revolution that would lead to hysterical reactions just about everywhere. He knew full well he'd be making a difference. Why else do it?

The "changes" led to all sorts of reactions - mainly booing and stamping of feet. From the UK came the cry heard around the world. 'Judas' echoed through the Manchester Free Trade Hall, a well-documented "rock 'n' roll moment". And, for some, the reaction to the tour was even more far-reaching and character-defining, as Q journalist Phil

flow. I quickly became festooned with stories on all sorts of subjects. Like how he was or how he wasn't influenced by Dylan Thomas in the choice of his name. By the legend that he signs his autograph with his left hand even though he is right-handed. With the story that when he appeared in '65 with the Butterfield Blues Band at the Newport Folk Festival, diehard traditionalists Alan Lomax and Pete Seeger attempted to cut the multi-core cable (if such a thing existed then) in order to stop his "blasphemous" performance.

Truth or suspicion, speculation or just tall stories, everyone it seemed had some information to impart, no matter how trivial or seemingly ill-informed it might be.

DEAN, *Rack House Primary School, Manchester (aged nine)*
"He looks like he'd be a good singer but his hair's too messy."

MICK JAGGER *(rather older)*
"Bob Dylan is a good lyricist - without qualifying it too much. Bit obvious that..."

In 1999, Dylan's kudos and credentials is probably more legendary than ever. He's never out of the news, even when he's trying his hardest to avoid it. Any star elevated to the realms of fame has a connection . For example, there's chart-topping Country crooner Garth Brooks and lauded Welsh belter Cerys Matthews of Catatonia:

GARTH BROOKS
"I kinda missed him and he never influenced

As Dylan prepares to enter his fifth decade as a role model, icon and definer of music, his profile is shifting from fallable pop star, to statuesque roots legend. As the '90s spiral to a close, Bob Dylan is regarded with the same reverence as John Lee Hooker, Jimmy Witherspoon and Jimmie Rodgers.

CHRIS ROLLASON, *Co-organiser, 'Bob Dylan Critical Corner' website (http://www.geocities.com/Athens/Oracle/6752)*
"With Dylan the musician, I feel too much emphasis is often put on his rock aspect and not enough on his role as continuator of a very ancient tradition - American folk music, with its roots in the traditional song of the British Isles - and as cross-fertiliser of that tradition with blues and country influences. Much of Dylan's work is straight in the line of Woody Guthrie, Robert Johnson, Jimmie Rodgers and the performers on the recently reissued 'Anthology of American Folk Music'."

'The Anthology Of American Folk Music' elevates the likes of Dock Boggs, Blind Lemon Jefferson, Blind Willie Johnson, The Carter Family, Uncle Dave Macon and Sleepy John Estes to much-deserved legendary status. It is a beautiful document that captures several pieces of history in its grooves, providing an instant and quite moving snapshot of a time. In the very same way, Bob's legacy delivers a cold chill, goosepimples even, when 'Blowin' In The Wind' is dusted off, or 'The Times They Are A-Changin'' rolls around again. You don't have to dig too far to turn up the grit and gravel of real America.

PATRICK HUMPHRIES, *author*
"Even if you can't stand folk music, Bob Dylan, harmonicas or acoustic guitars and you're into Public Enemy or Gay Dad, you still owe a debt to Bob Dylan because he took pop music from being saccharine and anodyne and he made it into something potent and powerful and revolutionary."

"Bob Dylan made music into something potent, powerful and revolutionary."

me. Then I saw him once at the Grammies. He sang a song and I didn't understand one word. But when he got up to accept his award from Jack Nicholson, he said, 'My daddy told me you can never get into something so deep that you can't pull yourself out.' That really helped me. Boom! I dug this guy."

CERYS MATTHEWS
"I never liked people like Donny Osmond when I was growing up. I always liked older men, like Bob Dylan. My father used to make me up tapes of his songs. The thing I really liked about Dylan was that you'd save all your money and skive off school to see him when you were 17. And he was shit. Then you'd hate him for a year or two but then you realise that he's fallible and he's got disorders and imperfections and at least he isn't trying to sell you this perfect two-dimensional product."

DISCLAIMER
This book isn't meant to be conclusive. It can't cover every session, every nuance and every meaning - there are already some excellent books out there doing that incredibly well. It also doesn't spend any time tracing the various Bob side projects and collaborations.

What I hope it does do is paint a picture of Bob through the stories of others. Some of the people who told me their own personal recollections aren't famous at all. They're just normal people, like me or you, who heard something in some lyric, or turned themselves around when Bob reached the chorus. Not everyone's life changed, not everyone was moved to tears - but a lot of the people I talked to certainly were.

Is Bob there?

Song to Bobby...

I'M A lover of music. A consumer often knowingly swindled by brightly-coloured record sleeves that look the part. I like new sounds that aggravate old taboos. Whether it's the sweetest melody or something "thunk up" by the harshest ruler-twanging eccentric.

I'm also a lover of the generation gap and the effect it has on musical creativity and, in turn musical excellence. No, really. And, when young turks storm the barricades, kick over the statues, let the shit hit the fan or just go firestartin', the result can only be good. It either shakes up the old guard, magnifying their fallacies or, like some strange, formulaic, osmosis-type thing involving drums, bass and guitar (and maybe on occasion a power drill), it sets off a butterfly effect that eventually means we thrill to things we used to think were an abominable load of old tosh.

Some people live through the changes. Some, just simply give up, stick with their 'record collection so far' and, well, don't bother with anything new. Sometimes those changes happen on a monumental scale. And when that happens, it's fantastic. But you have to be there and you have to invest. Spend. Get out the plastic. That makes it personal. And it makes those razor sharp witticisms, howling improvisations or succinct pluckings your own.

It's a long-standing thing with me. I need to touch vinyl on a regular basis and relate to things that are circular and square. I have an insatiable appetite but limited finances. I suppose have a problem.

LAST YEAR, if you'd have asked me my favourite ten bands of all time, they might have included (purely for pretentiousness in some places), er, Giant Sand, The Flying Burrito Brothers, The Dillards, The Byrds, Dennis Wilson, David Blue, Uncle Tupelo, Mickey Newbury, Phil Ochs and some obscure northern soul act. I would never have said Bob Dylan. Probably not even if I'd have been limited to the letters B and D.

In the spring of 1998, I was trying to get Bob Dylan to come to the Q Awards in the following October. I was also expecting that the debate about his attendance would go down to the wire and, in my role as the man who "does" the programme and looks after the daily paper for the Glastonbury Festival, I might even have to carry out some of the negotiation for his attendance while on site, mud-soaked and inevitably worse for wear, as I'd heard he was set to play the afternoon slot on the Sunday.

It was, then, essential that I learned to love the man. To understand his every nuance, to get inside his skin. Real deep cover stuff. I might have only one chance to beg him to be there and, if he threw me a bizarre one-liner, as legend would have him do, I'd better be ready for it.

It was already apparent that Glastonbury Festival organiser Michael Eavis was having to do a lot of smooth talking with Dylan's agent as Sunday headliners Pulp had requested at least three "new" acts between themselves and the legend. Dylan's agent was feeding back a feeling from Dylan's managers that, perhaps, the UK didn't even want him to play. This wasn't going to be easy.

I KNEW from the off that there was enough information out there to help me 'understand' Dylan. Well over a hundred books have been written. Many, many fanzines exist and endless web sites languish in the netherworldliness of time, speaking a 'languish' that only Bob himself can understand at times.

They comprehensively cover the why's and wherefore's of Bob's every utterance as they hyperventilate in cyberspace.

It would be a long job just skimming through some of the Bob bulletin boards and conversations that were taking place on a daily basis but they would surely bear fruit. Out there, whole theses were being spun out on the significance of his off the cuff remarks, like the impromptu reply he made in London in 1965. To the kind of question usually reserved for visiting Martians; 'What is your message?', Dylan quipped: "Keep a good head and always carry a light bulb." The shares of Osram quadrupled and a thousand pens wagged.

The converted have already over-analysed their own version of the teachings, lyrics and interactive spats of Bob. Even the analysis has been analysed. And, in my attempt to research the man, I expected I'd be on a collision course with fanatics, Fatwa-placers and people whose lives had simply been taken over by the man.

I even knew one of the latter group. My friend Chris had announced, on hearing of Dylan's heart problems the previous year, that he and his school-chum Paul, now located in Australia, were going to be there for Bob. They had immediately been in pan-global discussion and decided that, if the situation got worse, if Dylan's health deteriorated, they would be 'on the plane', from opposite sides of the world I grant you, to lend support. I can only assume that this meant that they were prepared to spend innumerable hours standing outside a hospital somewhere in downtown USA, leaving loved ones and indeed jobs for their temporary vigil. Thankfully, Bob got better.

But, it's that kind of eccentric behaviour that further fuelled my interest in Dylan. These were grown men, in their 40s, who would have dropped everything - new baby in Paul's case, freelance paid-by-the-job career with over-hanging mortgage for Chris. And there were lots more of these people out there.

On the .net, there was someone who was offering cut-out clothes for the different phases of Bob. There was also a man convinced that Bob had met aliens and witnessed a UFO. There were numerous guides on how to live your life by his lyrics and endless interviews that underlined the exquisite beatnikery he'd utilised in a variety of one-on-one interviews that gave little away.

For example, get a load of these onions from an interview, in 1965, where Nora Ephron and Susan Edminston, the 'It' girls of their day, tripped the triple tongue with Bob...

Dylan: "I collect things too."

Nora: "Monkey wrenches?"

Dylan: "Where did you read about that? Has that been in print? I told this guy out on the coast that I collected monkey wrenches, all sizes and shapes of monkey wrenches, and he didn't believe me. I don't think you believe me either. And I collect the pictures too. Have you talked to Sonny and Cher?

Nora: "No."

Dylan: "They're a drag."

In true Steve Martin-style, Bob was officially a wild and crazy guy. I knew I was going to enjoy finding out more. And, I sort of felt like I knew him. After all, I'd heard lots of his songs. (Or so I thought.)

Q MAGAZINE'S attempts to lure Dylan to the Q Awards had been going on since day one (1990), long before my time. In fact, my predecessor Mark Ellen had tried to cajole anyone who'd listen to respond the previous year. At a time when Dylan's new album 'Time Out Of Mind' was hot to promote, it would have been perfect for everyone. I mean, why wouldn't Bob Dylan want to outwardly promote this new studio album, his first for umpteen years, by accepting a Q gong, receiving the plaudits of the assembled throng and then being featured far and wide in a cross-pollination of TV, radio, glossy and quality papers? He could do all his promotion in one swoop and have a hoot along the way.

So the story goes, inroads and requests to his managers, Jeff Rosen and Jeff Kramer, had been made. But, they were unsure if the UK liked Bob's new album or, indeed, Bob himself. Something of a recurring theme that was already creating a "will he/won't he" talking point at Glastonbury.

Contact with Sony Music Europe MD Ged Doherty had been slightly more fruitful. He was keen, and a phalanx of Sony top brass were set to attend a Bob performance in New York in the hope that he might consider Concording over. But, Dylan didn't even meet up with his UK label when they skulked backstage and, as the song says, 'nothing was delivered'.

The Q Awards was instead honoured with an appearance from Phil Spector. Complete with 'Back To Mono' badge, Mr Spector's well-prepared speech resounded around the world for months to follow and, immediately after the ceremony, I whisked a copy of the Awards issue of Q off to Dwarf Music, Dylan's office, to suggest that next year, maybe, things could be different.

The response was not a no no. But it was not a yes yes, just a maybe maybe. There was work to do. But, maybe maybe, next year would be different.

In preparation, I decided to delve deep into Dylan's back pages, to tug on my resources and find some good reasons why Mr Dylan should be there and pre-empt objections before they could be thrown at me. How complex could Bob Dylan be? Pretty complex, as I scanned yet more classic Dylan confrontations on the .net.

Phil Spector at the Q Awards in 1997 (Bob just out of shot, allegedly)

December 24, 1997

Mr. Dave Henderson
Q Magazine
Lincoln Court
1 Lincoln Road
Peterborough PE1 2RF

Dear Dave,

Thank you for your invitation for Bob Dylan to appear at the Q Awards. It's hard to know what Mr. Dylan's schedule will be that far in advance. Please drop me or Jeff Kramer a line as the event approaches.

Best regards,

Jeff Rosen

r/llr

THE AUSTIN INTERVIEW,
September, 1966

Reporter: What do you consider yourself? How would you classify yourself?
Bob Dylan: Well, I like to think of myself in terms of a trapeze artist.

THROUGH THE mess of Dylanologists, astrologers for Bob, rune-holding mystics who hail his every utterance and psycho-analysts who have examined his "intense" lyrics, I quickly realised that there was no simple way to tap into the Dylan psyche.

I'd begun reading a wodge of books about my "tar-unretouched portrait of Dylan that emerges; a tormented man who, in the author's view may be "clinically insane", a disastrously unhappy figure who denied his Jewishness and, deliberately cultivating a ruthless mythomania, advanced his career by "building a character that would sell"."

Sure, that's a pulp novel spiel but it worked for me. I had to read more. And, in Scaduto's biography Dylan did seem to covertly style himself and creatively embellish his past in the early days. Thinking about it, though, doesn't every aspiring teenager? Scaduto is sharp enough (he used to be a detective) and, yes, Dylan was calculating, but no more calculating than any teen wannabe.

up with Nick Drake biographer Patrick Humphries to trace the Dylan legacy, recount some of those legendary apocryphal tales and put some perceptive perspective on things, I found more wide brush-strokes that added further colour to my sketchy memories of Dylan.

During the book's comprehensive and informative trek, which takes in the major Bob events and includes a set of fascinating detailed, point-by-point lists at the end, Humphries pontificates "The battle for the soul of Bob Dylan has raged for nearly a quarter of a century, with dozens of different Mephistopheles each claiming possession."

Now, although I found this a startlingly sci-fi-styled

get" to further my understanding and quickly became inebriated with the factual foibles of Dylan's middle-class upbringing in Hibbing, Minnesota, right through to the superstar outlandishness of his 30 Year Anniversary at Madison Square Garden and beyond.

The Madison Square show was the event where Sinnead O'Connor was booed off by a hostile, God-fearing American crowd. It was a special evening where Bob's label, Columbia Records brought out 100 stars (count them!) to recognise the fame of Bob. So, what did Bob do? Well, his fame recognised, the man sat in his car while the show went on. He sat in his car. Outside. Didn't go in until he was about to go on stage himself. Now, that's someone who's got to be hard to get to. Cool. Calculated.

My view was compounded by the back cover of Anthony Scaduto's 1970 biography, the publishers Abacus enthuse: "What makes Scaduto's study exceptional - and undoubtedly controversial - is the

In fact, I remember vividly my next-door neighbour Alan Lawrie's attempt to out-hip me in the Dylan stakes when we were at school. It happened during a particularly heavy Byrds phase I was going through. Earnest in the extreme, Alan mooched into our house sporting Dylan-esque shades and uncombed hair and, in a tempered search for one-upmanship, he extolled the virtues of the great man, announcing him to be pronounced 'Bob Dylon' (a well known British wool dye trade name). He then claimed he'd written the best half of the Byrds' songs anyway and stubbed his toe on the hallstand before exiting in a slew of swearing.

Of course, he may have been right about The Byrds, but never, not ever to a Byrds' fan. There was certainly no need to mention it.

In the mirthfully-titled Oh No! Not Another Bob Dylan Book (1991, Square One) in which the late Dylan expert and Q contributor John Bauldie teamed

quasi-religious and rather wordy revelation at first, in hindsight it's pretty well observed. I was trying to come to terms with an icon who'd been regarded as such from the drop of his first plectrum. Dylan, if John Lennon will excuse me, is bigger than Jesus. He had cult status from the get-go. Even back at college. Before he made it to Greenwich Village.

LES CRANE,
The Les Crane Show, February 17, 1965

Crane: I think you represent to America and to American youth something very, very vital and the last guy that had this kind of impact on the youth of this country was James Dean ...
Dylan: Aahh.
Crane: And I don't want you riding around in any hot sports cars.
Dylan: OK! I won't. I won't, Les! (audience laughter).

NAT HENTOFF,
Playboy magazine, published 1965

"For the nation's young, the Dylan image began to form: kind of a singing James Dean with overtones of Holden Caulfeld; he was making it, but he wasn't selling out."

FOR A teen world entering a new age at the start of the Sixties, Bob Dylan was James Dean (with a harmonica). Right place, right time, right jeans. He was the clever one who combined image with message, setting the unformed feelings of a nation into song. He was really saying something and, as his bandwagon trundled on through Newport, around the globe, he became more vocal about it. But on the second lap it all changed.

At the intersection where Dylan switched from folk "finger pointing" to electric power-chords, he was greeted by a hail of boo boys. Meanwhile his over-zealous manager, Albert Grossman was trying to make sure that the road would go on forever. In an environment where there were enough drugs to keep sleep at bay until the end of the decade spontaneous combustion was inevitable. On cue, Dylan came off his motorbike in Woodstock and, rumour had it, he was either dead, abducted by aliens, unable to strum or worse.

There are numerous anecdotes about what actually happened. Conspiracy theories include the idea that the post-accident Bob isn't the same as the pre-accident Bob. Whatever manifestation "the accident" took, it resulted in a pretty long lay off. Dylan being Dylan, he added to the mystique by not really telling anyone anything. He then spent over a year recuperating, a virtual lifetime for someone who'd by that point already racked up seven albums in four years. Columbia were supportive, they released a 'Greatest Hits' package. Bootlegs followed. In fact, the whole bootleg industry started there and then. And, Dylan decided to get his head together in the country. It was all new, innovative stuff for the time.

Prior to the shunt, Dylan had played in the UK at the end of a tour that had seen him roundly chastised and extensively quizzed by confused journo's around the globe. His two-part set consisted of an acoustic flurry, followed by a fully miked-up barrage. The faithful folkies removed their hands from their ears en masse to accuse him of "selling out" as the power grid collapsed.

Tangible, over-the-counter evidence of those shenanigans came late. In fact, it was in the late summer of 1998, that Columbia finally decided to release the much-bootlegged double album 'Live 1966', as part of the Bob Dylan bootleg series. Billed as 'Live At The Royal Albert Hall' and rumoured to be in the presence of The Beatles, the tapes in fact came from the Manchester Free Trade Hall and included participatory slow handclapping prior to an as loud as hell catcall of 'Judas' midway through the electric set.

Now, this is the stuff of legend and, yes, in my Dylangate investigations I'd read about such antics but until I heard the album I'd no idea of the absolute

The Bootleg Series Vol. 4
BOB DYLAN LIVE 1966
The "Royal Albert Hall" Concert

shock/horror gravitas of the situation. I, of course, tried to explain it to other people, my wife included, but was given either that knowing withering look or one of the shortest pieces of shrift imaginable.

But to me, as to anyone else hearing the colossal noise of Dylan accompanied by the nucleus of what was to become The Band, this was a monumental release.

KEITH CAMERON, *NME*

"It's an indictment of our decrepit cultural condition that the best new album of recent weeks is 32 years old. Make no mistake: Bob Dylan's 'Live 1966: The Royal Albert Hall Concert' is a revelatory experience. Its hys-

terical highlight, when an incensed Dylan turns to The Band and instructs them to "Play fucking loud!" as the opening strains to 'Like A Rolling Stone' vie with the heckling folky Stalinists for ascendancy, represents nothing less than the birth of modern rock 'n' roll."

DAVID FRICKE, *Rolling Stone magazine*

"It's hard to believe that a country then up to its eyeballs in electric R&B (the Stones, Animals, Pretty Things, Who) was so absurdly parochial about an amplified Dylan.

"The self-righteous goon who yelled 'Judas!' put the show in the history books. The music is the reason that Live 1966 is still epic theatre. Play it fuckin' loud."

TO ADD to the occasion's magnitude, CP Lee, an attendee on that fateful night in Manchester who went on to be a member of Alberto Y Los Trios Paranoias before becoming a student of music, had his story of the show, Like The Night published, complete with never-seen-before pictures by Paul Kelly showing a grainy Dylan leading the charge. It's an epic snapshot, a personal revelation offering an exceptional insight courtesy of scene-setting travelogue en route to Manchester, and a song-by-song show run-through, punctuated with the comments of several audience members.

AUDIENCE MEMBER ONE
"I couldn't believe it. It was so loud it physically hurt me."

AUDIENCE MEMBER TWO
"It was all your worst nightmares coming true. He looked like Mick Jagger posturing and strutting. It was all the worst elements of Pop."

THERE ARE lots of positive comments too but the overall feeling was one of mild terror, which you can virtually hear as you play the album now. There's a bristling power and expectancy in the air that makes it hard to catch your breath as Dylan and group career through a new version of 'I Don't Believe You' before unleashing 'Leopard-Skin Pill-Box Hat' and 'Like A Rolling Stone'.

In 1966, a heckler's cry of 'Judas!' summed up the outrage of folk fans furious that Bob Dylan had gone electric. Now a CD of that concert has finally been released. It is, says **Andrew Motion**, a revelation

WHEN THE TIMES A-CHANGED

WELL, were you there — at the famous Albert Hall concert in May, 1966, when Bob Dylan's folk supporters booed him for converting to electric music, and one of them shouted out: "Judas!"

Anyone answering yes to that is a liar. Dylan did tour England in the spring of '66, and he did play at the Albert Hall, but the notorious "Judas" episode happened in Manchester, at the Free Trade Hall. For some reason (though it's not surprising Dylan's life is thickly encrusted with mysteries) the two events got muddled up in the years immediately following. And it was only when an exceptionally good-quality bootleg recording of the Manchester gig — now available for the first time officially — began to circulate that people started getting their facts straight.

It was well worth the effort, and the wait. With a single angry word, an unknown heckler described a crucial moment in the life of a great artist, and also distilled a large argument about traditionalism and modernism, small-scale integrity and mass-market appeal.

The trouble that overflowed for Dylan in England had been brewing for a while. During the previous four years, he'd been feeling increasingly hemmed-in by the very things that had done more than anything to stage his style in the first place — the folk traditions which, as rock'n'roll began to take off, became truer and more inverted and self-protective.

Dylan, whose early songs had massively intensified certain aspects of the folk inheritance (in particular, the value it attached to protest-singing) had been given the combined role of messiah and guru. At the same time,

his most increasingly insistent pieces, like a *Rolling Stone*, which he described as "a long piece of vomit", adding pointedly: "I knew I had to sing it with a band."

When the band later the Band eventually turned up and plugged in their instruments, the reaction was just as Dylan had expected. At Newport — the "Mecca of the American Folk Revival", as CP Lee calls it in *Like the Night* (Helter Skelter, 1998) — his set was greeted with tears of rage. When he began a world tour in February 1966, playing in America and Ireland before coming to Britain in May, the same thing happened. His change of direction was a "betrayal".

In Liverpool, someone shouted "Where's the poet in you? Where's your conscience?" In Sheffield, he heard: "Traitor. We don't need you! Go and play with the Rolling Stones!" "Judas", clearly, was an insult waiting to be hurled.

Dylan has a reluctance to "explain" his work that would have done Philip Larkin proud. But he has said some very good things about his music generally, including this: "The closest I ever got to the sound I hear in my mind was on the individual bands on the *Blonde on Blonde* album. It's that thin, that wild mercury sound. It's metallic and bright gold, with whatever that conjures up."

Blonde on Blonde was released in the same month as the Manchester gig, and, although its studio qualities are inevitably smoother than those generated in a live performance, they nevertheless help us to see what Dylan was trying to achieve on stage. It's a sound that reinforces the paradoxes of his lyrics: driving but deliberate, visceral but scrupulous, but startling, exploratory but stunning. The Manchester gig polar-

> The dissent gradually accumulates, rising through catcalls and slow hand-claps to general barracking

A recently rediscovered picture of Bob Dylan at the Free Trade Hall, Manchester, May 17, 1966 — the day that fans rounded on the messiah of folk music. He had felt increasingly constrained by the purists' expectations; electricity offered a way out

> "**The self-righteous goon who yelled 'Judas!'** put the show in the history books. The music is the reason that Live 1966 is still epic theatre."

ANDREW MOTION, *The Daily Telegraph*

"Listening to it (Live 1966) we follow Dylan the protest singer into a storm of protest, knowing by this time that he will emerge triumphant. Does that make the value of the music sound too dry, too purely historical? It would be a pity if it did. Because what's "interesting" about the album, can't be separated from what is simply unforgettable: the tremendous beauty and subtlety of the songs, and the matchless voice that sings them."

AFTER HEARING it I was hooked. It opened the floodgates. It made me want to find Dylan even more. It made me want to find my Dylan albums too. I wanted the scam on the folk clubs of Minneapolis. I wanted to follow Woody Guthrie to New York. To hear Dylan playing at Gerde's with John Lee Hooker. Then to see how he got to Newport. To Newcastle with Joan Baez. And then to ride through those early electric storms. Maybe even sit beside John Lennon in the back of a Limo while Bob threw up.

Then, later that same interlude, maybe I could take off to Nashville and hear the duet session with Johnny Cash, perhaps I could even get some purchase on those religious albums before winding up with 'Time Out Of Mind'.

To me, the music was the key to Bob. That was what touched me on '1966'. That was what gave me goosepimples. But, as I delved into Planet Bob, amid the opinionated and intellectual overviews of the life and times of Dylan in books, fanzines and on the .net, I was already drowning. It seemed to me that people were almost ignoring his songs and treating Dylan like he was already in a glass casket. The money lenders had already set up camp in the temple, dealing in bootlegs, trinkets, rare photos and theories. (And various other Biblical analogies.)

I quizzed Chris again: "So, do you sit at home and, well, listen to Dylan? Like, all night?" He looked sheepish. "Yeah. Sometimes I've just got to sit down and listen to 'Slow Train Coming'. It's just so... emotional."

OK. I can understand that. We all still cry at 'It's A Wonderful Life', don't we?

But, what if Chris is just a nice bloke on the surface and as mad as a box of spanners underneath. It's hardly quality market research relying on a captive audience of one. I decided to spread my net further.

To my surprise, just about everyone I encountered had a wide-eyed, Dylan-related story etched on their heart. From being turned on to dope to all-night queuing for tickets. The inevitable mis-hearing of lyrics and the hatching of lengthy plots to secure the great man's autograph. Everyone had something to relate, most of them had a special song.

In fact, I now know young men who have worked into the night on brittle coat hangers, in an attempt to turn them into harmonica holders. I've met people that have taken a year off work to learn to play guitar and sing at the same time, while their hair developed a dishevelled fright wig appearance as some sort of visual extension of their desire. I've heard about people listening to 'Mr Tambourine Man' and deciding that's exactly what they want to do (enter Billy Bragg) and about numerous others who've already selected a Dylan song to play at their funeral.

Bob Dylan songs, I guess, just mean that much more. They can lie dormant at the crux of a relationship and then, for apparently no reason, just flare up. Uncontrollably. I remember very well at my pre-wedding goodbye from work drink up how one friend, Paul was publicly humiliated by his girlfriend for buying 'The Bootleg Series 1-3'.

"What's the point of that?" the softly-spoken Siobhan goaded. "What's the point of spending all that money on a Bob Dylan album that Bob Dylan didn't even want released?" Fair comment, I suppose. But, as Paul looked at me with a 'she just doesn't understand' face, we bonded in a very special way.

DISCOVERING Bob was just something I had to do. Like a previously unrealised part of my rites of passage as a, well, bloke who buys records and reads all sorts of life-changing stuff into them. I wore the facade of "researching it just for the Q Awards", but hell, I was just plain fascinated already. How could one man mean so much to so many?

Obviously through The Byrds I'd heard a lot of Dylan and as I went through my collection I realised I had a veritable cornucopia of Dylan songs but very little actually by Bob Dylan. I'm sure I used to have lots of Dylan records. I know I did. But, through a dozen house moves and various pre-nuptial disagreements my Dylan collection was now limited to a meagre handful of singles.

This was now a challenge I could warm to. Any consumer-turned-collector worth their salt needs a big project to work on. Alongside the inevitable list of those really mouth-watering but obscure items that you always need to keep an eye open for but invariably never see, this was a real challenge.

Discovering Dylan would be like any other improbable self-set task. Like listening to the full six CD 'John Coltrane At The Village Vanguard' Box Set in one sitting, or crouching on the floor eating falafel's in pitta bread as you played 'Woodstock' and 'Woodstock II' back-to-back, or even spinning every Buzzcocks' single in chronological order, playing both A and B sides. It's something that just has to be experienced first hand. I had to go through it to get it!

And, if by listening to 40-plus albums, viewing several films, and reading a book that no-one understands, I could remix my yin and yang, hear new melodic structures or uncover the meaning of life, then... well, why not? It'll have been well worth it. Oh, yeah, he might even come to the Q Awards.

Of course, I run the risk of over-intellectualising a subject that's already wantonly over-intellectualised - however my lack of O-levels should temper that. I also run into another dreaded gauntlet, the shark-infested waters of the financially-challenged zone. I knew before I accepted this mission that beyond those meagre 40 or so albums, there's a million bootlegs, foreign editions, deleted EPs and God knows what just waiting to asset-strip.

AND, THEN THERE'S THE COVER VERSIONS. For a man who's already built a sizeable stack of Beatles interpretations by strange and sulky subterraneans there was bound to be trouble.

My initial collection run-through revealed, in a similar way, that I own a whole host of interesting versions of Dylan songs. Readings that had obviously affected the careers of many would-be Dylans. But, how many more were out there? How many more thrills were likely to be uncovered. Are there any more like William Shatner, aka Captain Kirk from Star Trek! What on earth was he thinking about (or indeed which planet was he was on) when he recorded 'Mr Tambourine Man'? That is one unreal experience.

My initial investigations revealed that Kirk is just the tippermost tip of a very large iceberg that's sailing away with Dylan's musical legacy transmutilated beneath. Hark to these, carefully alphabetised coverers of that old chestnut 'Blowin' In The Wind: Steve Alaimo, Eddie Albert, Ronnie Aldrich, Ed Ames, Eddy Arnold, Chet Atkins, Joan Baez, The Banjo Barons, Bobby Bare, The Mike Batt Orchestra, Bibi Music, Ray Bryant, Sebastian Cabot, The California Poppy Pickers, Glenn Campbell, Ace Cannon, Castaway Strings, Cher, Bill Collins, Judy Collins, Ray Coniff Singers, Sam Cooke, Cormie Folkswingers, Dick Dale & The Daletones, Bobby Darin, Cliff Davis Sextet, Jackie DeShannon, Dennis & Rogers, Martin Denny, Barbara Dickson, Marlene Dietrich, Rob van Dijk, Dixie Drifters, Bobby Doyle, Dave

Dudley, Dorinda Duncan, Duane Eddy, Joe Enloe, Les & Larry Elgart, Duke Ellington, Roky Erickson, Percy Faith, Marianne Faithfull, Julie Felix, Flatt & Scruggs, The Folk Four, The Folkniks, The Folkswingers, Fontana Concert Orchestra, The Four Seasons, David & Dylan', Slim Gaillard, Galloway Singers, Charles Geller, Stan Getz, Jimmy Gilmer, Bob Gilroy, The Golden Gate Strings, The Gotham String Quartet, The Greenwich Village Migrants, Roy Hamilton, Oscar Harris, Ralph Harrison, Bob Harter, Edwin Hawkin Singers, Ted Hawkins, Robert Hazard, The Hollies, The Holy Light Singers, Hooters, Lena Horne, The Les Humphries Singers, Brian Hyland, Peter Isaacson, Chuck Jackson, Jerry Jackson, Mahalia Jackson, Walter Jackson, Etta James, Spike Jones, The Joyful Noise, Bill Justice, The Kingston Trio, Billy Larkin, James Last, Latin Souls, Enoch Light, Living Guitars, The London Sound & Art Orchestra, Trini Lopez, Arthur Lyman Group, Ed Lyman, The Mad Hatters, Johnny Maddox, The Maestro's All Steel Band, Junior Mance, The Johnny Mann Singers, Mantovani, Linda Mason, Chas McDevitt, Rod McKuen, Bill Medley, The Melodysingers, The Merrymen, Middle Of The Road, Mickey & Bunny, Mitch Miller, Chad Mitchell Trio, Hugo Montenegro, Jerry Murad, Johnny Nash, Nashville Sounds, New Christy Minstrels, The New Seekers, New World Singers, Nina & Fredrik, The Gene Norman Group, Odetta, Paul & Margie, Peter Paul And Mary, Peter Sue & Marc, Frank Pourcel, Power & Light, Elvis Presley, Leontyne Price, Cliff Richard,

Billy Lee Riley, The Rivals, Johnny Rivers, Danny Roberts, The Rockridge Synthesizer Orchestra, John Schroeder, Pete Seeger, The Seekers, Diana Scott, Bud Shank & Folkswingers, Sidewalk Swingers, Sierra Sand, The Silkie, Harry Simeone Chorale, Simon Sisters, Patrick Sky, Soul Stirrers, Sound Of Church, The Sound Symposium, The Spotnicks, The Staple Singers, Lucille Starr, Stars Of Faith, Billy Strange, Strings For Pleasure, The Supremes, The Swinging Blue Jeans, Johnny Tillotson, The Troubadour Singers, Stanley Turrentine, The US Navy Steel Band, The Ventures, The Village Stompers, Wagon Masters, Dionne Warwick, The Wayfarers, Bradley Wayne, West Country Three, Marion Williams, Williams Singers, Stevie Wonder, O.V. Wright, Martin Yarbrough and Neil Young.

Who the hell are they all? Sure, we know Joan Baez is an ex-Mrs Dylan, Chet Atkins is a country strummer, Arthur Lyman is a vibes playing lounge lizard, Rod McKuen is a moody poet, Frank Pourcel is entertaining in a lift near you, Patrick Sky was one of Bob's old compadres in Greenwich Village, The Edwin Hawkins' Singers are a soulful Gospel act and so on and so on. But, The Banjo Barons? The Greenwich Village Migrants? The London Sound And Art Orchestra?

Suffice it to say, that Dylan is not going to be short of a few bob. Everyone above has put in their ten penneth. The effect of Dylanwarming is global. He is omnipresent, strutting through everyone's lives, touching people who are enormous - Mr Presley is listed - or indeed minuscule - Bobby Doyle, anyone?

SOMEHOW, THROUGH ALL THIS HE REMAINS a pretty private man. There are few in-depth interviews. There's no first-hand biography. It's all heresay and interpretation. If you consider that The US Navy Steel Band interpreted 'Blowin' In The Wind' in a quite different way to Neil Young on 'Weld', then just about everyone has their own view of Bob and what he's doing.

Ten years ago, Dylan had had enough of the gesticulating, theorising and marginal Hari-Kiri-styled

"Everyone seems to come to Bob at different times and in different circumstances."

eccentrics. They'd become stranger and, probably, more intriguing than him. All Dylan wanted was to get out and play. So, in 1989, Bob turned down the cover of Rolling Stone magazine, saying, "You should get someone off the street and interview them about Bob Dylan, that would be more interesting."

It sounded like good advice. My search, then, was not going to be yellow-brick-road-like, leading to his Malibu mansion with all problems solved as a consequence, it was going to be a variation on Michael Morris's Roger And Me, a round the houses quest that might deliver either the Holy Bobgrail, a Dylan plectrum or a large Mastercard bill. Perhaps all three.

The people I had already encountered all had their own stories to tell and I realised I couldn't find out about his story without hearing and understanding theirs. Just among my friends there were wild enough tales of Bob-related nonsense. And each one of those friends seemed to have another friend who knew someone with an even larger story to unload. This was already becoming never-ending, like chain-letters of Bob coincidence stretching out to, well, who knows where?

So, let's start at the very beginning...

As I was pondering on how to unravel these stories and attempt to make sense of it all, I was by chance listening to 'Dynablob', which I eventually realised was a strange anagrammatical collection of songs by John Wesley Harding, a Hastings-born singer/songwriter whose talking blues style and impressive guitar playing had blossomed erratically over several albums. On 'Dynablob' there were some nice songs but there were also some truly amazing anecdotal Bob-related epics. One of these was 'Talking Great Folk Scare Blues', which extolled the virtues of Woody Guthrie, much in the same way the teenage Bob must have done, with the line "Woody Guthrie's guitar killed fascists and crime, but in Hastings, West Sussex, South of England, my guitar killed time."

The Guthrie experience, the rampant guitar, it all seemed to fit. On the same album, Harding painted a poignant picture which, undoubtedly, a lot of Dylan fans and indeed myself, could relate to on 'Phil Ochs, Bob Dylan, Steve Goodman, David Blue And Me'.

Now, I've interviewed John Wesley Harding in the past, and I reckon that the scene for this song is this: Harding narrates from his bedsit, festooned with albums and empty coffee cups (one of them undoubtedly has mould on or in). Singing to a photograph of some girl he's probably been dumped by, he tells the story of his four walls-turned-downtown cellar club. Maybe, I've over-romanticised a bit, but here's what he sings:

> *"Bob was there last week as well,*
> *He's a quiet guy, but he's got stories to tell.*
> *Our hero sits and listens without asking why,*
> *Teaches Bob A minor with a glint in his eye*
> *Well, Bob used it on 'Hollis Brown',*
> *But that was some time ago."*

And, then, he moves to the chorus:
> *"This is the only thing that really matters,*
> *Keeps me going, retains my sanity*
> *The nights I spent alone when there's just*
> *Phil Ochs, Bob Dylan, Steve Goodman,*
> *David Blue and me."*

I've seen that movie too. Definitely. I know it. I have the first David Blue album where he's trying really hard to remake 'Highway 61 Revisited'. It's superb. Excellent. A bastard version of Bob's art, bastardised because Dylan has affected David Blue so. Of course, David Blue sadly died, a virtually unsung hero. As did Steve Goodman. As Harding was quick to note...

> *"Stevie died and David died*
> *But only to the papers that lie outside*
> *Last Thursday they were in the room where he sits*
> *Laughing about their meagre obits..."*

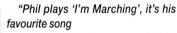

But to John Wesley Harding, and me, David Blue was every bit the troubadour Bob was. As was Phil Ochs. But don't listen to me, let's let JW take it away again.

> *"Phil plays 'I'm Marching', it's his favourite song*
> *And Bob plays harmonica but he gets it all wrong*
> *Stevie harmonises, like he did with John Prine*
> *David just sits and looks blue all the time."*

The song gives Bob the halo of normality. It places him in context with his pals who didn't make it, the people he knew long before he was strung out on the road. Harding relates this slice of 'Dynablob' with a very light, personal touch and the more people who were explaining their version of Bob to me, a snapshot of a Man for all reasons slowly developed. I don't mean this like he's the Messiah, but Bob is all things to all ears. He's touched so many souls whether he intended to or not. He seems to leave a lasting impression.

Everyone seems to come to Bob at different times and in hugely different personal circumstances. It's intensive stuff and to understand the life of Bob I knew I'd have to first flick furiously through his back pages. By doing that there would be at least some kind of understanding, some comprehension, of the Bob ethos. It would also put an order to things before I dived deeper into the swirling miasma of his back catalogue. Only then could I begin to justify to my wife why I was spending all this money on CDs by someone she considered to be a moaning fool.

I read the books about Bob - Scaduto, Shelton, Bauldie, Heylin, Humphries - then went back. Back to 1960. Cue swirly lights and backmasked strings. Imagine the scene, the young Bob is at college, struggling with literature and, undoubtedly, members of the opposite sex. He is already a deft strummer, brought up on high and lonesome radio faves and old blues legends. He bought a harmonica and, well according to rumours he threatened the people of Minneapolis with it.

1960

Bound for glory...

S O IT seems that Bob was bored with schooling - in typical rock 'n' roll style. Robert Allen Zimmerman had soaked up his influences from Little Richard's rock 'n' roll through blues players like Jesse Fuller and Big Bill Broonzy to country legends like Hank Williams. And then he picked up his guitar. Playing Minneapolis clubs The Purple Onion and The Scholar, he fast developed a workmanlike repertoire of dustbowl ballads courtesy of his main emotional squeeze Woody Guthrie. Having been introduced to Woody's biog, Bound For Glory, by the other, winning, male in a brief love triangle, the fledgling Dylan (the name change was imminent) placed

nose to grindstone and fast outgrew the folk-lite of The Kingston Trio and Harry Belafonte.

As 1960 rolled on, Minneapolis University wondered what Zimmerman or, indeed Dylan, looked like, as the be-denimed Bob sailed farther from the mainstream. His voice cracked and his flatpicking style matured. With a hint of harmonica, he was almost the real thing and, in search of more jigsaw, he announced that he would not only ingest the Woody Guthrie songbook but he'd travel to New York to visit the man and seek approval. Before he went, the majority of people in Minneapolis weren't taking him seriously.

STEVE BARD, *now a Minneapolis lawyer*

"He was the kinda kid you always used to pick on at high school. You know, the wimpy kid to make fun of."

BY HIS own admission, Bob had become "like a walking Woody Guthrie jukebox". And, by the time he hit Wisconsin, en route to the Big Apple, the people he met had trouble understanding just why. He met Jennifer Warren. She was not impressed.

"He knew more Woody Guthrie songs than Woody knew. He had the Guthrie accent, and it sounded like phoney shit. I remember thinking, 'Why the hell would a kid his age want to be somebody else?'."

But Bob had taken the call. It was, indeed, a religious thing. From Woody to Bob. And, the story has become legend. Even today's Bobyoung, surfing the internet for reasons to be revolutionary, can visit

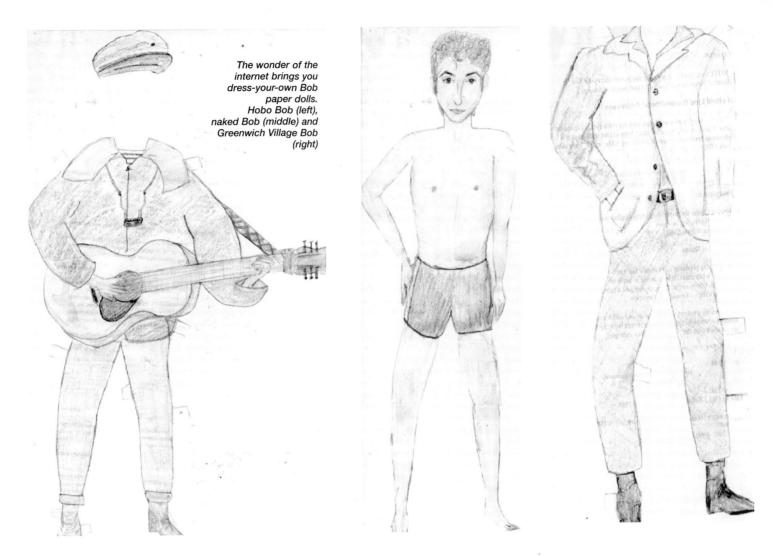

The wonder of the internet brings you dress-your-own Bob paper dolls. Hobo Bob (left), naked Bob (middle) and Greenwich Village Bob (right)

Geocities, and read a twisted variation on Bob's Big Apple sortie. It strangely, goes like this...

THE ADVENTURES OF BOBBY DYLWEED VOLUME 1:

BOBBY'S JOURNEY TO NEW YORK CITY, Part 1: Bobby Dylweed Gets a Telegram

A long time ago, in the late 1950's, in a place up north called Minnesota, there lived a boy named Bobby Dylweed. Now, Dylweed wasn't his real name mind you, his real, full name was Robert Allen Zigazigah. He changed his name for a lot of reasons, one of which was that when your last name starts with "Z" you're always last in every-

thing, last in roll call, last in line at graduation, etc.

Bobby wanted to get away. FAR away from where he was. Bobby was stuck at the University of Minnesota, taking up space. It was BO-RING. The teachers were mean, the work was hard, and he had no friends there. Well, maybe two, Dirty Maxx and Harry Joe. The three lived in a small, roach-ridden flat in Dinqueytowne, a pretty bitchin' part of Minneapolis, actually. The flat was located above a coffee house, where instead of studying and writing research papers, Bobby would play the guitar and sing in a beautiful, lilting tenor voice. He also played the harmonica a little bit too. You see, more than anything else Bobby Dylweed wanted to be a folk singer.

One day, Bobby received a telegram from his old friend and mentor, Woody Guthrie. They had been good friends ever since Bobby was thirteen. Woody was the one who taught Bobby how to play the guitar and to rebel against the establishment. The telegram said: BOBBY. MUST COME TO NEW YORK NOW. NEED TO SEE YOU. VERY URGENT. WOODY.

OK, IT'S a cartoonish interpretation, but in true Big Brother style, for all any new Bobverts know, it's as close to the truth as fact. Just add the "it was snowing when Bob Dylan arrived in New York" part that's in all the accepted books and, don't forget, that on his first night he played at Cafe Wha? in Greenwich Village.

No Direction Home

A-RAMBLING from his homebase of Minneapolis to New York City (taking in Muddy Waters live in Chicago along the way), Bob finally hooked up with the ailing Guthrie in New Jersey. With a couple of hundred Woody originals in his repertoire, Bob was still finding his own voice and gaining plaudits in the process. Infiltrating the Greenwich Village coffee house circuit, playing Cafe Wha?, the Gaslight and Gerde's, Bob was scooped for a one-off harmonica session with Harry Belafonte. Meanwhile, his live shows brought in imminent girlfriend Suze Rotolo,

HAMMOND SiGNS DYLAN

Having signed young newcomer Bob Dylan to blow harmonica on three tracks ('I'll Fly Away', 'Swing And Turn Jubilee' and 'Come Back, Baby') on a recording date for folk stylist Carolyn Hester, producer John Hammond (who discovered Billie Holiday, Bessie Smith and Count Basie among others) was so impressed by Dylan's raw talent that he immediately signed him to Columbia as a solo artist for the unprecedented royalty rates of four per cent.
NME, September 1961

future manager Albert Grossman and enthusiastic New York Times' journalist Robert Shelton. The word, although still a tad thin, was spreading.

Later, at a Carolyn Hester recording session, producer John Hammond checked Bob's credentials, spotted some potential and a deal was inked with Columbia to capitalise on Bob's penmanship, which was by then ably melding (if that's a real word at all) his roots background and the emerging interpretations he'd heard on the Greenwich circuit. A brace of covers were recorded, alongside Bob's homage to Guthrie, 'Song To Woody' and a wordy recollection of his arrival in the Big Apple 'Talkin' New York'.

DAVE BERGER *musician and writer*
"I was driving to New York and he wanted a ride. We drove straight through without stopping and he was singing all the way. It was annoying, that weird monotonic kind of style with Woody's twang. It was a pain in the ass. Eventually I just told him to shut the fuck up."

NAT HENTOFF *Playboy magazine*

"Some found his flat Midwestern tones gratingly mesmeric; others agreed with a Missouri folk singer who had likened the Dylan sound to that of 'a dog with his leg caught in barbed wire'."

IN New York, Dylan's back pages and Guthrie's Thesaurus broke the ice. He quickly ingratiated himself with the folk fraternity. He was very wordy, very clever. But he was not immediately the much-liked new kid in town...

DAVE VAN RONK *fellow Greenwich folk singer*

"Dylan was always vicious from time to time. This was no lollipop singer, you know. The only trouble about his viciousness, until he became famous, he couldn't get away with it."

THE SUPPORT of The New York Times' journalist Robert Shelton was essential. In fact, his words were so positive that Dylan read out his first review before he played one night.

LIAM CLANCY *of The Clancy Brothers*

"Shelton more than anyone was responsible for Dylan. He thought he was a tremendous poet."

PATRICK HUMPHRIES *author*

"I think Robert Shelton's quite an amazing character and I feel his role in the Dylan story is just really underplayed. This was a man who went to Gerde's Folk Club to see John Lee Hooker and came out praising the support act. Now most journalists don't even see the support act and he knew, right away that Bob

Dylan was going to be something really major. I suppose the talent would have come through at some point but Shelton discovered if, even if he did say that Dylan discovered himself.

"Whatever people say, Shelton was there with Dylan from when he was the Guthrie jukebox through to the wild Messianic acid-frizzled-haired God who broke his neck. That period was the furnace and Shelton and Dylan were inseparable. And, if you read No Direction Home, which took 20 years to finish, the period up to 1966 it's fantastic. The fly-on-the-wall stuff is just superb. After that it all falls apart but that key period, up to the end of '66 is just fascinating."

CAROLYN HESTER *singer/songwriter*

"Dylan impressed me as being totally absorbed with the music. It seemed to me that he didn't put his guitar down hardly ever."

JOHN TOBLER *journalist, label owner*

"As proprietor of a small independent record label, I have got to know Carolyn Hester, who is widely credited with a key role in the emergence of Dylan: she had met him at Gerde's Folk City in New York, where he was effectively doing floor spots, and she was a headliner. He heard her soundcheck one day, when she sang 'Lonesome Tears', a song written by Buddy Holly, and he asked her where she had learned a fairly obscure Holly song. When she told him that she had been taught the song by Buddy himself (both Holly and Hester were produced extensively by Norman Petty), Dylan could hardly believe that he was talking to someone who had actually known Buddy Holly (and also recorded with him, although sadly, nothing has ever been released).

"At the time, Hester was in the studio with the legendary John Hammond (Senior) producing her first album for CBS in 1961. She asked if Hammond would mind if she used a

harmonica player on a couple of tracks, as her father had done on her first album (produced by Petty). Hammond, basically a jazz expert, who later confessed to a very limited knowledge of folk music, said OK, and asked if she knew anyone. "I know this fellow who plays at Gerde's" she said, and had him audition for Hammond in a flat in Greenwich Village. Hammond was gobsmacked, and signed him immediately."

DYLAN'S DEBUT album was recorded in three days with Hammond at the controls. Virtually all first take stuff, the sessions included 'Baby, Let Me Follow You Down' which Dylan had learnt from another aspiring folkie Eric (Ric) Von Schmidt, plus Dave Van Ronk's arrangement of 'House Of The Rising Sun'.

ERIC VON SCHMIDT *singer/songwriter*

"We got together in my apartment and I played him stuff like 'He Was A Friend Of Mine', which I got from the Library Of Congress and 'Baby, Let Me Follow You Down', which I learnt from Geno Foreman, the son of Clark Foreman, the Civil Rights leader."

DAVE VAN RONK

"We had a terrible falling out about 'House Of The Rising Sun'. He was always a sponge, picking up on everything around him and he copped my arrangement for the song. He asked if I minded if he recorded my arrangement and I said that I wanted to do it. Then he asked me again later and said, 'Ooops, I already recorded it and Columbia want it'. For a period of two months we didn't speak."

LIAM CLANCY

"The only thing I can compare him with was blotting paper. He was ready to suck up anything that came within his range."

PHIL OCHS *protest singer*

"The first time I heard him sing a few songs, I thought 'This guy is it. He's the best writer, the best singer, that anyone has ever heard'."

Talkin' New York Blues

AS THE Greenwich scene simmered, Broadside magazine was launched to recognise its patron saints. Issue one featured Bob's 'Talkin' John Birch Society', an overview of a political hot potato which confirmed Bob's folk credentials. 'Blowin' In The Wind' was eeked out and fast became his battle cry for the new album. His elevation to role model was complete.

Grossman's careful management ensured that Columbia couldn't over-expose the songwriter as he immediately started work on his second album, 'The Freewheelin' Bob Dylan'. This time the album was overflowing with Bob originals, a world away from his just-out first single, 'Mixed Up Confusion', an upbeat rockabilly howl which suitably confused America which chose to ignore it. With throbbing harmonica and tinkling piano it swang like a 'Highway 61 Revisited' out-

ST81054

Lord Buckley

a most immaculately hip aristocrat

Bob Dylan

Tracks: She's No Good, Talkin' New York, In My Time Of Dyin', Man Of Constant Sorrow, Fixin' To Die Blues, Pretty Peggy-O, Highway 51 Blues, Gospel Plow, Baby, Let Me Follow You Down, House Of The Risin' Sun, Freight Train Blues, Song To Woody, See That My Grave Is Kept Clean.

Released March (June in the UK).
Produced by John Hammond.

SLEEVE NOTES: *Columbia Records is proud to introduce a major new figure in American folk music - Bob Dylan. Excitement has been running high since the young man with a guitar rambled into a recording studio for two sessions in November, 1961. For at only 20, Dylan is the most unusual new talent in American folk music.*

WHAT THE PAPERS SAID (first US review) *Young Bob Dylan is the most gifted poet to appear on the American scene since Woody Guthrie. His output is prodigious, his language direct, personal and of high literary quality.*

WHAT DYLAN SAID *"I wasn't even me. I was still learning language then."*

IN A NUTSHELL *The frost bites hard during Bob's story of his first few months in New York on 'Talkin' New York'. His hokey Okie accent, hillbilly references and pointed humour is perfectly set off by a rolling harmonica. Bukka White's 'Fixin' To Die Blues' is spat out, the succinct guitar on 'Highway 51' throbs and his Jimmie Rodgers howl on 'Gospel Plow' is jaw dropping. The opening of 'Baby, Let Me Follow You Down' beckons you to the edge of the stage as he tells the tale of hearing the song while visiting Ric Von Schmidt at Harvard University.*
Its delivery is almost like an intimate passage of secrets, with Dylan whispering around the chords. The album's an epic field recording that reverberates with passion and stark realism. If it was released in 1999, it would be hailed as better than Beck and an innovative trip back into authentic roots music, much as it was then.

SINGLES/EPS/ETC *Mixed Up Confusion/Corrina Corrina (single, US only)*

take. And, he hadn't even thought of that yet.

With Suze Rotolo on sabbatical in Italy, Bob - who's now legally Dylan - heads for London to perform in a BBC play called Madhouse On Castle Street. "The only reason I want to go to London, is to look for Charles Dickens." he claimed. Obviously. And, the British press were fascinated by the young folknik whose style was further developed after he spent several nights locked in a room studying the idiosyncrasies of the beat poet Lord Buckley, a Greenwich Village regular who'd died as Bob hit town. Buckley was a natural progression, the beat influence having arrived through Suze Rotolo, with

Lawrence Ferlinghetti's monologue style a mainstay of Bob's earlier talking blues deliveries.

BOB BROWN, *ABC TV, 1995*
"Dylan was greatly impressed by the beat poets that he encountered in New York City's Greenwich Village. The coffee house circuit boasted the likes of Allen Ginsberg, Geoffrey Corso, Jack Kerouac and his favourite Lawrence Ferlinghetti."

R GILBERT, *The 'Scene' magazine, London*
"Dylan is the most exciting white folk and blues singer, the experts say, America has produced. He writes many of his own songs, sings them 'consciously trying to recapture the rude beauty of a southern farmhand musing in melody on his porch' and accompanies himself on guitar and harmonica."

THE LISTENER *on Dylan's performance in Madhouse In Castle Street*
"(Dylan) sat around playing and singing attractively, if a little incomprehensibly."

BOB DYLAN DEBUT RELEASED

CBS Records have released a self-titled debut album by Bob Dylan. Of the 22 folk and blues tracks he recorded with just his own guitar accompaniment between November 20 and 22, 1961, a total of 13 songs are premiered. Most of young Dylan's influences are in evidence: 'You're No Good' Jesse Fuller. 'In My Time Of Dyin' (Jesus Gonna Make Up My Dyin' Bed)' Blind Willie Johnson. 'Man Of Constant Sorrow' (trad arr). 'Fixin' To Die' Bukka White. 'Pretty Peggy-O' (trad arr). 'Highway 51' Curtis Jones. 'Gospel Pillow' (trad arr). 'Baby, Let Me Follow You Down' Eric Von Schmidt. 'House Of The Risin' Sun' (trad arr). 'Freight Train Blues' (trad arr). See That My Grave Is Kept Clean' Blind Lemon Jefferson. Plus Dylan's own 'Talkin' New York' and 'Song For Woody'.
NME, March 1962

1963

Down The Highway

THE TRIBULATIONS of acting behind him, Bob headed for Italy to find Suze Rotolo. They miss each other. Literally, as she had returned to the USA. Back on 4th Street, the couple are photographed for the cover of 'Freewheelin' as Bob's shows got bigger (900 at the New York Town Hall on April 12) and he almost played on the Ed Sullivan TV Show - he pulled out at the last minute when his song, 'Talkin' John Birch Paranoid Blues' was canned.

Dylan's progress took him to the Monterey Folk Festival where he met Joan Baez, the undisputed Queen of Folk. Several shared bills later an affair developed as folk music came of age at the Newport Folk Festival. Now recognised as a social spokesman, Dylan played in front of 400,000 on the March On Washington, which culminated in Martin Luther King's legendary "I Have A Dream..." speech. 'Blowin' In The Wind' was a civil rights anthem and Bob set to work on his next album. His relationship with Suze Rotolo was ending and he moved to California to be near Joan Baez. But, whatever happened to Suze Rotolo who hugged the arm of Bob on the cover of 'The Freewheelin' Bob Dylan'?

PATRICK *via the internet*
"It just happens that Suze Rotolo is my cousin, although the way her and Carla (the "other sister") have been acting towards the rest of the family I probably don't have much more info than the rest of you. To the best of my knowledge, she still lives in the Village and is a freelance artist. She married a guy named Enzo whom she met on the famous trip to Italy towards the end of her relationship w / Bob and has a son who by now is probably 18 ."

And Ed Sullivan? John Birch? That stuff. I'm sure the bastion of broadcasting (that's Ed), who was allegedly nervous about The Beatles, wouldn't have allowed Bob to play a satirical political song. Or would he?

ED SULLIVAN *bastion of US broadcasting*
"We fought for the song. Said that everyone had the right to be kidded. But the network had had problems with the John Birch Society already and they didn't want to risk it again."

THE FREEWHEELIN BOB DYLAN

DAVID BLUE

"He was very upset. He disappeared for three days or so. I remember Suze, Van Ronk and Terri all asking if I'd seen him."

MATT CARSON,
Meadville,
Pennsylvania, 1999

"A couple of years ago, I was into the Beatles. While watching the Beatles Anthology and reading some info on them, I found that one of their biggest influences was Dylan, especially his album 'Freewheelin''. So I bought that CD. That night I had a report I had to do on protest songs. I wrote the entire paper on the very album I had bought a few hours

doesn't like him, every time I get a new CD or tape he rolls his eyes and complains about it. The girl across the hall thinks it's great that I'm so in tune to the '60s, even though I wasn't a part of it, although the only song she likes is 'Like A Rolling Stone'."

EYOLF, *Upsalla, Sweden*

"I do have a special relationship with 'Freewheelin'. It was not my first album; I bought it when I was 20-21, and that was all I played for more weeks than my partner could stand.

"The impact it had on me was the result of a combination of things: first of all - of course - the immediacy of the music-making itself. The

player and 'Masters Of War' fills the room. All of a sudden the world becomes cold and hard, with 'I'll stand over your grave 'til I'm sure that you're dead', etc. Growing up, facing the world, I guess you could call it. The description of the protagonist's listening experience was so vivid that I expected it to be merely literary, but the wonderful thing is that when I actually bought it and heard for myself, it was exactly like that.

"I think that's the most important effect that 'Freewheelin' had on me: the growing up thing, and the stunning fact that I was 21 and so was he, and he had done THIS, and I had done nothing."

By 1963, the Baez/Dylan interface was beginning to gain momentum. The pair were constantly playing live shows and nurturing a cause or two. What's more, they were just about an item. They were folk music's King And Queen and when their Royal Court convened at The Newport Folk Festival their body language spoke volumes. Dylan was excited.

Nearly half a million people headed for the Lincoln Memorial where "folk singers sang **protest songs of the '60s,** while Mahalia Jackson sang hymns of oppression."

before! It was amazing; I couldn't believe I could squeeze a paper out of only a couple of songs (mostly 'Blowin' In The Wind' and 'Masters Of War'). In the next year, I became the biggest Dylan maniac in the school, I had over 30 CDs, 10 records and about 25 bootlegs of his music. It was strange though, I found that I was one of the only true fans of my age. I don't know anyone at my college who likes him."

"I've been asking people what they think of my 'Dylan fetish'. First semester I had a music class, and I would always talk about Dylan. I did so much that the students in the class started calling me 'Dylan'! (which I thought a honour). Also, every time his name came up (like in Billy Joel's 'We Didn't Start The Fire') the teacher would look at me! My room-mate

crudeness, harshness of the singing appealed to me, in the same way and for much the same reasons as he describes in the liner notes to 'Joan Baez In Concert Volume Two'. It exposed nerve-endings.

"Then the discovery of how hilariously funny a lot of the lyrics are. What particularly comes to my mind now, is 'Oxford Town'. The character of the singing/playing is lightly mocking, with tongue-in-cheek humour in a way, which makes the cruelty of the text stand out even more clearly. 'It sticks in your throat.'

"My first impression of 'Freewheelin' comes from literature - from a Norwegian book called *Beatles* about four kids growing up in Oslo and following the Beatles heart and soul. One of the greatest scenes in the book is when they are playing 'Please Please Me' and a big brother comes in with a new album, puts it on the

Witness his enthusiastic programme notes:

"The folk songs showed me the way
They showed me that songs can say
something human
Without 'Barbara Allen' there'd be no
'Girl from the North Country'
Without no 'Lone Green Valley' there'd
be no 'Don Think Twice'
Without no 'Jesse James' there'd be
no 'Davy Moore'
Without no 'Twenty one Years' there'd
be no 'Walls A Red Wing'
Hell no."

Joan Baez first at Newport, continued the trend for bringing him to the stage mid-set, enthusing thus: "This is a young man who grew out of a need. He came here because he had an ear on his generation. And he set a pace on many people and now in the same way there are many others who are joining him. I don't have to tell you, he's yours... Bob Dylan."

AFTER NEWPORT, BAEZ AND BOB were travelling partners. Hobo-ing to gigs with Bob guesting for Joan at every opportunity. Author Greil Marcus recalls seeing Dylan, courtesy of another Baez guest slot.

"It was the summer of 1963, in a field somewhere in New Jersey. I'd gone to see Joan Baez and after a bit she brought out a scruffy-looking guy with a guitar. He looked dusty. His shoulders were hunched and he acted slightly embarrassed. He sang a couple of songs by himself and a couple with Joan Baez. I barely noticed the end of the show; I was transfixed. I was confused.

"When the show was over I saw him trying to light a cigarette. I went up to him. I was just dumbfounded enough to open my mouth: 'You were terrific,' I said brightly. He didn't look up. 'I was shit,' he replied."

"How many roads must a man walk down before you call him a man? How many seas must the white dove sail before she sleeps in the sand? How many times must the cannon balls fly before they are forever banned? I'd say the answer, my friend, is blowing in the wind.' The answer is blowing in the wind.'

The growth of the Civil Rights Movement coincided with Dylan's progress and undoubtedly propelled his new found politicism to new, welcoming ears. The importance and poignant imagery of 'Blowin' In The Wind' was soon adopted as the movement's anthem.

On August 28th, the Great March on Washington culminated with a speech by The Reverend Martin Luther King. Nearly half a million people, chaperoned by the army, headed for the Lincoln Memorial where "folk singers sang protest songs of the '60s, while Mahalia Jackson sang hymns of oppression."

Martin Luther King's immortal 'I Have A Dream' conclusion was set to resonate for generations accompanied as often as not by Bob's anthemic protests.

SHERYL CROW *singer/songwriter*
"When I was a kid writing really bad songs, I'd go down to the drug store and buy magazines like Creem and Rolling Stone with people in them like Bob Dylan and Joan Baez, a whole generation of musicians who were outspoken about the Civil Rights movement. That's what I wanted to be like."

PATRICK HUMPHRIES
"You know when you hear these things in Dylan songs, that you haven't heard before, when you get the spark, see the light? Like, when you hear "In the wild cathedral evening" and you think, 'what an amazing image'. I remember talking to Robert Shelton about 'The Ballad Of Donald White' and at that Bob and his fellow folk circuiteers were all going on the same marches, they were all getting upset about the same things. But only Dylan was able to turn the stuff around and write things that were so pointed and so timeless. You'd hear 'Only A Pawn In Their Game' and you knew that this song was going to be around forever."

DYLAN: VOICE OF PROTEST 1963
WITH THE 'FREEWHEELIN' BOB DYLAN' having sold in excess of 250,000 copies, Dylan has become acknowledged as America's foremost folk singer.
Peter, Paul And Mary have transformed two 'Freewheelin'' tracks - 'Blowin' In The Wind' and 'Don't Think Twice It's All Right' - into Top 40 hits and protest movement anthems, Joan Baez features many of Dylan's songs in her concert repertoire and is frequently joined on stage by the singer/composer.
As the protest movement gathers momentum across the United States, Bob Dylan makes his position clear, in words and music.
NME, August 1963

RED FOLKIE SCARE
With Peter, Paul And Mary's interpretations of two Bob Dylan songs, 'Blowin' In The Wind' and 'Don't Think Twice It's All Right' chartbound on both sides of the Atlantic, it has been left to UK music writer Derek Johnson to go boldly into print and publicly dismiss as rubbish scare stories in Britain's more lurid Sunday tabloids which claim that the current world-wide folk music trend masks subversive tactics by the Kremlin to 'poison young minds'!
NME, November 1963

The Freewheelin' Bob Dylan

Tracks: Blowin' In The Wind, Girl From The North Country, Masters Of War, Down The Highway, Bob Dylan's Blues, A Hard Rain's A-Gonna Fall, Don't Think Twice, It's All Right, Bob Dylan's Dream, Oxford Town, Talking World War III Blues, Corrina, Corrina, Honey, Just Allow Me One More Chance, I Shall Be Free.
Released May (November in the UK).
Produced by John Hammond.

SLEEVE NOTES *Of all the precipitously emergent singers of folk songs in the continuing renacence (sic) of that self-assertive tradition, none has equalled Bob Dylan in singularity of impact. As Harry Jackson, a cowboy singer and painter, has exclaimed: "He's so goddamned real, he's unbelievable".*

WHAT DYLAN SAID *"I wish I could write like 'Girl from the North Country'. You know, I can't write like that any more." (1966 Austin interview)*

WHAT THE WORLD SAYS
MARK EITZEL, *singer/songwriter, formerly of American Music Club "I've just been listening to it for the first time (1996) in my life. When I was a kid people would play it and I'd say, 'folk shit!', but God it's great, it's so fucking amazing."*
MEAT LOAF, *"That Dylan record with 'Blowin' In The Wind', on it was the first record I ever bought."*

IN A NUTSHELL *'Blowin' In The Wind' still resonates profoundly on an album that's deeper in tone than its predecessor and, this time around, all self-penned. Between the politics and a rasping harmonica, there's some simple country blues and matter-of-fact storytelling. Dylan's version of 'Corrina Corrina' is a cool jazz shuffle with an underplayed guitar, an unbelievable contrast from the long shadow-casting 'Masters Of War' and the poignant story that is 'Oxford Town'. Bob calls on Big Joe Williams' influence for the brooding 'Down The Highway', while 'Bob Dylan's Dream' owes a debt to Martin Carthy's 'Lord Franklin', which Dylan had heard back in 1962. In addition there's mentions of Brigitte Bardot, Elizabeth Taylor, bagels and pizzas for good measure.*

SINGLES/EPS/ETC *Blowin' In The Wind/Don't Think Twice It's Alright (single, US only)*

1964

No, no, no... It Ain't Me, Babe

TO SIGNAL the end of his time with Suze Rotolo, Bob wrote the downbeat 'Ballad In Plain D' which turned up on his next album 'Another Side Of Bob Dylan'. The split with Suze was not unexpected.

Meanwhile, pining for some kind of Kerouacian experience, Bob headed out with his road manager and renowned chess roadie in later days Victor Maimudes, singer Paul Clayton and writer Pete Karman, zig-zag driving across the country before winding up, road-weary and wasted in New Orleans.

Meanwhile, Peter, Paul And Mary had charted with 'Blowin' In The Wind' and others were keen to follow. Johnny Rogan's Byrds biog Timeless Flight

quotes producer Jim Dickson: "Dylan was a very adept record plugger. His biggest successes had come from Peter, Paul And Mary, not his own records. He came down and charmed The Byrds. He got them to like him." 'Mr Tambourine Man' was eventually recorded but it remained in the can until the following year.

A one-off show at the Royal Festival Hall in London was preceded by the quickfire recording of the next album. Bob was beginning to move away from the political spokesperson of old, a departure which was mirrored with Dylan's appearance at the Newport Folk Festival. People were not amused. In something that would become a trend for

Bob, the audience was dumbfounded by his latest shirt and hip new personality.

Whatever. Bob didn't seem to mind. And backstage he returned to his roots sitting in with bluegrass rebels The Dillards. Singer Rodney Dillard recalls, "We were just four boys from the Ozarks who'd been signed to Elektra and sent down to Newport to play. It was like letting a dog loose with a load of hens. After we'd played we were strumming some old country songs backstage and Dylan sat down and played with us. He knew all these old back porch songs. I think it was the first time I saw him smile that day. He was a really serious guy."

MITCH JAYNE *The Dillards*
"Rodney heard something in Dylan's music and the way he sang that he thought would add a new dimension to what we were doing. So, we took our rural sound and added a Dylan-styled vocal, we covered 'Walkin' Down

DYLAN: NEW ALBUM, NEW PRODUCER

Although Bob Dylan's SRO New York Carnegie Hall concert of October 26, 1963 was recorded for release (and given the catalogue number 77110) it has remained unheard. In the interim Dylan's new manager, Albert Grossman, has unsuccessfully attempted to re-negotiate his client's original royalty deal with CBS. In the course of much unpleasantness, Grossman secured Tom Wilson instead of John Hammond (who discovered and signed Dylan to CBS) to produce Dylan's third studio album, 'The Times They Are A-Changin''.
Recorded in August and October 1963, it comprises of ten Dylan originals.
NME, January 1964

The Line' and it's been a regular in our set for the last 35 years."

AFTER THE FESTIVAL, somewhat distraught, Dylan retired to Woodstock for the second half of the year, only being enticed back to New York to turn The Beatles on to dope, as you would, before playing a major show at the Philharmonic Hall.

On the other side of the Atlantic, a few spanners were at work. The Beatles were tuning in, according to Mark Lewisohn's The Complete Beatles Chronicles: "'I'm A Loser', written mostly by John shows a definite shift in direction away from the 'hand-holding' songs to a more autobiographical and introspective slant, influenced by Bob Dylan."

The Fabs were keen to meet up with Dylan and when they visited New York, Lennon asked mutual friend Al Aronowitz to organise a rendezvous.

AL ARONOWITZ *journalist*
"One of the biggest laughs of my life was when The Beatles first smoked marijuana. It was at the Hotel Delomonico on Manhattan's Park Avenue on August 28, 1964. John had asked that I bring Dylan down to meet them and when we arrived, I asked Dylan to roll the first joint. John offered it to Ringo, then everyone had their own joint and was smoking them like cigarettes. In the adjoining room, radio and record people, Peter, Paul And Mary and The Kingston Trio were waiting to meet the group. They were all being incredibly polite but they must have wondered why everyone was just collapsing in heaps laughing at each other."

MARGARET CHIN *Dylan fan*
"When I was 12, I wrote a story about a denim-clad guy who roamed the countryside, cast out of society, but free of its restrictions. He was my fantasy and I longed for him to come along and take me away from my strict Calvinist family and grim grammar school in the small, miserable town where I lived.

"Then, I saw Bob on TV. Not only did he fit my fantasy man's image, he articulated thoughts that I'd had about life, love, politics and society.

"I played his records and I felt spiritually-inspired, moved by his passion and turned on by the skinny, snaky hips and tousled curls on the record sleeve. It was a heady mix.

"The anti-war anthems, like 'Masters Of War' and 'With God On Our Side' and the social commentary of 'The Ballad Of Medger Evans' a murdered black activist in the south, told me things about the 'free' world that never turned up on the six o'clock news. His songs were the catalyst that made me devour all sorts of radical and alternative writing. It formed the bedrock of my social and political awareness.

"And, of course, he wasn't just some kind of Marx in music, he had emotion too. I loved the smouldering wistfulness of 'Boots Of Spanish Leather' and the humour of 'I Shall Be Free', which my parents particularly tutted at for lines like 'he smelled like a skunk' and 'she rolls me over and kicks me out of bed'. Perfect.

"Bob seemed to live in the same world as I wanted to, permeated with the popular culture of the day. I was longing to be old enough to join in."

The Times They Are A-Changin'

Tracks: The Times They Are A-Changin', Ballad Of Hollis Brown, With God On Our Side, One Too Many Mornings, North Country Blues, Only A Pawn In Their Game, Boots Of Spanish Leather, When The Ship Comes In, The Lonesome Death Of Hattie Carroll, Restless Farewell. Released January (May in the UK).
Produced by Tom Wilson

SLEEVE NOTES *Made up of a lengthy stream of consciousness titled '11 Outlined Epitaphs', the sleeve mentions virgin girls, Hibbing, Woody, a wasteland wind (whistled), zombie strollers, the Russians, Adolf Hitler, Robert E Lee, Eric (Von Scmidt), Terri and Dave (Van Ronk), Brecht, Behan, AL Lloyd, Piaf, Dietrich, Paul Clayton, Ginsberg, Mondigliani, William Blake, Miles Davis and many more.*

WHAT DYLAN SAID *"Those songs were all written in New York. I would never have written - or sung any of them in that way - if I hadn't been sitting around listening to performers in New York cafes."*

WHAT THE WORLD SAYS MARTIN CARTHY, *"I was at the Festival Hall in London when Dylan played the most amazing concert. He sang 'Hattie Carroll' and I was scarred for life. I couldn't believe that a song telling a story could be that powerful, it drew me into narrative songs." (Martin Carthy does his version of 'Hattie Carroll' on the 1998 album 'Signs Of Life')*

JENNA, via e-mail *"Ever since I first heard 'The Times They Are A-Changin' I was captivated by his every word and rhythm. Although I wasn't born in the generation that his music is linked to, I feel that I can somehow relate."*

JON LANDAU, writer *"This song ('When The Ship Comes In') is truly frightening in its righteous zeal. It is vengeful in the Old Testament sense of the word. It is the work of a profoundly religious mentality."*

IN A NUTSHELL *The pace of 'The Times They Are A Changin'' is more controlled, slower, more considered. It's the work of a champion storyteller, bringing the audience in and leading them carefully through each moving episode. The painfully sad 'North Country Blues', the clever perspective of 'Only A Pawn In Their Game' and the loneliness of 'Boots Of Spanish Leather' all have their tragic appeal. Even when the tempo lifts for 'When The Ship Comes In' there's no slacking for Dylan's melancholy prose. The monumental nature of the title track dictates the timbre and the majestic delivery of 'With God On Our Side' and the couplet-cascade of 'The Lonesome Death Of Hattie Carroll' are powerful support.*

"**Bob seemed to live in the same world as I wanted to, I was longing to join in.**"

BRIAN WALKER

"I remember being in someone's house in about 1964 and this guy said to me, 'You gotta hear this' and he pulled out 'The Freewheelin' Bob Dylan' and I remember thinking this was something really different and refreshing and I really liked the songs a lot."

DAVID HEPWORTH

"I can distinctly remember the first time I heard him because strangely enough I was at school and he was a name that we'd read about in the Record Mirror and the NME. He was a person who was namechecked by people that we admired.

"Me and my friend both thought he was called Bob Dylon and we were surprised to find out that there was to be a recital of Bob Dylon's music in the Geography room, mounted by the Grammar School's Folk Club. We went along and I remember distinctly Richard Hughes, from the Sixth Form, conducted a little lecture orchestrated by songs by this man that we were shocked to hear was called Bob Dylan.

"He played us stuff from the first album and the second album, then pointed out that with 'Another Side Of Bob Dylan', that Dylan had exhibited a new form of maturity. Now, the whole concept of maturity was something that was quite unknown to us in terms of pop music."

THE SOUND OF DYLAN

CBS RECORDS

Bob Dylan NEW SINGLE RELEASED ToDay

'THE TiMES THEY ARE A CHANGIN''
c/w 'Honey, just allow me one more chance'
201751

C B S RECORDS · 104 NEW BOND ST · LONDON W1

Another Side Of Bob Dylan

Tracks: All I Really Want To Do, Black Crow Blues, Spanish Harlem Incident, Chimes Of Freedom, I Shall Be Free No. 10, To Ramona, Motorpsycho Nitemare, My Back Pages, I Don't Believe You, Ballad In Plain D, It Ain't Me Babe.
Released August (November in the UK).
Produced by Tom Wilson.

SLEEVE NOTES *More poems, including rhyming prose about jack o'diamonds, drug store dope, shoeboxes, crackers and fishermen, bleeker street, Jesus Christ and Francois Hardy. With few capital letters in evidence.*

WHAT DYLAN SAID *"The songs are insanely honest, not meaning to twist any heads and written only for the reason that I myself me alone had wanted to write them."*

WHAT THE WORLD SAYS CHER *"My first hit was his ('All I Really Want To Do'), but I haven't seen him for years. If I never see him again, I don't really care, but it was interesting to know him at one time and be around him and Sara and the kids."*

IN A NUTSHELL *The madcap irreverence of 'I Shall Be Free No. 10's talking blues, with its perfectly crap self-analysis of 'I'm a poet, I know it, Hope I don't blow it' and its denuncia-tion of Bob the role model, is a wonderful tongue-in-cheek observation. It contrasts perfectly with the opening troubled love song, 'All I Really Want To Do', which has Dylan caught in a throat-warbling vibrato on the chorus, and the classic emo-tional sketch of 'It Ain't Me Babe'. Elsewhere, there's the mer-cilessly undernourished lilt of 'To Ramona' next to the B-movie propaganda of 'Motorpsycho Nitemare', which bears the dia-logue-ramble of classic Bob, like a string of limericks waiting for a punchline. In addition, the chilling 'Chimes Of Freedom' and the vitriolic 'Ballad In Plain D', plus the sombre 'My Back Pages', make 'Another Side' an emotional minefield.*

SINGLES/EPS/ETC *Blowin' In The Wind EP (EP, European) All I Really Want To Do EP (EP, European)*

1965

On The Road Again

A QUANTAM leap beckoned as 'Bringing It All Back Home' was instigated with the inventivenss and wild flair of a small boy with a dangerous chemistry set. Lyrical and musical boundaries were breached and a suitably eclectic electric team were brought in for the imminent journey. Plugged in, Bob then unplugged to embark on an English tour which took him back to the acoustic basics. Only madness could possibly follow. DA Pennebaker was along to film every quip and canoodle for the film Don't Look Back, with Joan Baez attending but failing to make second fiddle.

Back in America, the electricity was turned back on. 'Like A Rolling Stone' was unleashed and the Newport Folk Festival was creamed. A steadfastly unready Butterfield Blues Band made history. By the Autumn Bob was backed by The Hawks (later to be The Band) who then began the long haul, with acoustic strummery followed by raucous rock

rebel rousing. A modicum of audience outrage followed.

Dylan's reasonably well-protected personal life was exposed on Don't Look Back and by year end he'd married his latest flame, Sara, much to the chagrin of Joan B, Warhol starlet Edie Sedgwick and a world of teeny Bobbers. Of course, Bob stayed aloof. His every opinion was gospel and, at a press conference in San Francisco, a young George Lucas attempted to get Dylan to talk about the "symbolism of the motorcycle in (his) poetry." Indeed, on both sides of the Atlantic, people were smitten with Bob. And the parents? Well, they were worried.

EXAMPLE ONE:
JENNY DE YOUNG and PETER ROCHE *Sheffield University Paper, representing the UK's view of Bob*

"I try to harmonise with songs the lonesome sparrow sings," sang Bob Dylan, alone on the stage at a packed City Hall last Friday: Dylan is himself sparrow-like - a thin, faded, ruffled sparrow - but one that sings to the tune of £2,000 per concert. His dark-circled eyes seemed to peer above the conglomeration surrounding him (two microphones, a table with two glasses of much-needed water and a harmonica cradle round his polo-sweatered neck), while his penetrating songs convinced even the most cynical that Bob Dylan is worthy of the mound of superlatives which has been heaped upon him and under which his earlier followers feared he might suffocate."

EXAMPLE THREE
JOSEPH HAAS,
Chicago Daily News, speaking for parents everywhere

"When the 24-year-old performer sings his original compositions, in his highly distinctive way, millions of young people listen—at concerts and on his best-selling long-playing albums and single recordings. Wise parents, who want to understand what the younger generation is thinking, would do well to listen to him, too. "

PATRICK HUMPHRIES

"The first time I heard him, I remember very clearly listening to pirate radio, probably Radio London and I heard 'Mr Tambourine Man' and I thought it was Donovan at first, before I realised it was Dylan. I couldn't believe the song, there was just something in it that was so emotional and it's remained my favourite song. It was the summer holidays in 1965, it was coming out of a tinny transistor radio and there was just the extraordinary world weariness that seemed incredibly sophisticated and other-worldly to the ears of a 12-year old. It's so immediate and you can even hear that it's done in one take as he reaches the end of the harmonica solo and catches his breath before carrying on. It's just a moment. A really vivid moment.

"Much, much later he did Tambourine Man' at Brixton and I just found myself standing at the back with all these other grey-haired gentlemen with beards just drying their eyes. It's just a very extraordinary and provocative piece of music."

Don't Look Back followed Dylan as he slam-dunked through the press, through ex-Animals keyboard player Alan Price, through Donovan and, sadly for Joan Baez, through Joan Baez. It was the end of the affair. The Queen of folk had gone on the tour expecting to guest but Bob had other ideas. Or just plain forgot.

The two drifted apart. Baez became seemingly obsessed with Dylan's songs, almost lingering in his moods and mind's eye after she couldn't have Bob himself. She recorded dozens of them over the following years, including a double album, 'Any Day Now' all of the royalties for which went straight to Bob's Woodstock retreat. She even wrote about him. 'To Bobby' from 'Come From the Shadows', 'Diamonds And Rust' from the album of the same name and 'Time Is Passing Us By' from 'Gulf Winds' all featured Dylan. And there was much more that never reached vinyl.

JOAN BAEZ

"Dylan I can never really talk about because unlike other people, about whom I think I have some kind of sense, I never understood him at all. Not a tweak."

EXAMPLE TWO:
NORA EPHRON AND SUSAN EDMINSTON *representing the USA's view of Bob*

"(For the interview) He was wearing a red-and-navy op-art shirt, a navy blazer and pointy high-heeled boots. His face, so sharp and harsh when translated through media, was then infinitely soft and delicate. His hair was not bushy or electric or Afro; it was fine-spun soft froth like the foam of a wave. He looked like an underfed angel.
Q: Where did you get that shirt?
A: California. Do you like it? You should see my others. You can't get clothes like that here.

PEOPLE WERE DEFINITELY LISTENING. But the knives were out. Especially in the kitchen of Les Claypool's house according to Paul J Robbins from the LA Free Press: "A local disc jockey, Les Claypool, went through a whole thing on Dylan one night, just couldn't get out of it. For maybe 45 minutes, he'd play a side of Dylan and then an ethnic side in which it was demonstrated that both melodies were the same. After each pair he'd say, "Well, you see what's happening ... This kid is taking other people's melodies; he's not all that original."

"**Embracing Dylan** was like marrying a monster from outer-space."

While Baez felt betrayed, the world was buying into Dylan's forthright messages of life and indeed love. Everyone was writing themselves into the lyrics and the power of his words became a new international language...

JOHNNY BLACK *journalist and broadcaster*
"I came to Bob Dylan very early for a Brit via my elder sister Suzie. We lived in Penicuik, outside Edinburgh. Suzie was just on the '60s end of being a beatnik, and I suppose I was a proto-mod evolving into a hippy.

"The first thing I remember was that she bought the EP with 'Corinna Corinna' and 'Blowin' In the Wind' and 'Don't Think Twice' on it, when it came out. It had a drawing of Dylan on the cover, I think. To someone who had grown up with Tommy Steele and Billy Fury as his idols, then replaced them with Beatles, Beach Boys and Stones, discovering and embracing Dylan was like marrying a monster from outer space. The voice, the sparseness, the words - it was all alien. I think Suzie had got to him first because her natural haunt was folk dens in Edinburgh.

"Anyway, the upshot of this was that when The Byrds did Tambourine Man, I was bristling with the horrified, disgusted, outraged heebie-jeebies that only a prattish, holier-than-thou sixteen year old can muster by this bastardisation of my idol's artistic vision. No wonder everybody at school avoided me. Actually, there were three of us in Penicuik High (or should that be in Penicuik, high) who 'got' Dylan, and we hated everybody else just as much as they hated us. They were incredibly stupid. We were insufferably right. They were buying Billy J Kramer, The Supremes (hell, my mother bought The Supremes) or some such and loving it. It took hearing 'Eight Miles High' coming out of a music shop on Leith Walk some time later before I realised that The Byrds were the finest musical aggreggation ever to have walked the planet (until I discovered the Velvets). I digress. And how long it took me to get to The Supremes, I can't imagine.

So it was that, somewhere in the mid-'60s, I found myself in a youth hostel in the Lake District, on my first real outing from Scotland. I'd gone camping with chums Dave Watterson and Ernie Whiteoak.

"There was a very pretty girl, Mama Michelle model, in the hostel. Only one. All us boys lusted after her. Late in the evening we were sitting round with acoustic guitars singing songs, and a chubby French lad was essaying 'She Belongs To Me'. When he reached the line "She's a hypnotist collector" he shot a knowing glance at her and then at me. Instant communication. Instant response - I sang the next line "You are a walking antique" with as much vitriol as I could muster, glaring back at him. Hell! Ain't no Johnny Onion coming over here and stealing our fair maidens. Direct hit. He was suitably deflated, and I felt wondrous smug. As it happened, the comely wench had not the vaguest interest in either of us, and who can blame her? "

JOHN LECKIE *seasoned producer*
"My favourite track has got to be 'She Belongs To Me' from either 'Live 1966' or 'Bringing It All Back Home'. The way it swings in on the

UK TOUR SELL-OUT FOR FOLK FAVOURiTE DYLAN

Announcements of British tour by Bob Dylan, acknowledged as the world's leading folk singer, have resulted in a rapid sell-out and the addition of extra dates to the original itinerary. Promoter Tito Burns announced: "Without a single poster having been printed, every ticket was sold for Dylan's concerts in Manchester on May 7 and the Albert Hall three nights later. His other appearances, at Liverpool, Leicester, Sheffield, Birmingham and Newcastle are almost sold out already. "I have to cable him this week to advise him that if he wants to avoid riots in London - and my blood being shed - he must do an extra date at the Albert Hall."
While in the UK, Dylan will film his own TV special, and Burns is currently deciding between offers from two of the four major ITV companies for its screening.
NME, March 1965

intro and the delivery of the first line is so confident. I know this girl she's singing about, she's every girl I've ever met and wanted to meet. The song is about the mystery of women or as singer/songwriter David Gray once told me, Dylan's singing about his "muse" on this one. I know the words off by heart."

Dylan's love songs were not only aching hearts, they were providing wordy social commentary that was stretching the understanding of teenage rites of passage. Even years later Bob's incisive lyrics were as cutting as the sharpest knife in the drawer.

ANDREA FALESI
"When I discovered Bob Dylan in 1977, I was 11. My sister, she's 13 years old than me, owned a little record shop in Sienna, the town where I live here in Italy. She loved Dylan since the 60s. I loved to listen to 'easy music' like Boney-M. I was never interested in adult music like Dylan, the Stones, or The Beatles.

"One beautiful day, my sister brought back home some defective LPs, to send back to the distributor. One of those records had a guy with a strange shirt and a motorbike on the cover. He had sunglasses in his hand and he looked at me in a strange way...

"That copy of 'Highway 61' had an off-centre hole and so it played with a lot of flutters. I fixed the problem with Scotch tape and I played it on my old not so hi-fisystem: The snare banged, a man started to sing words that I couldn't understand with a voice... such a voice... nothing was the same for me after that. "Anyway, the LP wasn't fixed completely, and I had thought for many years that the guitar on 'Queen Jane' was out of tune only on my copy. Eventually all the tracks on it went out of tune too. So, I began to buy all Dylan's LPs and I bought a book too: the Scaduto biography and it also changed my life.
"Now, after 22 years I have got hundreds of LPs, singles, CDs, books and magazines, sheet music, badges, stickers and everything else. I even have a serious problem storing it all in my house. And my collection grows everyday.

"I've seen Dylan in concert many times, but sadly I never met him. But I don't care so much, 'cause I built my own idea about him, and for me, it's enough to know him through his music."

Bringing It All Back Home

Tracks: Subterranean Homesick Blues, She Belongs To Me, Maggie's Farm, Love Minus Zero/No Limit, Outlaw Blues, On The Road Again, Bob Dylan's 115th Dream, Mr Tambourine Man, Gates Of Eden, It's Alright, Ma (I'm Only Bleeding), It's All Over Now, Baby Blue.
Released March (May in the UK).
Produced by Tom Wilson.

SLEEVE NOTES *More Bob beatnikery, with erotic hitchhikers wearing Japanese blankets, people claiming to be in The Supremes and Gertrude Stein and James Dean sharing column inches with Tolstoy, Bach and Mozart.*

WHAT THE WORLD SAYS JACKSON BROWNE, singer/songwriter *"'Bringing It All Back Home' is the one. It was that transcendental moment when he sang 'Gates Of Eden', 'Mr Tambourine Man', 'It's Alright Ma (I'm Only Bleeding)' - these really long, magnificently-crafted, literary songs. They were close to beat poetry - 'Maggie's Farm', 'Subterranean Homesick Blues' - but backed by a real cacophonous band made up of New York smoothies and Chicago blues guys like Mike Bloomfield and Harvey Brooks."*
WALTER BECKER, singer/songwriter, Steely Dan *"I'd read in Downbeat magazine various derogatory comments about Dylan, how he couldn't sing, couldn't write. I heard a song on a free-form FM station that could only be by him from the descriptions I'd read, it was pretty cool, so I went out the next day and bought 'Bringing It All Back Home'. I listened to it over and over until I knew all the words and I remember answering a question in my English Literature exam by writing the entire lyrics to 'Mr Tambourine Man'."*
MARTIN AMIS, rather successful novelist *"I was compared to him by one critic and I was pleased to see it. And I did plagiarise him in The Information; the lines "You get sick, you get well, you hang around the ink well." You know, that great sequence where he says, "Get born, stay warm, short pants, romance." 'Subterranean Homesick Blues'. Without a doubt, it's as good as anything Shakespeare ever wrote... the Seven Ages Of Man... He's a great poet."*
BILLY BRAGG, singer/songwriter, new folk luminary *"The record that changed my life was 'Mr Tambourine Man'. I first heard it in the listening booth in the basement of Guy Norriss's Record Shop in Station Hill, Barking. I suppose I must have been about 13 or 14 and I realised songs didn't just have to me verse/chorus/ I love you, all that sort of poppy stuff."*

IN A NUTSHELL *'Bringing It All Back Home' of course remains a masterpiece. From 'Subterranean Homesick Blues' which lasts an hour in your mind (2.23 on the album), to the collapsed laughter at the start of 'Bob Dylan's 115th Dream', the original 'Mr Tambourine Man' and the epic closer 'It's All Over Now, Baby Blue'. Bob's worldview goes slightly south of off-kilter and enters the disturbingly dreamlike. Every line has its own identity, each tells a story. The quips are breakneck fast - "I asked for some Suzette and I said could you please make that crepe" - like a thousand cartoon edits jotted next to diary notes and half forgotten travelogue. On its release in 1965 it must have been like inhaling laughing gas at the dentist, 32 years on it still retains that wild mercurial glow.*

KEN BROOKS, *author*
Taken from 'The Girl In The Leopard-Skin Pillbox Hat - Edie Sedgwick

"It was at the Kettle Of Fish restaurant that Edie first met Bob Dylan. Bob said after, to Bob Neuwirth that he 'had to meet this terrific girl.' He did and the threesome toured the clubs and restaurants of New York in late 1964.

"Edie was one of eight children who'd grown up in on an oil-bearing ranch before being

carved out a career as a sculptor which set her up for her meeting with Andy Warhol in January 1965. That clandestine union took place at Lester Persky's club in Manhattan, where she sported the legendary leopard-skin pillbox hat and Warhol became besotted.

"Ensconced in the Warhol Factory scene, she did photo shoots with Mick Jagger and developed her drug habit in the early days of The Velvet Underground with whom she'd

JONI MITCHELL: "'Positively Fourth Street' just stopped me in my tracks. I thought, 'Oh My God, we can write about anything now'."

occasionally sing. Warhol had begun his filming projects and John Cale recalls how 'Dylan came along and sat around for half a day while Andy filmed him'.

"Bob also viewed Edie from the periphery and wrote 'Just Like A Woman' about her.

"With her relationship with Warhol and her drug problems making working difficult, Edie signed with Dylan's manager Albert Grossman and efforts were made to find a film script for a Bob and Edie film.

"By now Bob was dating the unconventional Sedgwick and managed to outstrip her antics by marrying Sara Lowndes during the courtship.

"With Edie's depressive history rekindled, she sank into the seedier side of New York nightlife and, after a brief bout in rehab met up again with Bobby Neuwirth. The two became an item, Dylan was back on the scene and 'Leopard -skin Pillbox Hat' was penned to reflect the madness and loose times. Eventually the relationship with Neuwirth soured and she skipped onto a selection of art scene hopefuls before succumbing to a barbiturate overdose in November 1971.

ostracised by her father after she discovered him in the throes of advanced canoodling with a woman that wasn't her mother. Put on tranquillisers and sent to a mental institute by her father to cover his trail, the going was always going to be stormy.

"But, by the time she met Dylan, Edie had

Highway 61 Revisited

Tracks: Like A Rolling Stone, Tombstone Blues, It Takes A Lot To Laugh, It Takes A Train To Cry, From A Buick 6, Ballad Of A Thin Man, Queen Jane Approximately, Highway 61 Revisited, Just Like Tom Thumb's Blues, Desolation Row.
Released September 1965.
Produced by Bob Johnston.

SLEEVE NOTES *More riotous flow of tide thinkage from Bob, with a keen William Burroughs- styled wave to Andy Warhol and the WIPE-OUT GANG at the Insanity Factory, various beautiful strangers, Vivaldi's green jackets, the Cream Judge and the clown, Savage Rose and even quazimodo. The company he kept!*

WHAT THE PAPERS SAID
'Like A Rolling Stone' was voted 19th best single of all time by the readers of Q magazine in January 1999. Q summed up the best bit thus: "(0.56) the snare drum and tambourine-battering build-up to the first howl of "How does it feel?"

WHAT DYLAN SAID *"I'd quit singing and playing, and I found myself writing this story, this long piece of vomit, about 20 pages long."*

WHAT THE WORLD SAYS JOHN MELLENCAMP, singer/songwriter, painter and performer *"To this day I'd say that it's the best record ever made. It combined folk and rock, you could dance to it, but the lyrics were listenable and had a kind of intelligence that was lacking in pop music. In an era when hit songs were less than two minutes, his were six minutes plus. He broke all the rules and crossed all the boundaries. When I realised that I wanted to do music, it became my standard of excellence."*
PHIL OCHS, singer-songwriter and Greenwich contemporary *"When I put it on I laughed. It's ridiculously good. It can't be that good. I walked away and didn't listen to it again right away because I thought this was too much. How can a human mind do this?"*

IN A NUTSHELL *The second groundbreaking album in one year? And, opening with the everlasting 'Like A Rolling Stone' before the adrenalin-motormouth tirade 'Tombstone Blues', with its cast of characters fresh from any art house freakshow. With Mike Bloomfield's stinging guitar and plenty of keyboards to add a hokey '20s feel, the album wanders into saloon after saloon to check how the participants are coping with the night. In the aftermath, Bob flees town via 'Desolation Row', struggling with theories, religion, life, a hangover for the times. It's a startling piece, as graphic as any film the Coen brothers have released. The simple, emotive guitar plays variations on a tiny scale, leaving the vocal line plenty of room to take the melody, wilfully taking the album miles from the urban squalor where it began.*

SINGLES/EPS/ETC *The Times They Are A-Changin' (45) Subterranean Homesick Blues (45) Maggie's Farm (45) Like A Rolling Stone (45) Positively 4th Street (45) Can You Please Crawl Out Your Window (45) It Takes A Lot To Laugh (EP) Subterranean Homesick Blues (EP) Dylan (EP) Like A Rolling Stone (EP European) Positively 4th Street (EP)*

1966

Stuck Inside Of Mobile

CONDUCTED AT hyperspeed, life was, well, rampant. (Chew, chew.) Dylan's marriage had to compete with a panoramic world tour, a second film project which he wanted to direct himself and the recording of a double album with a completely different set of musicians. Easy wasn't an option. 'Blonde On Blonde' was created in Nashville with seasoned pro's, before Bob took the Hawks to Australia (controversial) and Europe (controversial 2).

Pennebaker was back behind the camera, someone in Manchester shouted 'Judas' and The Beatles and the Stones came along to the Royal Albert Hall performance. Bob was under the influence of too much life and his obscure and obtuse press conferences added to the boo boys' venom before the tour finally wound down. Home in Woodstock, Bob celebrated by falling off his

Plugging in: Dylan at the "Royal Albert Hall" concert in May 1966

ANOTHER SIDE OF BOB DYLAN
RARE 1966 CONCERT DOCUMENTARY HITS THEATERS FOR THE FIRST TIME

BOB DYLAN IS NOT A MAN WHO IS EASILY EMBARRASSED. "EAT THE DOCUMENT," A LONG-BURIED film about his 1966 tour of England, is finally seeing the light of day – and it brings new meaning to the term "warts and all." Director D.A. Pennebaker made *Eat the Document* as a follow-up to his acclaimed Dylan study *Dont Look Back*. *Document* was originally intended for – but then rejected by – ABC-TV. Later, Pennebaker's version was re-edited by Dylan and cameraman Howard Alk; only now is it getting a limited theatrical release. Pennebaker followed Dylan on his second European tour with the Hawks (who would soon become the Band), filming them onstage and off in a jittery, hand-held *cinéma vérité* style. Like Dylan's music at the time, the resulting *Document* is raw and restless, revealing and riveting.

Plugging into an electric guitar pushed Bob Dylan to a musical peak; it also created a huge controversy among his reverent folkie followers. Throughout *Eat the Document*, Dylan is defiant, almost reveling in the taunts and catcalls from the audience. A succession of fans castigate the former folkie as a

bike, damaging his neck and entering a lengthy period of convalescence during which he managed not to complete any of his scheduled projects and fell out with Grossman. Good man.

People were not very happy with Bob during 1966. First of all there was Bill Diehl, columnist for the St. Paul Evening Dispatch. Diehl wrote, "He (Dylan) is... bitter or extremely conceited. (During the set) the audience started to whistle between the long delayed selections. Dylan said into the mike, 'I'm just as anxious to go home as you are. Don't you have any newspapers to read?'"

Then there was the press conference in Melbourne, Australia. (Read copy as Robert Downey Jnr character in Natural Born Killers.)

"Beneath his mop of shaggy hair, Dylan,

the acclaimed 'king of folk music', rocked backwards and forwards on his feet as if feeling faint from the onslaught. His voice was barely audible. Some of the queries he threw back at the questioners, others he shrugged off as if they weren't worth the physical effort of answering, and for a few he wove long answers of fairyland fancy from the beat world - nonsensical, but sharply amusing."

In Australia, according to Anthony Scaduto's biography, an un-named actress was certainly touched by the hand of Bob...

"I came to believe that Dylan was Christ revisited. I felt that everything fitted, without being Christian-religious or anything, I felt that what he had to say about living and communication with people was the truest, most honest and most Christ-like thing I've ever heard."

The the whole shebang swiftly moved on to Europe. First stop Sweden and Klas Burling, a Swedish DJ.

"I had a terrible time with Dylan." he told Mojo magazine. "He was very unresponsive. He wasn't really interested."

"What would you call yourself, a poet or a singer, or do you think that you write poems and then you put music to it?"
Dylan: "No ... I don't know ... It's so silly! I mean you can't ... You wouldn't ask those questions of a carpenter, would you? Or a plumber?

"What do you think Mozart would say to you if you ever come up to him and ask him the questions that you've been asking? What kind of questions would you ask him, you know, 'Tell me, Mr Mozart ...'."

Then it was Copenhagen, where NME correspondent Sven Wezelenburg tried his best.

Sven: "Why did you laugh at the start of 'Bob Dylan's 115th Dream'?"
Dylan: "I don't remember ... well, wait a bit ... yeah ... somebody entered the studio disguised and looking like my mother. Yes, that was it. I just started laughing."

In London, the conversation wandered further afield, according to the NME's Keith Altham who was skulking at the back.

"Bob, your hair has got me worried", said one lady reporter, "How do you get it like that?"

"I comb it like that."

BRIAN MITCHELL
Gig departee, Cambridge

"Who were these people who walked out of Dylan's 1966 tour? Let me step forward from the guilty shadows. How did I end up in the pub next door to the Bristol Colston Hall? Walking out seemed like a powerful act of defiance. Years of shame have followed of course."

(1966)

Blonde On Blonde

Tracks: Rainy Day Women Nos. 12 & 35, Pledging My Time, Visions Of Johanna, One Of Us Must Know (Sooner Or Later), I Want You, Stuck Inside Of Mobile With The Memphis Blues Again, Leopard-Skin Pillbox Hat, Just Like A Woman, Most Likely You'll Go Your Way And I'll Go Mine, Temporary Like Achilles, Absolutely Sweet Marie, 4th Time Around, Obviously 5 Believers, Sad Eyes Lady Of The Lowlands.
Released June (August in the UK).
Produced by Bob Johnston.

SLEEVE NOTES *There aren't any, just lots of pictures. However, Q's 'Sleevenotes' series, which focused on the classic albums of our time produced their own insert which included a quote from Al Kooper who played the keyboards on the sessions: "The amazing thing about cutting that album was the first-hand knowledge that we were making history."*

WHAT THE PAPERS SAID *"(This 1966 album) represents an artist at the peak of his powers."* Martin Aston, Q 1995 on its re-issue.

WHAT DYLAN SAID *"At the time of 'Blonde On Blonde' I was going at a tremendous speed."*

WHAT THE WORLD SAYS
MARK KNOPFLER *"I was hugely influenced by him at the age of 14. Going round to girls' houses, drinking coffee, smoking cigarettes and listening to 'Blonde On Blonde'."*

BOB DYLAN *Blonde On Blonde*

JASON RINGENBERG, Jason And The Scorchers
"My sister went off to college an innocent little farm girl and she came back in a mini skirt with beads and a copy of 'Blonde On Blonde' under her arm. When I heard that, I couldn't believe anything could be that good."
HOWARD MARKS, writer *"My favourite album of all time is 'Blonde On Blonde'."*
LOUDON WAINWRIGHT *"I was attending drama school. I just have an image of my friend George and I hunched near some speakers, under the influence of SOME substance, and trying to figure out what Bob was saying, particularly one sentence "the country music station plays... soft" or is it "Sartre?". But we kept going back and forth, because we couldn't figure out which... "No, man, it's 'soft'"... "No, man, it isn't, it's 'Sartre', what's the matter with you? Listen to it again." George and I never tried to come up with 'What is the song about?' We revelled in its mystery, really. This album has a real speedy feel to it, it has a cocaine feel to it, to be honest. It feels that kind of brittle... it's not flowers and strawberry fields, yellow submarines, and diamonds in the sky - it's gritty, dirty streets and being 'up for five days'.* ➤

CP LEE author of Like The Night

"The anticipation was so high because the press had been debating the electric issue in advance (of the show at the Manchester Free Trade Hall). His acoustic set was politely applauded, then he came back out with The Hawks and the sound was huge, like a jumbo jet taking off. As we left the hall, people were arguing and scuffles were breaking out. That's how radical it was."

ANDY KERSHAW broadcaster

"If I had to pick just one track, it would have to be 'Like A Rolling Stone' from the Manchester Free Trade Hall gig in 1966. Why did anybody think there was any point in making rock 'n' roll after that?"

THE DAILY TELEGRAPH

"Bob Dylan is beginning to show signs of a man who doesn't care if he communicates or not."

The tour was nothing if not controversial. People stamped their feet. They threw tantrums. They slow-handclapped. They tutted very loudly. And a lot of them just walked out. From Manchester, the tour moved onto France.

Le Figaro: **"BOB DYLAN SHOULD STOP SINGING ALTOGETHER... OR STOP TAKING BARBITUARTES."**

And Paris Jour: **"BOB DYLAN: GO HOME."**

The tour closed at the Royal Albert Hall in London, in front of The Beatles and chums, as annotated by Mark Lewisohn in The Complete Beatles Chronicles. "John and George attended Bob Dylan's legendary "electric" appearance at the Royal Albert Hall, cheering as the crowd jeered the folk turncoat. Earlier in the day Dylan and John Lennon were filmed in the back of a chauffeured limousine, driving to central London from John's house in Surrey. Without a script and with no apparent direction, the two muttered a lot of 'stoned' gibberish before Dylan announced he was about to puke."

JOHN LENNON

"Whenever we used to meet it was always under the most nerve-wracking circumstances. And I know I was always uptight, and I know Bobby was. I'd always be too paranoid or too aggressive, or vice versa."

Back in America, well, nothing happened. Until it did. And, Joan said she saw it coming: "I always pictured Bobby with a skull and crossbones on his forehead. I guess it's because I've seen him be destructive to himself and other people." And, after the accident things got stranger still. Enter Tiny Tim. He came down to one of my shows just after his motorcycle accident. We talked about the Greenwich Village days when we were both on the circuit and I said, 'Mr Dylan, you are today what Rudy Vallee was to the people back in 1929'."

MYSTERY OF THE MISSING BOB DYLAN

A mystery is deepening over the whereabouts and condition of Bob Dylan, who is now three months into a complete disappearance. In August he reportedly had and accident on his motorbike, sustaining broken neck vertebrae and concussion, and it was said that a couple of months' convalescence would be necessary before he could resume his normal engagements. However, Dylan did not simply retreat home to nurse his injuries, but dropped out of sight completely, Many of his closest friends do not know where he is, or how badly he is hurt.

Such a total absence of news, over such a lengthy period, is now leading to widespread speculation that his accident - and the injuries - were far worse than originally suggested, and that his career is over. His manager Albert Grossman dismisses such suggestions as nonsense, but can give no definite news of Dylan, or when he is likely to re-emerge.

To further fuel these rumours, the publication of Dylan's book Tarantula, previously scheduled for this autumn, has been postponed indefinitely, while a TV special originally slated for mid-November is now cancelled.

It is believed that only two people have known Dylan's whereabouts since the accident, the determinedly silent Grossman, and the singer's close friend Allen Ginsberg. In mid-October, the World Journal Tribune tracked down a hideaway where Dylan had been staying - a rambling old house miles off the beaten track on the Cape Cod peninsula in Massachusetts.

The paper challenged Ginsberg with this information, and he admitted visiting Dylan there and taking him some reading material. However, when a Tribune reporter called at the house, nobody was prepared to say whether or not Dylan was still in residence. Until this cloak-and-dagger behaviour ends, just what has happened to Dylan will remain a mystery.

NME, November 1966

"Bob Dylan is beginning to show signs of a man who doesn't care if he communicates or not."

1967

Down Along The Cove

COCOONED IN Woodstock with Sara and a slowly growing set of children, Bob spent his time avoiding the outside world. An attempted law suit to stop the publication of Daniel Kramer's book of photographs failed and Bob spent his waking hours writing songs with The Hawks who'd moved up to nearby West Saugerties in a house they imaginatively called Big Pink. It was big and pink.

The daily routine included lengthy writing sessions, followed by recording marathons in the basement of The Hawks' house. Mountains of ferric rolled out and were eventually bootlegged as 'The Basment Tapes', a watershed which led Bob to a new kind of storytelling and delivery for the cleaner-cut, Nashville-recorded 'John Wesley Harding'.

With little or no public profile you might have suspected that shares were low in Dylanco, but the radio was resounding to Bob's 'Greatest Hits' and a jumble sale of cover versions were acting as support. Ensconced in Woodstock the songs began to flow. In fact, Bob's only public appearance was on the sleeve of Sergeant Peppers where he filled the top right hand corner next to avant garde sculptor Simon Rodia and just behind Sir Paramhansa Yogananda. And the tapes? Well, previously unknown songs by Dylan, The Band and a couple by Tiny Tim were mothballed by the label and only snook out illegally or through friends of friends.

RICHARD THOMPSON

"We were lucky to fall in with Joe Boyd in the early days of Fairport Convention, he'd been the stage manager at Newport when Dylan went electric and had recorded the Paul

John Wesley Harding

Tracks: John Wesley Harding, As I Went Out One Morning, I Dreamed I Saw St Augustine, All Along The Watchtower, The Ballad Of Frankie Lee And Judas Priest, Drifter's Escape, Dear Landlord, I Am A Lonesome Hobo, I Pity The Poor Immigrant, The Wicked Messenger, Down Along The Cove, I'll Be Your Baby Tonight.
Released December (January UK). Produced by Bob Johnston.

SLEEVE NOTES *Featuring a bizarre story involving three kings, Terry Shute - the alleged theses writer, whose diatribes about the beard as part of Dylan's life have been cast on the .net and included in various books (see main text), and Frank, during which the narrator claims that Dylan's new album doesn't contain any songs written by Dylan. Obviously.*

WHAT THE PAPERS SAID *"This is Dylan's quietest, most modest album in years. It's an outlaw tale, like Woody Guthrie's 'Pretty Boy Floyd', filled with the acceptance of the bizarre - 'I Dreamed I Saw St Augustine' and 'All Along The Watchtower' for instance. It's an intensely religious record, one that owes almost as much to country music as it does to rock." Rolling Stone*

WHAT THE INTERNET SAYS *"I've had trouble getting into this, but some of the material is strong: the rambling 'Ballad Of Frankie Lee And Judas Priest'; the gently rocking 'WickedMessenger'; the straight-up country number 'I'll Be Your Baby Tonight' (complete with steel guitar, courtesy of Nashville legend Pete Drake); and, of course, 'All Along The Watchtower'." JA, Wilson - Alroy Record Reviews*

WHAT DYLAN SAID *"I could have sung all of it better. I'm not bragging I just don't think that I did it justice."*

WHAT THE WORLD SAYS ANTHONY SCADUTO *"'John Wesley Harding' is infused with a belief in God, with self-discovery and compassion. It is Dylan's version of The Bible, songs written as parables describing the fall and rebirth of one man - Bob Dylan."*

IN A NUTSHELL *'John Wesley Harding' catches Dylan, hobo-like at another crossroads. Like a story told in black and white, mixing legend and tradition wit almost vaudevillian wordplay. Bob, back from the accident, has a different voice. A different tune. The harmonica is fluid, like a waterfall, it seems to avoid notes and present a wash of sound when needed, while Bob has adenoid considerations to think about. The hoarse delivery makes the songs more rounded, like a circus barker's schtick, pronounced and to a set formula that follows the storylines. The result is a less definable, unique sound, very different from the psychedelically-enhanced flash frames of before, almost like it rained during the whole recording and the deluge is contained within.*

SINGLES/EPS/ETC *Leopard Skin Pill-Box Hat (45) If You Gotta Go Go Now (45) John Wesley Harding (45) All Along The Watchtower (45)*

Butterfield Blues Band, so he seemed the right man for the job. He had a lot of sound input and turned us on to a lot of music that we would later cover. He actually knew Joni Mitchell and Phil Ochs, that connection was important to us.
"At that time, we took pride in finding obscure imports of Jim And Jean, Phil Ochs, or obscure Dylan material - we had stuff from his publisher that no-one else had at that time, which eventually became 'The Basement Tapes'."
The Fairports' 'Unhalfbricking' in 1968 and included three Dylan covers, one of which was a French translation of 'If You Gotta Go, Go Now', titled 'Si Tu Dois Partir', which became a hit for the group.

Other British groups also had huge success with their covers of Bob tunes, unreleased or otherwise. In fact, Manredd Mann were elevated from R&B shouters to cultured unilateral storytellers.

MANFRED MANN
"The whole thing with Dylan is really a big myth. None of us have ever met him. It's just a business thing where his publisher sent a tape to us."

Meanwhile, the film of Bob Dylan's 1965 UK tour, Don't Look Back was premiered in San Francisco. Dylan subsequently denounced the film and filed a court injunction to prevent it being shown. It immediately became legendary, mysterious and unshown. (The film was finally released on video in the UK in the Autumn of 1988.)

JAN STACY *from Rockin' Reels*
"This vehicle was important because it was different, almost hostile to the audience. Dylan's look and demeanour were totally different from previous rock stars. This was art meets rock 'n' roll"

DA PENNEBAKER, *Don't Look Back director*
"I was never interested in educating people about Bob Dylan. I don't know enough about

him. Who does? Don't Look Back is about the Sixties, and the man who got us through them."

The cast and contributors were all put through Bob's own kind of ironic casting during the shooting. The mayoress: "He was a very nice boy, he wrote me a lovely letter." No-one seemed to know what was true and what was not. Paranoia reigned. Irony came a close second.

JOAN BAEZ
"I should never have gone on that tour. I don't know what had happened in Bobby's mind and he wouldn't ask me onto the stage to sing. I was very, very hurt. I was miserable. I was a complete ass. I should have left after the first concert."

TERRY ELLIS, *student newspaper journalist*
"I wasn't meant to interview Dylan. I didn't have a ticket and I told the man on the door, 'I've come to interview Dylan' and he just let me in. Then I got ushered into Dylan by his roadie, like a lamb to the slaughter. In retrospect, I don't think he was being cruel to me, he was being quite pleasant. I must admit, I do squirm if I see the film now."

Bob Dylan Greatest Hits
UK version. Tracks: Rainy Day Women #12 & 35, Blowin' In The Wind, The Times They Are A-Changin', It Ain't Me Babe, Like A Rolling Stone, Mr Tambourine Man, Subterranean Homesick Blues, I Want You, Positively 4th Street, Just Like A Woman.
Released January UK (December 66 US, with different tracks)
US version, issued in 1998 in the UK at Nice Price.

Tracks: Blowin' in the Wind, It Ain't Me Babe, The Times They Are A-Changin', Mr Tambourine Man, She Belongs To Me, It's All Over Now, Baby Blue, Subterranean Homesick Blues, One Of Us Must Know, Like A Rolling Stone, Rainy Day Women #12 & 35, I Want You.

1968

All Along The Watchtower

THE PACE slowed. With 'John Wesley Harding' completed, Bob returned to Woodstock to continue sporadic Hawking and professional married life. In the wake of The Beatles' 'Seargeant Pepper' the world began to read things into 'John Wesley Harding'. It's religious. The Beatles are secreted in the sleeve. It's Pepper for America. It's Bob's personal journey out of/or into bondage.

DENNIS J GREEN *via the internet*
"'Sgt Pepper's Lonely Hearts Club Band' was released at the end of June, 1967. It was the background music for the Summer of Love. 'John Wesley Harding', was released six months later, the end of December, 1967 and WAS VERY MUCH Dylan's answer / response to 'Sgt Pepper'. Dylan used 'Sgt Pepper' as a paradigm for 'John Wesley Harding' which has been overlooked / not realised by many Dylan fans over the years.

"To explain, first the album's concept. In 'Sgt Pepper', The Beatles are transformed into a Victorian era, uniformed, bandstand musicians. (See the animated movie Yellow Submarine for more). The album is a concert show put on by these very British entertainers.

"In 'John Wesley Harding', Dylan transforms himself into an American stereotype: a Western frontiersman, preacher, itinerate type of fellow (usually alcoholic) which could be seen played occasionally by a guest character actor on the many TV westerns of the '50s and '60s.

"Dylan's 'John Wesley Harding' had a G added to him; G = GOD. Indeed John Wesley HardinG lives up to his Christian name: John Wesley was a devout British clergyman who founded the Methodist branch of protestantism. However, Dylan's 'John Wesley Harding' is only almost God: his

initials, J W H are only 3 of the Tetragrammaton (JHWH); out of fear / respect, Jews would not write God's name, Jehov(w)ah out fully. The concept and songs of 'John Wesley Harding' is the American gospel of Bob Dylan (not God) as told by John Wesley Harding."

PATRICK HUMPHRIES
"I remember listening to John Peel the first time he played 'John Wesley Harding' and it was just so different. Before the crash he'd been playing these long 12-minute epics and the he came back and sounded like Johnny Cash."

His only public appearance took place at the end of January when he played at the Woody Guthrie Memorial Concert - Guthrie had finally succumbed to illness in 1967. Dylan played with the newly-named Band at his first live show since his accident,

sporting shorn locks and powered by a handful of Guthrie songs.

'John Wesley Harding' reached number one in the UK as Dylan continued his country-flavoured muse, recording 'Lay Lady Lay' which was intended to be included in the John Voight and Dustin Hoffman film Midnight Cowboy. But, the song was completed too late for inclusion.

CHRIS BINDING *Bobfan*

"My problem was I couldn't afford Bob Dylan - and perhaps in some ways that added to the attraction. His career was well under way in the wealthier world when I heard my first batch of Dylan songs at a school party in 1966. I was 14 and ready to accept a hero into my life. Dylan filled that void perfectly. I loved the way adults hated him. I loved the way he sang - such arrogance, such confident bitterness. The words sometimes made me shiver.

"But records were way out of my

reach and anyway, I didn't have a record player. I couldn't ask my parents for pocket money because they simply didn't have it. I had to have a plan and over the next couple of years one came to me. Almost naturally.

"Then, one day, my father handed me a tape recorder. I think someone was throwing it away and he salvaged it. It was a monstrous thing, all teak

veneer and silver knobs. But it worked.

"And then I did a terrible thing. For Bob, of course.

"There was, in my school year, A Boy Who Had Everything - everything, including all the Dylan albums, all in pristine condition with shiny covers, protected by those plastic sleeves you could buy in Boots. He had them because he was rolling in money, not because he liked Dylan.

"You know the sort, smart-assed bastard. Dylan could have written a great song about him.

"Yes, I hated his guts - but, to my eternal shame, I pretended to be his friend in order to get at his record collection. The deception makes me feel ill even now, 30 years later.

"So, I loaded my monstrous, second-hand embarrassing tape recorder into a big bag and cycled the six miles to his massive luxury house and set it up in his disgustingly huge and ridiculously well-equipped bedroom to tape everything I could get my hands on.

"He had a fabulous hi-fi, but of course, my steam-driven tape machine wouldn't connect up to it. So the recordings were done by propping a microphone against one of his huge, pulsating speakers. Then I'd cycle home again, simultaneously happy and thoroughly ashamed of myself. The friendship lasted until the last track of the last LP.

"Bob Dylan, you could say, twisted my honesty a little, but I recovered. And anyway, I was older then. I'm younger than that now."

1969

One More Night

SPRINGTIME FOR Bob saw him back in the studio fertilising his country roots and Ol Opry upbringing on 'Nashville Skyline'. The album included the finally completed 'Lay Lady Lay', alongside some aching ballads and a rag workout. Even though he'd failed to get 'Lay Lady Lay' finished for Midnight Cowboy, Dylan was asked to provide the whole soundtrack for the impending Peter Fonda, Dennis Hopper and Jack Nicholson cult epic Easy Rider. Bob was keen, but his insistence on script changes stalled the project and even his song, 'It's All Right Ma' was delivered by Roger McGuinn on the soundtrack.

Back at the 'Skyline' sessions, Bob performed a series of duets with Johnny Cash, one of which was a return to 'Girl From The North Country'. Cash had been a close ally since Dylan first joined Columbia and laid down over a dozen songs with Dylan during the recording of 'Nashville Skyline', which have been roundly bootlegged over the years.

And, remaining in the illegal department, the very first rock bootleg saw the light of day as 'The Great White Wonder'. It featured tracks from Bob and The Band's 'Basement Tapes', plus some medieval acoustic cuts from the early '60s. To curb this exploitation, Bob set about compiling 'Self Portrait', an album of out-takes, oddities and covers. In mid-compile, he was persuaded to play at The Isle Of Wight Festival in Britain over August Bank Holiday weekend. Depending on which reports you believe, an estimated 200,000 (or 250,000, receipts weren't fully disclosed) attended. Whatever the number, the island didn't sink.

BRENT HANSEN *President MTV Europe*
"My favourite Dylan track of all time is 'Girl From The North Country', with Johnny Cash duetting with Dylan. I really love 'Nashville Skyline' and its crossoverness, if that's a word. That signifies the tip of an iceberg and a direction that he could have taken."

Nashville Skyline

Tracks: Girl From The North Country, Nashville Skyline Rag, To Be Alone With You, I Threw It All Away, Peggy Day, Lay Lady Lay, One More Night, Tell Me That It Isn't True, Country Pie, Tonight I'll Be Staying Here With You.

Released May (November 1970 UK). Produced by Bob Johnston.

SLEEVE NOTES Johnny Cash writes of Bob: *"This man can rhyme the tick of time, The edge of pain, the what of sane, And comprehend the good in men, the bad in men."*

WHAT THE PAPER'S SAID *"Dylan opted to mix throwaway country jaunts with some masterful crooning on subdued erotic ballads like 'Lay Lady Lay' and 'I Threw It All Away'. The lyrics are often banal, sometimes sublimely so, but the duet with Johnny Cash on 'Girl From The North Country' and Dylan's celebration of love as one who's tried to do without it, remain masterfully evocative."* Mark Cooper, Q on its 1988 re-issue.

WHAT DYLAN SAID *"These are the type of songs that I always felt like writing when I've been left alone to do so. The songs reflect more of the inner me than the songs of the past."*

WHAT THE WORLD SAYS DAVID BLUE, Greenwich singer/songwriter, melancholy meanderer *"Nashville Skyline took him to where he wanted to be, sitting with his wife and kids in the country."*
ERIC ANDERSON, another Greenwich Village contemporary *"He said he'd learned to sing for the first time in his life. He knew something about music, about how to sing and play, and he was proud of it."*
GRAM PARSONS, the grandpappy of alternative country *"I knew Dylan was going to get around to it (country music) sooner or later. Cause I mean, nobody loves Dylan more than I do. I love his sense of humour. The guy is a great writer, I wish that he could do the country thing better but he just can't."*
MADONNA (Doh!) *"I used to listen to that one record, 'Lay Lady Lay', in my brother's bedroom in the basement of our house. I'd lie on the bed and play the song and cry all the time."*
KRISTI, via internet *"The first time I heard Bob Dylan, I was riding in the car with my mom. I must have been about 5 or 6 and the song was 'Lay Lady Lay'. It was a pretty heavy song for a six-year-old, but I loved his voice."*
ELVIS COSTELLO *"'Nashville Skyline' is so overlooked. He's technically miles better than other pop writers. This uses stock images, like 'The Twelfth Of Never', but the sentiments are so lovely."*

IN A NUTSHELL *After toying with Nashville since 'Blonde On Blonde', it was only a matter of time before the high lonesome sound of Dylan's youth turned him onto a more mellow country sound. Relaxed in his private life, the voice was now tempered and the opening duet with Johnny Cash, as they revisit the classic 'Girl From The Country', opens the back porch to some old time balladeering. 'NashvilleSkyline' contains heartfelt ballads, songs of lost love and a yearning for a more genteel existence. Painting on such an epic scale and plain talking, Bob's soul is allowed to shine through on the churchy 'I Threw It All Away', the epic 'Lay Lady Lay', 'Tell Me That It* ➤

TOM PAYNE *IT Manager and pr-Bob virgin*

"I lost my virginity while listening to 'Nashville Skyline' (was that the album with 'Lay Lady Lay' on it? no pun intended - entirely coincidental). I kept my shoes on for a fast getaway as her light-sleeping grandparents occupied the next room. It was not a huge success but then I suppose the first time rarely is."

Perhaps the strangest event of the year was Dylan's appearance at the Isle Of Wight festival. With Bob in virtual live retirement, a group of would-be festival promoters on the island thought of who they'd most like to play and, well, just gave it a go.

VIC KING *Isle Of Wight rock fan*

"The concert was set up by the Faulks brothers who had put on an event in 1968 to raise money for a swimming pool and managed to bring in £10,000. They were sitting around in the pub and they were thinking who the most exciting person would be to get to a festival on the Isle Of Wight, someone who would bring in lots of people and money.

"Dylan hadn't been doing anything for some time and they figured that he would attract lots of people. So they made a video of the island and went to New York to show him. They persuaded him to come on the premise that he'd be able to get away from everything and have a holiday and they showed him pictures of a farmhouse they would put him up in. It seems like it was as simple as that.

"Dylan decided he wanted to do it which, when you think about t, was the strangest thing as it was about two weeks after the Woodstock Festival and that was virtually in his back garden."

JOHN MANNING, *fan, Suffolk*

"The first time I saw him was at the notorious 'Now you see him, now you don't' Isle Of Wight Festival. I got stoned with Lord Montague of Beaulieu and his entourage, only because they happened to be pitched in the arena right next to us. They had loads of food, booze, spliffs and they were mega generous with me and my two mates. So, really, my recollection of events is a tad hazy. But, I do remember Dylan's 'lemon' suit and his brief appearance was great. And there was lots of

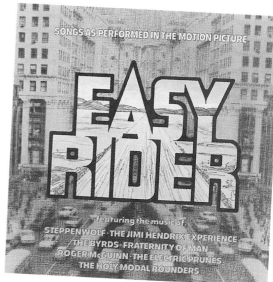

discontent and sacrificial bonfires when he left sooner than everyone expected."

PHILIP TALBOT *Theatrical director*

"It was the summer of '69, well, the autumn actually, but that doesn't quite have the same resonance. expelled from Great Yarmouth Grammar School For Boys, for daring to write a poem on an 'A' Level Maths paper, I was banished to the College Of Further Education with the rough boys.

"Being a radical poet, my first task on day one was to join the Student Union which occupied a large wooden shed at the far end of the playing fields. Having knocked on the door

DYLAN RECORDING WiTH CASH

Bob Dylan has completed the sessions for his next album in Nashville, using the same trio (Charlie McCoy, Pete Drake and Kenny Buttrey) who played with him 18 months ago on 'John Wesley Harding', plus three further session men. An unexpected development at the sessions was a series of duets with country star Johnny Cash - according to reports, the two of them 'just went into the studio and jammed', producing some 15 tracks. Some of these may make it on to the new LP, but there is speculation that whole album of Dylan-Cash duets may now follow later.
NME, March 1969

and been ignored, I went in anyway, and witnessed a primitive form of election in progress.

"The room fell silent.

"Where are you from?" I was asked and after telling them of my recent departure from higher, all-boys education, they decided that I must be a) brainy and b) perfect for the position of Vice President. What did I have to lose? Indeed, what did I have to do? Whatever, I was accepted and a hippy with formidably long red hair then proceeded to set up the Dansette and crash a wholesome slab of vinyl onto the turntable. This was hardly Grammar School behaviour but everyone seemed to be for it. And, as the first strains of Bob Dylan's 'Highway 61 Revisited' filled the room, this didn't seem like a bad place after all.

"By now I was corralled with the President, whose first strategic question was "Do you smoke?". Amid the Bob blare, I didn't want to offend and as he passed me what I could only presume was 'a joint', I replied, 'Well, I could try'.

"As the aroma filled the room, I pondered on this new form of education and, as I tugged deep into my lungs before returning the depleted stogie, I suddenly became aware of one other subtle change in my new scholastic arrangements. The room was filled with young women, something I'd not been in this close a proximity to since Junior School.

"As Dylan rambled on and enthused 'How does it feel?', I thought, 'Yeah, it feels pretty good, actually, Mr Dylan. Thanks for asking'."

"Yeah, it feels pretty good, actually, **Mr Dylan**, thanks for asking..."

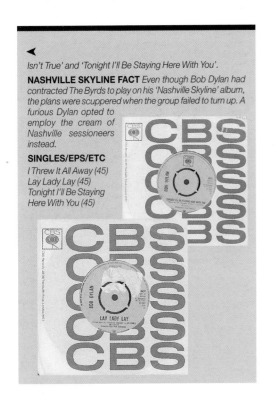

Isn't True' and 'Tonight I'll Be Staying Here With You'.

NASHVILLE SKYLINE FACT *Even though Bob Dylan had contracted The Byrds to play on his 'Nashville Skyline' album, the plans were scuppered when the group failed to turn up. A furious Dylan opted to employ the cream of Nashville sessioneers instead.*

SINGLES/EPS/ETC

I Threw It All Away (45)
Lay Lady Lay (45)
Tonight I'll Be Staying Here With You (45)

AND THAT WAS THE SIXTIES...

BY THE TIME THE '60S stuttered to a close, Bob Dylan had changed the face of music and youth culture. Not bad for a decade's work. He'd been around the world a few times, introduced a new generation of people to Woody Guthrie, marched on Washington, turned electric, sacked his manager, renegotiated his contract, moved to the country, invented country rock (sorta), survived a bike smash and several months in a basement with bearded men from The Band, written a book, starred in a film and summed up 'Attitude' with some seriously ironic press calls. Bob had become a role model and he'd brought his heroes, Cummings, Ferlinghetti, Ginsberg, Hank Williams, Ezra Pound, Camus, TS Eliot and Big Bill Broonzy along for the ride.

He'd produced monumental recordings. From the political clout of 'Blowin' In The Wind' and 'The Times They Are A-Changin', to the surreal travelogue of 'Subterranean Homesick Blues' and the evocative 'Like A Rolling Stone'. He'd done drugs, 'Rainy Day Women Nos 12 & 35', sex, 'Lay Lady Lay' and, of course, rock 'n' roll. Unfortunately, living in Carlisle,

a northern town devoid of industry and impenetrable to Radio 1, most of it had passed me by completely.

Me? I'd been at home. The Sixties for me were highlighted by England winning the World Cup in 1966. My parents had bought a small red leatherette record player from the Reader's Digest and their initial World Music Club selection of Nelson Riddle, Art Tatum and Stan Kenton, were quickly joined by Cliff Richards' 'Summer Holiday', The Beatles' 'I Want To Hold Your Hand' and albums by Jack and Tom Jones (no relation). All music seemed to sound like that and Radio 2's Sing Something Simple on a Sunday night merely confirmed it.

By 1969, my one album, The Beatles' 'Help!', a snip at 39/11d, was beginning to wear out. At the

The unforgettable Hank Williams mono

ripe old age of 13 I'd made the decision that music was more important than football and the first signs of this came with a selection of singles including 'Space Oddity' by David Bowie, 'All Along The Watchtower' by Jimi Hendrix, 'Magic Bus' by The Who (which of course I thought was about a magic bus!) and 'Mr Tambourine Man' by The Byrds.

Obviously, there were other less worthy sides, The Marmalade's 'Ob-La-Di Ob-La-Da' being one of them, but my head on collision with Dylan was pending and as I argued at break times about the supreme merits of Manfred Mann's 'Mighty Quinn', that song about Eskimo's, I was puzzled how they could write that then some old tosh like 'My Name Is Jack'. Little did I know that the hand of Bob was already forming my musical thinking. Of course, as the '70s started, I was off listening to Mungo Jerry, Atomic Rooster, Deep Purple and Frijid Pink.

But my time would come...

1970

Time Passes Slowly

I N A year of slow, controlled change, Bob replied to taunts from the press about inactivity by claiming he needed rest and family to soothe his soul. By the end of the year, however, he'd forsaken the solitude of Woodstock and moved back to New York. In the interim he was awarded a Doctorate Of Music by Princeton University, which he would later celebrate in song on 'Day Of The Locusts', which appeared on the third of his trilogy of sorta country-esque albums 'New Morning'. People were already reading too much into everything and Terry Shute, an alleged professor of, well, beards, was no exception as John Bauldie and Patrick Humphries' *Oh No! Not Another Dylan Book* reported. Of course, this must be complete baloney but, there again, people get grants for walking around with planks of wood on their head... well, they used to, anyway. So, who knows... Let Dr Shute tell us more.

"We've got Dylan back!"

Self Portrait

Tracks: All The Tired Horses, Alberta #1, I Forgot More Than You'll Ever Know, Days Of 49, Early Mornin' Rain, Search Of Little Sadie, Let It Be Me, Little Sadie, Woogie Boogie, Belle Isle, Living The Blues, Like A Rolling Stone, Copper Kettle (The Pale Moonlight), Gotta Travel On, Blue Moon, The Boxer, The Mighty Quinn (Quinn The Eskimo), Take Me As I Am (Or Let Me Go), Take A Message To Mary, It Hurts Me Too, Minstrel Boy, She Belongs To Me, Wigwam, Alberta #2.
Released June (October UK).
Produced by Bob Johnston.

SLEEVE NOTES *A lengthy list of perpetrators, including groovy acoustic guitar stylist Norman Blake, steel player Pete Drake, fiddle player Doug Kershaw, various Band members, plus the usual Nashville crew, Al Kooper et al, is the only key to where we're heading.*

WHAT THE PAPER'S SAID *"If 'Nashville Skyline' was a failed country album, then 'Self Portrait' was a disaster that crossed all generic boundaries. For the first time Dylan tried to interpret the songs of some writers that had followed him in the folk-rock movement, surrounding these with a batch of wholly uninspired originals."* Rolling Stone

WHAT THE INTERNET SAYS *"This record was slammed on release, and I figured the critics must've been exaggerating. But there's almost nothing (except for a few examples of his nicotine-free singing voice) to recommend this record."* DBW, Wilson - Alroy Record Reviews

WHAT DYLAN SAID *"I didn't live with those songs for too long. Those were just scraped together."*

WHAT THE WORLD SAYS CLARE ELLEN, artist *"Because he had already made some of the greatest records in the universe people were expecting something really earth shattering. They preferred him when he was dark and mysterious rather than when he was light and romantic."*

IN A NUTSHELL *I can't help but go against history and claim that 'Self Portrait' has its moments. Sure, it's messy in its construction, but some of the songs have a permeance and unreal sentimentality that's hard to beat. OK, he didn't write them, but Bob's versions of 'Days Of '49', 'Blue Moon', 'Let It Be Me' and 'I Forgot More Than You'll Ever Now' have stayed with me since I first heard them, nearly 30 years ago. It's his voice, a non-plussed but passionate drone. His take on Gordon Lightfoot's 'Early Morning Rain' has more warmth than the Canadian's and his own version of 'The Mighty Quinn', a live take of 'Like A Rolling Stone' and his Hank Williams-styled croon on 'Take Me As I Am (Or Let Me Go)' are like hearing a befuddled and somewhat distant late night Oklahoman radio station, as you bear down on the Grand Canyon.*

TERRY SHUTE *Regius Professor at the University of Delacroix from his doctoral thesis on 'Visions Of Hispidity In The Record Sleeves Of Bob Dylan'*

"'Self Portrait' has a self-portrait of Dylan on the cover, the painting is, of course, clean shaven, suggesting a return to the old persona."

OK, it's ridiculous, but it is an indication of what was to come. Dylan's periods of inactivity were not greeted with calm or attendant good humour, instead a world of probably stoned fans were rubbing their eyes and seeing Mickey Mouse and the Messiah holding hands.

New Morning

Tracks: If Not For You, Day Of The Locusts, Time Passes Slowly, Went To See The Gypsy, Winterlude, If Dogs Run Free, New Morning, Sign On The Window, One More Weekend, The Man In Me, Three Angels, Father Of Night.
Released October (November UK).
Produced by Bob Johnston.

SLEEVE NOTES *Not as such. However, the back sleeve did feature an archive shot of Bob at a session with blues legend Victoria Spivey. Just why? We'll probably never know (unless there's a web site about just that).*

WHAT THE PAPERS SAID *"We've got Dylan back again."* Ralph Gleason
"While the songs are occasionally exceptional - particularly 'Went To See The Gypsy', an obvious Elvis parable - the music is too diffuse to be really effective." Rolling Stone

WHAT THE INTERNET SAYS *"This is one weird record. It starts off with another simple, pretty country tune that would have fit on 'Nashville Skyline' ('If Not For You'), then heads for new territory. Then, there's a couple of lame attempts at beat poetry ('If Dogs Run Free' featuring Maeretha Stewart doing some wild scat singing, 'Three Angels') and a religious number presaging his later "born again" work ('Father Of Night'). The instrumentation is unusual - spotlighting his piano playing, which is surprisingly effective - with female backup singers, and an uncharacteristically professional and well-rehearsed band. DBW, Wilson - Alroy Record Reviews, via the internet*

WHAT THE WORLD SAYS Scott Gilbert, via internet *"'Day of the Locusts' has always done it for me - it gimme a cheeill. Don't know why, I think it's the combination of that voice, the evocative pianochords and imagery and the idea of Dylan tackling the meaning of "what it'sall about" and coming up with the nuclear family as an answer. I think I recall reading that the exploding head man was Norman Podhertz (I couldn't possibly make that up)."*

IN A NUTSHELL *Eight of the 12 tracks here have never been let out of the box live. This is Dylan caught in flux, between his country past, his cupboard-clearing and the next phase which was, quite frankly some way off. That's not to say that 'New Morning' is treading water, it's a comfortable album, like an old couch you can slouch on. These are stories of days passing with little in the way of life-evaluating theories necessary at all. In a way, as the title suggests, Bob just seems to be happy to have made it through the dark night. Certainly, the lead off track, 'If Not For You' is a besotted love song but through time and history. Olivia Newton John's version of the song has destroyed its resonance over the years.*

SINGLES/EPS/ETC
Wigwam (45)

I'm Just Sitting Here, Watching The River Flow

WHEN THE going got weird, the world spun faster. Back in New York, Bob fell foul of underground loon AJ Weberman who raided his dustbin and analysed the Bobtrash inside. AJ also recorded an interview with Bob on the telephone which he then tried to unsuccessfully release on the Folkways label.

As Bono so succinctly put it some time later, "Sure, we all want to be Bob Dylan, but we don't want AJ Weberman rooting in our rubbish."

Dylan followed his country idyll to the natural bluegrass extreme and teamed up with Earl Scruggs for a couple of songs before offering some self-analysis about his reclusive nature on

'Watching The River Flow' and he finally published his "officially mad" book Tarantula, some five years after it had been, er, typed.

In an effort to prevent Weberman from cashing in on the Dylantrash and a bookleg of the text, Bob decided it was time to publish and be damned. The cover claimed the contents were, indeed "poems" and that Dylan's interest in "the exploration of spontaneously occurring ideas" was at the core of things.

Tarantula had been on the official back burner since 1965, when Paul J Robbins from the Los Angeles Free Press stumbled on it in its earliest guise...

Robbins: "You wrote the book to say something?"
Dylan: "Yeah, but certainly not any kind of profound statement. The book don't begin or end."

That's certainly true and its publication resulted in a torrent of explanations and hyperbole, even the book Understanding Tarantula by a suitably guided hand. Journalist Robert Yates probably summed it up best when he wrote, on its reprinting, "The kindest way to assess Tarantula is to view the book as fragments of lyrics - some of them very fine - in search of music."

Dylan had already been acclaimed as 'poet laureate of young America' by the New York Times but his one book project had stalled. Written during 1965-66 it lay shelved. Earlier versions, one entitled Tarantula Meets Rex Paste are said to exist and although Bob claimed he'd scrapped the whole project, revises seemed to point to only minor adjustments. When it was finally published in 1971, Tarantula was hailed as a literary version of 'Highway 61 Revisited' in some quarters, as "surrealism on speed" in others.

In reality, Tarantula isn't that bad. It's very much in the cut-up style of William Burroughs and Bryon Gysin but, like the songs on 'Highway 61 Revisited' its tangents and characters pay only fleeting visits to the text. In book form this made the narrative hard to follow. The more workable travelogue passages owe a debt to the style of Jack Kerouac and the whole book is littered with one-liners that paint huge images, pinpointing vivid storylines that are never explored at the turn of a phrase. Holiday reading it is not.

And, so it went on. Bob went to Israel. Bob turned 30. Bob punched AJ Weberman for taking one empty milk carton too many. Bob recorded with Allen Ginsberg and some Tibetan Buddhists. Bob bought a big house in LA. Bob played for free.

George Harrison's Concert For Bangladesh preceded Live Aid by

some 14 years and, through his efforts awoke public concern about the flood and famine catastrophe which had hit the country at the start of the '70s. The concert was captured on album and film and eventhough Ravi Shankar was applauded for tuning up, the George Harrison, Eric Clapton, Billy Preston and Leon Russell axis was nicely rounded off by Dylan.

JOHN BAULDIE *reviewing the re-issue of the album in Q*

"Bob Dylan, making what was a rare live appearance, croons tunefully and flawlessly through his five song set."

Bob caught bang to rights by the Beat inspiration

More Bob Dylan Greatest Hits

Tracks: Watching The River Flow, Don't Think Twice, It's Alright, Lay Lady Lay, Stuck Inside Of Mobile, I'll Be Your Baby Tonight, All I Really Want To Do, My Back Pages, Maggie's Farm, Tonight I'll Be Staying Here Tonight, She Belongs To Me, All Along The Watchtower, Quinn The Eskimo, Just Like Tom Thumb's Blues, A Hard Rain's A-Gonna Fall, If Not For You, It's All Over Now, Baby Blue, Tomorrow Is A Long Time, When I Paint My Masterpiece, I Shall Be Released, You Ain't Goin' Nowhere, Down In The Flood.

Released November (December UK)

SINGLES/EPS/ETC *If Not For You (45) Watching The River Flow (45) George Jackson (45)*

MIKE FINK *"I was born in 1970 and was raised in a middle-income household in Southern California. My upbringing, while heavily tainted with religion and faith, was filled with typical California suburban experiences - with perhaps one exception, a stronger than normal interest in music. At 19 I served as a missionary, where I lived a conformist and restrained lifestyle. Upon my return I attended a university owned by my church where again conformity and homogeneity was the name of the game. For me, the one-two punch of a mission and attending a church-owned university gave me my fill of religion and church and faith; I began to break out. "While I was at school, I purchased Dylan's 'Greatest Hits' and loved how I could play those songs on my guitar and sing the interesting lyrics. It was also at school where I met the woman of my dreams who convinced me to purchase Bob Dylan's 'Greatest Hits II', even though I hadn't heard ONE song! "I remember the warm day sitting in her living room and listening to 'All I Really Want To Do' for the first time thinking how weird, raw, absurd, brazen, and funny it was. I thought, 'Who does this guy think he is!?' The seriousness and poetry of 'Hard Rain', the tenderness of 'Tonight I'll Be Staying Here With You', the stripped intensity of 'Watchtower' mesmerised me. Dylan's work, act, and persona, for me, represented the individuality and freedom awakening within myself at that time and that I revere presently. Years, several concerts, countless CDs and tapes, many Bob-friends, and a website later, I'm still listening to and appreciating Mr Dylan the artist."*

"I remember listening to 'All I Really Want To Do' and thinking how weird, raw, absurd, brazen it was."

1972

Still Blowin' In The Wind

NOTHING MUCH happened till late in the day in '72. Then Dylan recognised something in the so-called "new Dylans" and wound up playing, harmonising and harmonica-tooting with John Prine and Steve Goodman. Seemingly enlivened by music again, he then opted to go Tex-Mex with Doug Sahm and offered it to Roger McGuinn on his first solo album, supplying harmonica on 'I'm So Restless'. The track was co-written by Jacques Levy who Dylan would hook up with again in a later incarnation.

And, then, it all went rather haywire. Lured from hibernation by, of all people, blood-thirsty and really quite offbeat film director Sam Peckinpah to record some music for the western Pat Garrett And Billy The Kid, Bob ended up in the film. Deep in the heart of Mexico, the assembled cast found it hard to follow the script and even harder to follow Sam. Still, the music was good.

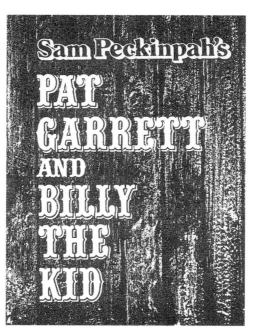

Eat The Document, the DA Pennebaker follow-up to Don't Look Back, filmed during Dylan's seismic 1966 European tour and featuring a brief Lennon/Dylan cab ride was finally released. Edited in extreme, the 55-minute clip has rarely had an outing subsequently, even though it featured footage from The Royal Albert Hall, including 'Leopard-Skin Pill Box Hat' and 'Just Like Tom Thumb's Blues'. In the wake of the release of 'Live 1966', Pennebaker's film was reported to be in the process of heading for a theatrical release by Rolling Stone magazine in their November 12, 1998 issue. In fact the Stone editorial revealed that the format features a "succession of fans castigating Dylan" in a series of vox pops, intercut with performance and Dylan lapping up the animosity.

DA PENNEBAKER

"Dylan didn't know what he wanted to do, so he said, I want you guys to go ahead and do a rough edit to get an idea of what you did,

EAT THE DOCUMENT

Scenes from a lost film: the less-than-expensive title-board

Camera-conscious dawn composition

Robbie Robertson, clearly under the Dylan spell

A luckless Danish girl and her boyfriend look baffled as Richard Manuel offers to buy her in Australian loose change

Dylan and Cash singing I Still Miss Someone

Searching for suitably *avant garde* locations, Denmark.

Spontaneous 'set-piece' with firearms

Ritual press baiting in Scandinavia

Dylan bizarrely mobbed by Danish schoolkids

Relentless *cinema verité*

Further floral shirt rese[...]

SINGLES/EPS/ETC
Blowin' In The Wind (45)

because ABC were keen to get it. So, me and Bobby Neuwirth started to edit something together."

"Dylan got pissed at everyone. He either thought ABC were putting too much pressure on him or that he was in competition with me. I could see nothing positive out of making the film."

"I think Dylan thought that he was going to be like Ingmar Bergman and make some new kind of film - which was terrific and I didn't want to discourage him from doing that. But it was the first time I'd seen him really happy with music so I felt you had to focus on the music on stage."

BOB DYLAN

"They made another Don't Look Back!" Dylan complained years later.

In a completely offbeat incident, Yoko Ono's sleevenotes for 'The John Lennon Anthology', released in 1987, recalled a strange Dylan-related moment during the otherwise seemingly serene John/Yoko union.

"In 1972, the night George McGovern lost the presidential election, John and I were invited to a party at an apartment in Greenwich Village. It was a gathering of New York liberal intellectuals, some artists, musicians and many journalists.

"John became totally drunk and pulled a woman into the next room and started to make love. Nobody could leave the party because all the coats were in that room. We were all sitting there, trying to ignore what was happening. The wall was paper-thin and you could hear the noise, which was incredibly loud. A considerate musician put on a Dylan record to offset the sound. But that did not drown out the sound coming from the room."

"I could see nothing positive about making the film."

Knockin' On Heaven's Door

STILL CLEANING the sand from his joints on a regular daily basis, Bob is uncomfortable with the film world and disillusioned with the madness of King Peckinpah. Back in LA, finally, the music was recorded, but Peckinpah cuts it into all the places that Dylan didn't think it was intended for.

Bob used his new western reasoning to renegotiate his contract with Columbia which was expiring. His six gun failed to bear fruit and a deal was instead inked with David Geffen's new Asylum label, while Bob is snapped up by Island in the UK. Dylan regrouped The Band for the 'Planet Waves' sessions, while Columbia raided the vaults to unleash 'Dylan', complete with a cover of Joni Mitchell's 'Big Yellow Taxi'. Perverse? Moi? The public's image of Bob became cloudier still and, of course, the beard concerns continued to grow.

DAVID EHRENSTEIN, *Rock On Film*
"Dry winds, director Sam Peckinpah's

BOB DYLAN
PLANET WAVES

MOONGLOW

**ACCOMPANIED BY THE BAND
ON HIS NEW ALBUM · PLANET WAVES**

Record ILPS 9261 Cassette ZCI 9261 Cartridge YSI 9261

drinking and an unhappy studio meant that the movie was edited into a 90 minute package and released with a host of Dylan songs throughout. James Coburn claimed: "It was almost like a musical". After Peckinpah's death, the Martin Scorsesse-acclaimed two hour director's cut was unearthed with a more tempered selection from Dylan and this is the edit that made the UK video release in 1998."

As any good director would do, Peckinpah disowned the film. Confusion ran riot and Dylan's soundtrack was acclaimed as "not the new Dylan album".

JAN STACY, *author of Rockin' Reels*
"Dylan is a natural before the camera, as you can see in Don't Look Back. In Peckinpah's disaster, he looks shy. I rushed to see this western because I love Dylan. What a letdown. It's like an Elvis picture without Elvis singing."

Pat Garrett And Billy The Kid

Tracks: Main Theme, Cantina Theme, Billy 1, Bunkhouse Theme, River Theme, Turkey Chase, Knockin' On Heaven's Door, Final Theme, Billy 4, Billy 7.

Released May (September UK).
Produced by Gordon Carroll.

SLEEVE NOTES
The cast and credits of the film with a picture of Kris Kristoferson 'getting his' on the back tells little of what's inside. The listed players include Booker T Jones, fiddle player Byron Berline and Roger McGuinn.

WHAT THE PAPER'S SAID *"The title song isn't much but 'Final Theme' and 'Knockin' On Heaven's Door' have an epic grandeur reminiscent of Dylan's best electric work, even though they are more modestly presented."* Rolling Stone

WHAT THE WORLD SAYS ROXY GORDON, author of a Billy The Kid novel *"(The album was) mournful and the past has always been mournful for me. I've kept it (the music) in my mind... the feel is right, a dark, Catholic, Spanish kind of atmosphere - a sound as dark and lonely as the place."*
BARRY O'BRIEN, music fan and former fledgling muso *"I loved 'Pat Garrett And Billy The Kid' and I really admired Dylan's part in the film but I hated 'Knockin' On Heaven's Door' with a vengeance. The problem was that the very first band that I was in could only play a few songs and that was one of them. Every time we played it, it seemed to get slower and slower. The memories of a hot summer and endlessly wading through the goo of 'Knockin' On Heaven's Door' still haunt me."*
DAVID LYNN, Glasgwegian record hoarder, an outdoor type *"Given my lukewarm reaction to Dylan's voice, it's hardly surprising that my favourite Dylan track is an instrumental. 'Final Theme' from 'Pat Garrett' does the trick for me. In the early '80s, I was an archaeologist in Orkney, where midsummer night amounts to two to three hours of twilight (the Simmer Dim). We used to go out to the outlying islands and build bonfires out of driftwood and drink home- brew and Highland Park, while we toasted sausages and marshmallows as the sun went down to a stunning backcloth of sea, islands, sky and puzzled seals. Then we'd rush round to the other side of the island, build more bonfires and watch the sun come up again. "All of this activity would be conducted as each of us played favourite tapes to each other. That's how I first heard 'Final Theme' - it matched the tranquillity and beauty of the setting perfectly.*

IN A NUTSHELL Perhaps the lack of focus evident on 'New Morning' gave greater depth to this collection of musical interludes for Sam Peckinpah's film. By fusing the ambience of Morricone's western soundtracks and lots of echoey drum effects, there's room for the guitars to track each other and create the kind of windblown emptiness that Mexico's mock-American desertland needed. Of course, there's the epic 'Knockin' On Heaven's Door' but this is mainly mood music that rolls through the film itself adding an extra dimension.

PAT FACT 'Billy Surrenders' a track Dylan produced while jamming with Terry Paul appears in the movie's two finished cuts but not on the album itself.

I distinctly remember the day I discovered Bob Dylan. It was around 1973, and I was about 13. I was lying in my parent's living room floor reading the sports section of the Washington Post. Normally I wouldn't look at any other section. On this day, however, I noticed an article about this singer, Bob Dylan, who I had heard was making a comeback or something, and it was apparently a real big deal. I read the article. I don't remember any of the details.

Even as a teenager I liked to read, but rarely my schoolbooks since they were almost invariably boring, so I used to hang out at the public library quite a bit, trying to find something interesting. I used to check out the library's album collection while I was there. I had acquired a mild taste for country music, having listened to my father's Johnny Cash and Marty Robbins albums a lot. Of course, like most teenagers, I also liked the current pop stuff. I remember Elton John was a favorite. Anyway one day, shortly after I had read the Post article, I was thumbing through the albums and came across a Dylan title, 'Planet Waves', the album that had just come out. I took it home.

When I got home, I looked over the album cover. Unlike any other album I'd ever seen, the sleeve of 'Planet Waves' didn't have a plastic coating. It was rough, like recycled cardboard, with a curious, sloppy, black and white portrait on the front, kind of like a Rorschach. The album's subtitle "Cast Iron Songs & Torch Songs" was scrunched into a little corner of the picture. On the back was a little essay that Dylan had written by hand, his sentences drifting up and down the page like a grade-schooler, mistakes scribbled out instead of erased neatly. "Furious gals with garters & smeared lips on bar stools that stank from sweating pussy". References to Victor Hugo, Baudelaire, Goya, vampires. Muscular prose that was startling to a 13-year-old used to Elton John records.

Next I put the record on my old Sears turntable. I loved it immediately. I really can't really explain the attraction, except to say that it really was like falling in love. Who can explain why they fell in love? You don't fall in love with someone just because they have a beautiful voice, or can compose wonderful verse.

Dylan

Tracks: Lily Of The West, Can't Help Falling In Love, Sarah Jane, Ballad Of Ira Hayes, Mr Bojangles, Mary Ann, Big Yellow Taxi, A Fool Such As I, Spanish Is The Loving Tongue.
Released November.

Original Recording Sessions Produced by Bob Johnston.

SLEEVE NOTES There are none. Merely a tinted picture of Bob's profile, swirling into oblivion.

WHAT THE PAPERS SAID
"'Dylan' is an act of vengeance, put out by Columbia while Dylan was recording for Asylum. It features Joni Mitchell's 'Big Yellow Taxi' and a version of 'A Fool Such As I', a hit for Elvis Presley, both guaranteed to net only horselaughs."
Rolling Stone

WHAT THE INTERNET SAYS *"Often there's a guilty pleasure in listening to recordings that an artist didn't want issued, but not this time: None of the tunes are Dylan originals, and they're uniformly less interesting than the cuts that made 'Self Portrait', which was lousy to begin with. There are no high points." DBW, Wilson - Alroy Record Reviews*

IN A NUTSHELL By no means is this a great Dylan album. And, indeed, according virtually all and sundry, it's not an album at all. What you get are the good, the bad and the pretty drab actually. 'Can't Help Falling In Love' is charming but unchallenging, 'The Ballad Of Ira Hayes has power but little real muscle and 'Sarah Jane' and 'Mary Ann' suggest that they know their way home. Undoubtedly 'Big Yellow Taxi' is a jesting jest and 'Spanish Is The Loving Tongue' has a haunted sentiment that reverberates around without really taking any prisoners. It's Flamenco rattle is the closest thing to emotion for a verse but then it descends into an ill-advised parody of Mexicala.

DYLAN FACTS
In a potentially- befuddled marketing move the French version of the album failed to mention that it was actually by Dylan.

SINGLES/EPS/ETC
Just Like A Woman (45) Knockin' On Heaven's Door (45) A Fool Such As I (45)

You fall in love because someone connects with your soul. Why 'Planet Waves' did that to me I'm still not all that sure.

Certainly the lyrics of the songs held some attraction. I was never a particularly good student, but I did like my literature classes, and had a limited appreciated poetry. The power of some of the lines, such as

---

"The tracks were not to be used, they were just warm up tunes."

"I went out on Lower Broadway and I felt that place within / That hollow place where martyrs weep and angels play with sin", were not completely lost on me.

But I think the more important attraction was the sound. Most of all, it was his voice, its rawness, authenticity. His voice on 'Planet Waves', or any other album for that matter, is not beautiful. It cracks, it's nasal, out of tune. But it gripped me unlike any other singer ever had or likely ever will. More than the voice itself, his phrasing saves even the most hackneyed lines, makes them interesting, keeps you guessing. He slows down, speeds up, emphasises the sound of a particular word or phrase in such a way that the meaning of the lyrics is defined more precisely, the emotion convey more compelling.

The music too was something remarkably new to me. It wasn't country music, although there was more than a hint of a country sound It certainly wasn't rock, at least not like any rock music that was playing on the radio at that time. I didn't know what it was, but it certainly was alive, loose, stinging, churning underneath Dylan's voice, adding an additional layer of meaning and emotion to the songs.

For a long time I didn't buy any other Bob Dylan albums, I just keep playing 'Planet Waves' continuously. I read an article by a rock critic who said that 'Planet Waves' didn't measure up to some of the other Dylan records. I didn't believe it. How could any album be better? It seemed impossible.

Eventually I bought all the albums, working my way backwards through the Dylan catalog, each album a revelation in itself. Later I sought out other artists connected to Dylan in same fashion: The folk singers, John Prine, Steve Forbert, Bruce Springsteen, Leonard Cohen, Phil Ochs, Joan Baez, Joni Mitchell. The filmmakers, Sam Sam Peckinpah, Martin Scorsesse. The writers, Sam Shepherd, T.S. Elliot, Lawrence Ferlinghetti, William Burroughs, Allen Ginsberg, and many others.

I still have that old album from the library. I never returned it. I played it so many times it's completely worn out, the grooves turned gray from so many listens. My mother, only half-jokingly, has always said that my discovery of Bob Dylan was my downfall. I suppose it was, if your goal was to raise a clean-cut kid, an All-American boy, with short hair a tidy house in the suburbs. But I know that finding Dylan helped me discover new musical, intellectual and spiritual realms that I may have never glimpsed if I hadn't read that newspaper article, if I had never listened to 'Planet Waves'.

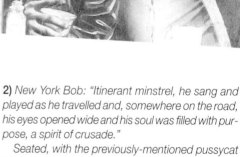

BOB GETS AIRBRUSHED

The cover of Guy Peelaert and Nick Kohn's Rock Dreams featured a clean -shaven, moody Bob, be-James Deaned in a diner with Mick Jagger, Elvis and Lennon. The book of airbrushed rock history was a real oddity which arrived in WH Smith's on the news stand-priced at a then-wallet-busting £1.95. Copies were ceremonially pinched and re-sold at our school gates so the history of Bob, alongside a variety of tragi-cases, was explained in four artwork plates that covered each phase till then.

These were summed up as:

1) *Robert Zimmerman, His Journeys And Adventures: Hobo Bob',* for which Nick Kohn romanticised: *"Very young and frail, Bob left his home one day and set forth to seek his fame and fortune, with his possessions knotted in a red spotted handkerchief and his pussycat at his heels."*

2) *New York Bob:* *"Itinerant minstrel, he sang and played as he travelled and, somewhere on the road, his eyes opened wide and his soul was filled with purpose, a spirit of crusade."*

Seated, with the previously-mentioned pussycat in hand in the back of a Limo, Kohn then recognised, only fleetingly, mind you:

3) *Superstar Bob:* *"Soon his fame spread and he toured, grew rich and was worshipped."*

And finally, there was:

4) *Country Bob:* *"However, even Messiahs must have hobbies, and Zimmerman's was his motorbike, which proved to be his downfall. One night he fell off and nearly died."*

It may have included some sweeping generalisations, but at the Carlisle Grammar School where I was failing maths for music, it was gospel.

Forver Young

1974

NOW SURELY some kind of madness was taking hold. After not playing live for what seemed like a lifetime, Bob embarked on 40 concerts in six weeks. Millions of dollars were posted for tickets in hopeless hopefulness. It was estimated that there were in excess of 15 million ticket applications. After the shows, to contrast and develop inwardly, Bob spent a couple of months dabbling with painting and philosophy in true renaissance-man style.

Off the boil but understanding more about his navel, Dylan was approached by "not marching anymore" protest legend Phil Ochs to play a charity concert for The Friends Of Chile. Unfortunately the Ochs'

strategy to ensure Dylan played involved locking him in a room with lots of wine, the result was an uncontrollable drunken slur of a performance. Hic.

The sobering realisation that he was probably better off with Columbia Records meant that Bob resigned and immediately set about recording 'Blood On The Tracks' the first indications of how stormy the collapse of his relationship with Sara was. In fact, an earlier version of the album was scrapped, the story emerging that it was just too close to the knuckle and that Bob was giving too much away. So, during the Christmas break, he decided the tracks weren't releasable and he went back into the studio with some local Minneapolis talent to re-do them.

"The album was redone because, according to popular myth, Dylan thought he was giving too much away."

Planet Waves

Tracks: On A Night Like This, Going, Going, Gone, Tough Mama, Hazel, Something There Is About You, Forever Young, Forever Young, Dirge, You Angel You, Never Say Goodbye, Wedding Song.

Released January.

sleeve NOTES Nothing much other than some hand-scrawled notes as to who played what and some quickly drawn "waves", of the planet variety, no doubt.

WHAT THE PAPERS SAID "'Planet Waves' sounds hasty, unfinished. He was once again recording with The Band but there was not enough quality material to produce a major work of the standard expected from an artist of Dylan's stature." Rolling Stone

WHAT THE INTERNET SAYS "Bob's reunion with The Band sounds unrehearsed and half-finished. There are good songs here, but apparently not much thought went into the performances.
DBW, Wilson - Alroy Record Reviews, via the internet
"Recorded in three days, and it sounds like it. The sloppiness and cacophonous overplaying is ironic, because the Band's own studio work was always immaculately rehearsed and complexly, but economically arranged." JA, Wilson - Alroy Record Reviews

WHAT THE WORLD SAYS REINHARD HOLSTEIN, Glitterhouse label owner "Dylan? Are you crazy? My first encounter of Bob was actually 'Planet Waves', but it didn't turn me on to Dylan, it turned me on to The Band."

CLINTON HEYLIN In Clinton Heylin's book Dylan: Behind The Shades, 'Wedding Song' is recognised as "A public declaration of overwhelming love" which Dylan penned for wife Sara, who he married in November 1965. However, within two years, Dylan had also written the "deeply troubled" 'Sara', which talked of the marriage in the past tense. Sara filed for divorce on March 1, 1977.

IN A NUTSHELL Out of his Columbia contract, Dylan revisited the basement and got back together with The Band. Their intimate interplay returned immediately with Garth Hudson's sweet organ rolling through Dylan's mainly sombre tones. Robbie Robertson's guitar chops through like a displaced soul man and Richard Manuel's piano adds an echoey resonance to the affair. The Band's own albums, since the players last sparred, reappear and dictate the flow on the likes of 'Tough Mama' and the second 'Forever Young', a hollering back porch swing punctuated by Bob's harmonica. 'Planet Waves' may have been, as the paper's of the time heralded, the union of two of the world's greatest acts. But, they didn't quite seem to be on tip top form.

PLANET WAVES FACT
This unique, none-Columbia Dylan album (now out on Columbia Nice Price) was nearly unleashed as 'Ceremonies Of The Horsemen' - a line from Love Minus Zero/No Limit. The cover had reached artwork stage when the change took place.

BILL PRINCE Dylan fan, indeed Bobcat

"Having started my Dylan thing with 'Hard Rain' then being introduced to the really overwhelming 'Blood On The Tracks', that became my favourite album. Then, like any overbearing fan, I heard that there was an even rougher, more emotive version of the 'Blood On The Tracks' album, which was closer to the actual split with Sara. The album was redone because, according to popular myth, Dylan felt like he was giving too much away and changed some of the lines and re-did it all.

I mentioned that I was keen to hear it to a couple of people I knew and within a week I'd been given a tape. The versions were probably fifth generation but it was simply stunning. I think Garth Hudson is playing with Dylan and the version of 'You're A Big Girl Now' is just phenomenal. The words are more cutting and the playing is just tremendous. In itself 'Blood On The Tracks' is a masterpiece but these outtakes are just phenomenal."

DYLAN-BAND CONCERTS HAILED

Bob Dylan's tour with The Band ended in Los Angeles on February 14, when the singer played to a star-studded audience at the city's Forum. Jack Nicholson, Carole King, Neil Young and Ringo Starr were among those who stayed to cheer. Dylan's recent concerts at New York's Madison Square Garden have been hailed by some as being among the greatest rock 'n' roll concerts of all time, Dylan opening with an acoustic guitar and rendering songs such as 'Most Likely You Go Your Way And I'll Go Mine', 'Lay Lady Lay', 'Just Like Tom Thumb's Blues', Rainy Day Women Nos 12 And 35', 'It Ain't Me Babe' and 'Ballad Of A Thin Man'.

He accompanied himself on piano for the last-named, returning after a Band set for an electric fling involving 'Like A Rolling Stone' and others.

He was forced back to encore on 'Maggie's Farm' and, finally, 'Blowin' In The Wind'. The tour encompassed 39 shows in 21 cities.

NME, February 1974

Before The Flood

Tracks: Most Likely You Go Your Way (And I'll Go Mine), Lay Lady Lay, Rainy Day Women Nos 12&35, Knockin' On Heaven's Door, It Ain't Me Babe, Ballad Of A Thin Man, Don't Think Twice, It's Alright, Just Like A Woman, It's Alright (I'm Only Bleeding), All Along The Watchtower, Highway 61 Revisited, Like A Rolling Stone, Blowin' In The Wind.

Released June.

Produced by, well, no-one claims it on the sleeve. Yet there are recording engineers, mixing engineers and many more.

SLEEVE NOTES Very little in the way of words, just the details of the 21 songs, plus some red-tinted shots of the main instigators, all in various stages of facial hair growth. The front cover's thousand hands holding lighters aloft shows something of the magnitude of the shows themselves.

WHAT THE INTERNET SAYS "All the Band's biggest hits are here, along with many of Dylan's 60's hits. Everything's transformed into the Band's ragged country-rock. For Band fans, that's probably a good thing; for me it's monotonous, as all the different Dylan periods are processed into one shoddy sound. Dylan himself is thoroughly unremarkable, shouting out his lines without much feeling, even on the short solo acoustic set. DBW, Wilson - Alroy Record Reviews

WHAT THE PAPERS SAID "This two record set followed 'Planet Waves' and featured Dylan reinterpreting all of his old material drastically, singing the lyrics as though they either mean nothing or something very different from what we've always understood them to signify." Rolling Stone

IN A NUTSHELL The second album (a double) from Dylan's brief tenure at Asylum/Island came from his first tour since his motorcycle debacle. The completely over-subscribed shows allowed the recently reunited Bob and Band to revisit their back pages. The music gushes like a keyboard-accompanied waterfall crashing onto the expectant crowd, from the first chugging stew of 'Most Likely You Go Your Way' the players add new dimensions to the classics. It's a good time show, the kind of revue format that big band, then R&B labels had perfected, with a slice of guitar acrobatics, some fevered quasi-religious arrangements and Garth Hudson's keyboards adding generous layers of curling sound behind Dylan's often-chirpy lead.

SINGLES/EPS/ETC
A Fool Such As I (45) On A Night Like This (45) Something There Is About You (45) Most Likely You Go Your Way (And I'll Go Mine) (45) All Along The Watchtower (45)

DYLAN STRIKES GOLD

Bob Dylan, in the middle of his first US tour since 1965, has received a gold record for his 'Planet Waves' album.

NME, January 1974

1975

Shelter From The Storm

WELL, IT seemed like a good idea at the time. Honest. Following a brief holiday where he'd been reading about the plight of jailed boxer Hurricane Carter, Dylan visited the man in chokey and, in a 'Rough Justice'-style, decided to draw attention to what had happened to Hurricane on a rather grand scale with a return to his protestations of old on the single 'Hurricane'.

After gatecrashing sets by a variety of acts to play new songs, Bob hit on the idea of a concert Revue, something instant and completely different to the monolithic rock shows that were becoming the norm. With 'Blood On The Tracks' on the racks, he undertook a 40-date straggle with a host of friends along to speed the plow.

SEAN BODY *Helter Skelter supremo*
"Without wanting to come over too Nick Hornby, at my school, following music was as partisan a pastime as following football. You had to decide whose side you were on: Led Zeppelin or Deep Purple; Rainbow or Whitesnake; The Clash or The Pistols and so on.

"By extension, even older artists such as Dylan provoked extreme views. While the school featured plenty of Dylan acolytes, I fell strictly into the Neil Young camp - and bizarrely, you couldn't really like both. Young appealed to me more anyway - he appeared more of a rebel; he was less well known, and could play guitar - he even tried when he was playing harmonica. Also, Neil would never have written anything as weedy as 'Blowin' in the Wind' - though later, I did realise that 'Sugar Mountain' and 'I Am A Child' were lurking in his closet to prove me wrong.

"Because of my absurd loyalty to Neil, I never really opened my ears to Dylan, and for a long time was unaware of his post 1964 oeuvre. I just didn't want to know. So, when my younger brother brought home a copy of 'Blood On The

Tracks', I saw it as an act of betrayal - he too was a Neil partisan up to that point. So, in a very grown up way, whenever he put the record on, I would leave the room.

"Finally one day, short on cash and tired of listening to all my own records - and most importantly, because my brother was out of the house - I decided to give 'Blood On The Tracks' a listen. I was immediately taken by the mysterious cover, but when I put it on, it truly was a moment of epiphany.

"'Tangled Up In Blue', first of all, and my ears pricked up - the voice! The old whiner was actually singing. By the time I had got through 'You're A Big Girl Now' - I was converted for life. The mesmeric finger-picking, the beautiful harmonica playing, and the aching vocals. When I found myself thinking, 'Wow, this beats the pants of 'Harvest'' another voice bellowed into the room, 'Et Tu Bob?'. I was found out.

"And so I had to revalue my life. I compared 'Blood On The Tracks' to 'On The Beach', and I realised I was in completely different territory! It would be a long time before I even got to the second side - so taken was I with the 'Simple Twist Of Fate', 'You're A Big Girl Now', and 'Idiot Wind' axis. But, when I did? 'If You See Her, Say Hello'? Absolute genius.

T-BONE BURNETT
guitarist on The Rolling Thunder Revue
"The first half of that tour could arguably be

ROLLING THUNDER REVUE

STARRING
BOB DYLAN
JOAN BAEZ · JACK ELLIOTT
BOB NEUWIRTH

BANGOR MUNICIPAL AUDITORIUM
Bangor, Maine
Thursday, November 27th   8:00 p.m.
Reserved Seating $8.50   Limit 4 tickets per person
On sale at Municipal Auditorium

ZEBRA CONCERTS, INC.   8.

said to be Dylan's best tour. It was really spiritual and really beautiful. On the second night Dylan started with a solo version of 'Simple Twist Of Fate'. I wept. It was so beautiful and so painful. There were lots of moments like that on the tour."

JONI MITCHELL
"Bobby and Joan Baez were in whiteface and they were going to rescue Hurricane Carter. I had talked to Hurricane on the phone several times and I was alone in perceiving that he was a violent person and an opportunist. I thought,

Blood On The Tracks

Tracks: Tangled Up In Blue, Simple Twist Of Fate, You,re A Big Girl Now, Idiot Wind, You,re Gonna Make Me Lonesome When You Go, Meet Me In The Morning, Lily, Rosemary And The Jack Of Hearts, If You See Her, Say Hello, Shelter From The Storm, Buckets Of Rain.
Released January.
Produced by Bob Dylan.

SLEEVE NOTES *What happened to the sleeve note concept? Too much scribbling too soon? The emotional disturbances of the songs inside and the sketchy Bob pic on the sleeve ensured that the packaging could do little to put over the tortured message within, so he didn't bother writing anything.*

WHAT THE PAPERS SAID *"A bitter chronicle of love affairs gone wrong. The two best songs, 'Tangled Up In Blue' and 'Simple Twist Of Fate' might have been better than anything he'd ever done if his band had offered him decent support."* Rolling Stone

"Blood On The Tracks turned the personal anguish of a collapsing marriage into a recurring saga of a wasted but unforgettable love. Suddenly Dylan seemed to be no longer straining to recapture the surreal poetic torrents of the mid-'60s but managing to both write from the heart and yet frame his own emotions in folk-based narratives and tunes that turned his own love's labours into a sorrowing but universal pilgrimage." Mark Cooper', Q on the album's re- issue in 1993

WHAT DYLAN SAID *"A lot of people tell me that they really enjoy that album. It's hard for me to relate to that, you know. I mean people enjoying that type of pain?"*

WHAT THE WORLD SAYS STEVE EARLE, the growling Bob, singer/songwriter *"Along with 'Freewheelin', it's my favourite. It's his marriage coming apart on this record."*
BETH ORTON, the folky female Bob, singer/songwriter *"'You're Gonna Make Me Lonesome When You Go' is a big feeling song and the whole atmosphere is incredible. I don't like all of Dylan's songs but there's a real magic about his greatest songs and this is one of them."*
BEN HARPER, the emotive vocalising Bob, singer/songwriter *"My mom and dad were huge Dylan fans. 'Tangled Up In Blue' is his mature songwriting. It's a blues cut, yet it's in a folk style. Perfect storytelling. 'Blood On The Tracks' showed how folk influenced blues and blues influenced folk."*

IN A NUTSHELL *After the excursions with The Band, Bob dug deep into his soul for 'Blood On The Tracks'. With his home life under scrutiny, he wrapped his feelings in some of his finest songs, capturing the bitterness, loss and misunderstandings that domestic collapse surely brings. The opening statement of intent, 'Tangled Up In Blue' throws caution to the wind, while the psychiatric session continues to the maudlin realisations on 'Idiot Wind' with it's perceptive exposition of the end of a relationship and the inevitable changing attitude to the relationship. Further on there's the mood swing of 'You're Gonna Make Me Lonesome When You Go' and the truly biting 'If You See Her, Say Hello'. If that weren't enough in between is another serving of Bob's Americana storytelling on 'Lily, Rosemary And The Jack Of Hearts', making this a truly awesome collection.*

The Basement Tapes

Tracks: Odds And Ends, Million Dollar Bash, Goin' To Acapulco, Lo And Behold, Clothes Line Saga, Apple Suckling Tree, Please Mr Henry, Tears Of Rage, Too Much Of Nothing, Yea Heavy Traffic And A Bottle of Bread, Crash On The Levee, Tiny Montgomery, You Ain't Goin' Nowhere, Nothing Was Delivered, Open The Door Homer, This Wheel's On Fire.
Released June (August UK).

SLEEVE NOTES *"'The Basement Tapes' are a bit like the phantom 1956 session that brought Elvis, Carl Perkins, Jerry Lee Lewis and Johnny Cash together for the first and last time. Despite the bootlegs and the cover versions, the Basement Tapes have always been more of a rumour than anything else." The cover shot of freaks, fans, fanatics and friends of the cause is as alluring as some circus side-show squirming into your back yard."*

WHAT THE PAPERS SAID *"The two record set that eventually appeared isn't even all-inclusive, and features many songs that feature The Band without Dylan, but it is a brilliant document nonetheless, made even more legendary because of the long delay between creation and release." Rolling Stone*

WHAT THE PRESS OFFICE DID (John Tobler)
Although we have never met, Bob Dylan certainly occupies a unique place in my history. Blown away by 'Blonde On Blonde', loved 'Like A Rolling Stone' (and was very excited to meet Al Kooper several times in the Seventies), became press officer at CBS (now Sony) at a time when Dylan was on Island, but was fortunate to work on 'The Basement Tapes'. This was pretty much the highlight of my career at CBS.
Mick Watts was assistant editor of Melody Maker at the time, and I knew him quite well through our mutual friendship with a legend literally in his own lunch time, Mike O'Mahoney, an Irishman who conceivably owned the factory where they manufacture blarney stones. Mike had also been press officer for CBS in the UK, but had managed to get himself transferred to the US. Anyway, I was informed that some kind of advance copy of the legitimate version of this legendary bootleg was available, and told to get a front page by offering an exclusive to either MM or NME - it had to be Mick Watts. We went to CBS Studios in Whitfield Street (now known as The Hit Factory, apparently), where it was played through once via studio monitors (which make everything sound wonderful), and Mick clearly enjoyed it. The result defied all expectations - the next week's MM had a picture from the album sleeve on the front cover. How many times has an album sleeve been the front page lead on Melody Maker ? The weekly marketing meeting gave me a round of applause, and that in itself makes the whole thing personally unforgettable.

IN A NUTSHELL
After the bootlegs, the rumours of Tiny Tim's involvement and The Band and Bob on tour, 'The Basement Tapes' was finally released and, through covers, versions and legend, the framework sounded more than vaguely familiar.
SINGLES/EPS/ETC
Tangled Up In Blue (45) Million Dollar Bash (45)
Hurricane (45) Mozambique (45)

'Oh, my God, we're a bunch of white, pasty faced liberals. This is a bad person, he's fakin' it'. "So, when we got to the last show, which was at Madison Square Garden, Joan Baez asked me to introduce Muhammed Ali. I was in a particularly cynical mood - it had been a difficult excursion. I said, 'Fine', what I'll say is - and I never would have - I'll say, 'We're here tonight on behalf of one jive-ass nigger who could have been champion of the world and I'd like to introduce you to another one who is. She stared at me, and immediately removed me from the introductory role. I thought then, I should go on in blackface tonight. Anyway, Hurricane got released and the next day he brutally beat up this woman..."

ROGER McGUINN

"It was a great big rolling party, two or three tour buses out there with all your friends. I sat next to Joni Mitchell on the bus and Joan Baez was there and T-Bone Burnett and Bobby Neuwirth and Mick Ronson and Ramblin' Jack Elliot. It was amazing, I wish I could conjure it up and relive it for a while."

HAVING MET UP WITH JACQUES LEVY again, the duo began writing for the 'Desire' album at a tremendous pace. If the impending live excursion, a new album and a new cause wasn't enough to keep his mind off the end of his relationship with Sara, then there were always other people's sessions to fill the time. Dylan wasn't choosy and he wound up working with Bette Midler who later talked of a near-sex experience in various magazine interviews. Nice.

"I wish I could conjure it up and relive it for a while..."

iS iT ROLLiNG, BOB?

While 'the new Dylan' is gathering all the publicity with the re-release of the legendary 'Basement Tapes', the old Dylan is embarking on an idiosyncratic tour with a selection of old and new friends under the name of The Rolling Thunder Revue. Among the friends - Joan Baez, Ronnie Blakely, Bobby Neuwirth, Ramblin' Jack Elliott, Allen Ginsberg, Bette Midler, Eric Anderson, Mick Ronson and Patti Smith. Most of this unlikely crowd piled on to a bus and headed to Plymouth, Massachusetts, to begin a series of small scale shows.
In typical Dylan fashion, they've decided to make a film at the same time to record anything that moves... and a lot of things that don't.
Just to give the whole adventure a focus, there's a campaigning Dylan single called 'Hurricane', in defence of boxer Hurricane Carter, imprisoned after allegedly being framed for murder.
NME, November 1975

58

1976

One More Cup Of Coffee

AS THE question 'Can music change the world?" was being puckered to the lips of the punk rock-loving press, Bob's Rolling Thunder Revue, in America's bi-Centennial Year, rolled into Houston for 'Night Of The Hurricane II'. Although the gig itself was officially a damp squib in attendance terms, Carter was granted a retrial within two months.

The tour had become public property and, at the second attempt in torrential rain, the event was filmed as 'Hard Rain'.

JOHN HARRIS *Writer and broadcaster*
"My favourite Dylan recording, which isn't really my favourite song, but it is a classic performance, is 'Shelter From The Storm' from the live album 'Hard Rain'. I think it's because of the fact that it's the most gloriously ragged, beautifully all over the place piece of music that I've ever heard.

"The story is that Dylan and the band he was playing with on the Rolling Thunder Revue had spent three days getting really drunk and when they got to the stadium it was really peeing down and they were all in danger of getting electric shocks. Dylan's marriage was in the process of breaking up and he was womanising like there was no tomorrow. So, he gets down to the venue, with all this going on and who should be there but his wife and, consequently the whole thing is done through clenched teeth.

"The song is also the only one to feature Bob Dylan on slide guitar. It's out of tune but it's really good. All in all, that's why you like him, it's not about technique or technical delivery, it's just about someone who really, really means it."

Bit-part work with Clapton and Cohen followed. The latter included a session with gun-toting producer

Bob: It's good to be back, hankie and all

Phil Spector, who snorted ferociously at Bob, while Allen Ginsberg looked on.

As the year drew to a close, the too brief career of The Band climaxed at the Winterland in San Francisco, with Bob and Band filmed for posterity in Martin Scorsese's The Last Waltz.

SHARON DEMARKO,
Pensacola News Journal
It seemed like fiction three weeks ago when

rumours circulated around the city that Bob Dylan's Revue, complete with Joan Baez, Bob Neuwirth, Kinky Friedman and a platoon of musicians, would stop in Pensacola. But, Wednesday night was one of nostalgia for approximately 5,000 folk-rock fans who paid $8.75 each to renew acquaintances with Dylan and Baez.

This was the final stop on Dylan's Florida tour which marked his first appearance since ending a 40-day series of engagements in the Northeast in January.

If anyone missed Dylan's presence on stage during the first hour it was unnoticeable. Then

MASTERPIECES

Tracks: CD1: Knockin' On Heaven's Door, Mr Tambourine Man, Just Like A Woman, I Shall Be Released, Tears Of Rage, All Along The Watchtower, One More Cup Of Coffee, Like A Rolling Stone, The Mighty Quinn, Tomorrow Is A Long Time, Lay Lady Lay, Idiot Wind. CD2: Mixed Up Confusion, Positively Fourth Street, Can You Please Crawl Out Your Window?, Just Like Tom Thumb's Blues, Spanish Is The Loving Tongue, George Jackson (Big Band Version), Rita May, Blowin' In The Wind, A Hard Rain's A-Gonna Fall, The Times They Are A-Changin', Masters Of War, Hurricane. CD3: Maggie's Farm, Subterranean Homesick Blues, Ballad Of A Thin Man, Mozambique, This Wheel's On Fire, I Want You, Rainy Day Women Nos 12&35, Don't Think Twice, It's All Right, Song To Woody, It Ain't Me Babe, Love Minus Zero/No Limit, I'll Be Your Baby Tonight, If Not For You, If You See Her, Say Hello, Sara.

SLEEVE NOTES
None at all.

WHAT THE PAPERS SAID
"This comprehensive Japanese release features a track from the legendary 'Royal Albert Hall' concert."

IN A NUTSHELL
"This comprehensive New Zealand-only release originally came out in 1976 and was indeed the first place to feature an official track from the legendary 'Royal Albert Hall' concert. 'Just Like Tom Thumb's Blues' is a ambience- challenged early mix of what finally appeared on 'Live 1966' with tape hiss optional. The rest of the package, for the time, was a real delight, with 39 tracks covering a variety of classic Dylan performances. And the album set, with its patchy sleevenotes is available at a knock-down price today. For around £15 you can get this three CD set which makes up in track selection for what it lacks in sound quality.

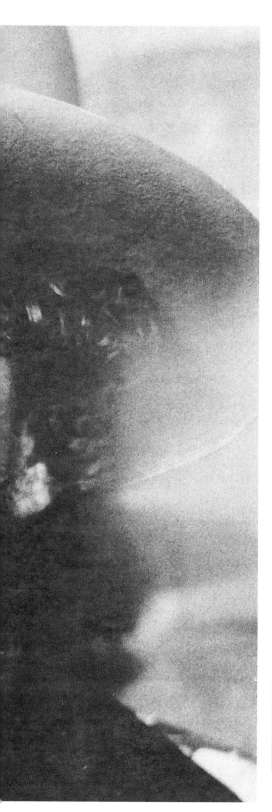

silently, amid the furore created by wildman Kinky Friedman, Dylan slipped on stage. He opened with 'Tambourine Man' and only the crackle of the voice cued spectators that this was their man.

He looked, as always, like a waif and sang like the mythological minstrel he has become. Hair scraggly, falling out from a sloppily-tied pink bandanna a rum- pled, khaki jacket over faded jeans, Dylan moved into 'Just Like A Woman'.

As in the past what Dylan has to say is better than the musical way in which he chooses to communicate. And, Dylan is at his best alone, without the band, without the amplification, relying solely on his inimitable power to mesmerise listeners. In a Dylan concert there is more magic than music.

Desire

Tracks: Hurricane, Isis, Mozambique, One More Cup Of Coffee, Oh, Sister, Joey, Romance In Durango, Black Diamond Bay, Sara.
Released January.
Produced by Don De Vito

SLEEVE NOTES *"Where do I begin... on the heels of Rimbaud moving like a dancing bullet thru the secret streets of a hot New Jersey night filled with venom and wonder."*
Allen Ginsberg drools through the songs and explains and kinda intimates about the Rolling Thunder Revue.

WHAT THE PAPERS SAID *"Ambitious in scope, 'Desire' lacks a good band. With love songs like 'Sara', such topical items like 'Hurricane' and 'Joey' and simple ironic rock songs like 'Mozambique' it could have been a masterpiece."*

Rolling Stone *"This could be the most commercial album of Dylan's career, thanks to its distinctly solid electric folk style. Time hasn't been kind to 'Hurricane', but 'Sara' and 'One More Cup Of Coffee' are still amongst his most bewitching performances."* Q on the album's re-release on CD

WHAT THE INTERNET SAYS *"This album, mostly written with novelist Jacques Levy, is well worth listening to, but I can't really say why I like it, aside from the brilliant 'Hurricane'. It's not as focused as its predecessor; it contains the 11 minute-celebration of a gangster, 'Joey' and Scarlet Rivera's monotonous violin on too many tracks.* DBW, Wilson - Alroy Record Reviews

WHAT DYLAN SAID *"That particular song, 'Sara', well... some songs you figure you're better off not to have written. There's a few of them lying around."*

IN A NUTSHELL
Like the patchwork collage of the sleeve and inner-bag, 'Desire' is a moment caught in time, where causes and curses lie next to emotional grief and song stories of heroes and villains. The Tarot cards and drooling dialogue inside tell something of Dylan's state of mind and where the album is going. A rolling violin propels the story of 'Hurricane' to the fore as the album begins and it's played like a riddling foil throughout the album. Sub-titled 'Songs Of Redemption', there's a religious zeal and a forthright search for honesty on 'Desire'. But it's an odd juxtaposition with seemingly throwaway thoughts lodged next to aching couplets, with Bob's heart tacked to his sleeve for the likes of 'Oh, Sister' (which includes a teetering duet with Emmylou Harris) and 'Sara', but absent in other areas.

Hard Rain

Tracks: Maggie's Farm, One Too Many Mornings, Stuck Inside Of Mobile With The Memphis Blues Again, Oh Sister, Lay Lady Lay, Shelter From The Storm, You're A Big Girl Now, I Threw It All Away, Idiot Wind.
Released September.
Produced by Don De Vito.

SLEEVE NOTES *Lists of lyrics are bookended by a moody Ken Regan black and white shot on the cover and a grainy colour screen grab of Bob's back, complete with tea towel on his head, as shot on the Rolling Thunder Revue.*

WHAT THE INTERNET SAYS *"The band here, loosely based on the 'Desire' line-up, included Mick Ronson and T-Bone Burnett. This marked the beginning of Dylan's commercial decline in the late 70's, peaking in the middle of the Top 40."* JA, Wilson - Alroy Record Reviews

WHAT THE PAPERS SAID

"'Hard Rain', from Dylan's 1976 tour, The Rolling Thunder Revue is simply inconsequential, without the differences that make 'Before The Flood' fascinating." Rolling Stone

IN A NUTSHELL
Featuring nine tracks, recorded live with Bob at his most rambunctious in the rewriting/reworking department, 'Hard Rain', remodels 'Maggie,s Farm', 'One Too Many Mornings', and 'Stuck Inside Of Mobile With The Memphis Blues Again, into swaggering cod-reggae. The arrangements are not delicate and the delivery is akin to a pick-up band who,re unable to unscramble their monitors. Similarly 'Lay Lady Lay, is overwhelmed by rattle and hum and it,s only when the tempo drops for 'Shelter From The Storm', and 'You,re A Big Girl Now', that any emotion is served up. The bluesy reading of 'I Threw It All Away, has all the histrionics of rock opera, while the closing 'Idiot Wind, adopts an over- wrought and rather heavy back-beat which throws the monologue into the realms of pub-singer over-dramatics.

RAIN FACTS
The album was created as an audio version of a TV special that tracked the Rolling Thunder Revue. However, the TV show was reshot and the recordings that were released actually came from a show a week after that.

SINGLES/EPS/ETC
Hurricane (45) Lay Lady Lay (45) Mozambique (45) Rita Mae (45)

1977

The Memphis Blues Again

AS THE punk foghorn blared across the Atlantic eruption, Bob spent his time wrestling with authorities. He got legal. The year was taken up with an ongoing divorce battle with Sara, which involved custody disagreements, analysts, psychoanalysts, counter-analysts, psychiatrists, armed bodyguards and detectives. A detailed TV movie has not as yet followed, but the shenanigans were rife for peak viewing.

Punctuating the brahuha, Dylan hung out with Allen Ginsberg prior to the release of Renaldo And Clara, a lengthy film covering the Rolling Thunder Revue and its surrounding circus. Ginsberg tried to put spin on the movie, but all was not well. Late in the year, Bob shuffled into a session for a new Etta James album in search of veteran producer Jerry Wexler who he wanted to help him with his next album project. Round, round, get around...

MUSIC WRITER JOHNNY BLACK'S DIARY ENTRIES - *1978*

Undated. On Friday night Angel and me went off to see the lengthy epic *Renaldo And Clara*. I enjoyed it thoroughly, although four and a half hours is a long time. Anyway, I feel Dylan has put the movie together much as he puts songs together. A succession of powerful and enigmatic images along with a number of charismatic and intriguingly mysterious people, who are also famous and talented. The only theme I could see in the movie was of the relationships between men and women. Especially broken ones. Johnny

Undated. Apart from the music, I thought this film was a load of rubbish. Anonymous

SIMON HOLLAND
Marketing Manager, Pinnacle Records

"Although nominally at Lancaster University, structured academia had given way to extensive research into the effects of drugs. Many hours were passed around elaborate bongs of increasing size and capacity; always with a suitable soundtrack of course, as music assumed a dominant position in our lives. Amongst the group of people who lived at 'The Farmhouse' (just six lanes of motorway from the Uni itself), was a guy called Chris.

"Chris fancied himself as a bit of a poet and he buried his head, when it could be found at all, in the writings of William Blake and the song lyrics of Bob Dylan. 'Blood On The Tracks' received constant attention on the house stereo as Chris Transcribed the lyrics into a notebook, regaling anyone who dared to still be awake with the worldly provenance of each and every line.

"Of course, Chris's enthusiasm was treated with good humour, which, with the passage of time, would eventually turn into hilarity as he transcribed a line from 'Jack Of Hearts', as we referred to it, as "Rosemary took a cabbage into town". He could have been right, he could have been wrong. Whatever. We rejoiced in the surreal imagery of the situation.

"Chris, of course, was adamant. Hours of pained and patient explanation turned into weeks of futile entreaties as the rest of us tried in vain to reason that a "cabbage" was a none

too mainstream form of transport and perhaps, maybe, only just slightly, it might have been a carriage that was townwards bound.

"In the end we had to admire his tireless zeal. His absolute refusal to give way. And, for all we knew, up the M6 from Manchester, many, many miles from Greenwich Village, Woodstock, Hibbing and, indeed Manchester, a cabbage might have been a beatnik term for something we knew nothing of. Or even a new model of Buick of which we were, quite frankly, completely unaware of.

"And so, it went unsaid. Unargued, His theory unsullied. Chris and Bob were at one on this and cabbage transport was suddenly something we were all about to aspire to."

SUZANNE VEGA *after getting into Bob in 1977*
"When I see those pictures of him in his oversize jacket and tight black jeans and so skinny in his little pointy boots and all pale and intense, that's the character I feel for. If I could have been anyone, that's who I'd want to be. It's not so much sexy as neutral and fascinating which I guess is kinda sexy in its own way. Very mysterious and cool."

SINGLES/EPS/ETC
Stuck Inside Of Mobile With The Memphis Blues Again (45)

Changing Of The Guards

THE RELEASE of *Renaldo And Clara* was met with mass disinterest. It was long. It was bizarre. It was a costume disaster.

In the middle of some rather less than upbeat reviews, Bob revealed its subject matter about alienation and life were very personal to him. The film was littered with vox pop interviews, disguises, bizarre storylines and fantasies, even at 232 minutes it failed to feature much music. And, even when cut to 112 minutes at a later stage it still dragged with precious little Dylan between the cameos from David Blue, Ramblin' Jack Elliot, Roger McGuinn, Allen Ginsberg, Arlo Guthrie and various others. It's said that collaborator Allen Ginsberg's first idea for the film was to sleep with Dylan. Thankfully filmic evidence was not forthcoming. But whatever was shot was certainly edited in. It was not easy going.

MEL HOWARD
Production team Renaldo And Clara, from Telegraph 46

"Sometimes he was totally inarticulate - he would clam up and not say anything. The joy and problem of being with Dylan is that everyone is so anxious to fill in the spaces, that if he's just silent for two minutes some assholes going to jump in and sing a song or do a cartwheel, and we all did.

"The film is another example of how Dylan is willing to upset his artistic conventions and fuck with his talent. He does versions of his songs that are tantamount to a dog's yodel."

THE TIMES
"It is difficult to understand why a man of his sensibilities has allowed such a hotch potch of unfinished, rambling jumble to appear under his name."

In search of guidance in the post-Sara void, Dylan went out on the road again, relying on a psychic adviser for guidance. Said psychic, Tamara Rand had

Zimmie shows artistic integrity by stifling a yawn during Renaldo and Clara.

Bob caught uncomfortably unawares in Renaldo mode

revealed that Bob's previous lives included high times in the Roman empire. As he circumnavigated the globe on tour, like a centurion on a route march, he

Street-Legal

BOB DYLAN

Tracks: *Changing Of The Guards, New Pony, No Time To Think, Baby, Stop Crying, Is Your Love In Vain?, Senor (Tales of Yankee Power), True Love Tends To Forget, We'd Better Talk This Over, Where Are You Tonight?*

Released June.
Produced by Don De Vito.

SLEEVE NOTES The seemingly-candid inner sleeve black and white shots of Bob eating dinner present a completely different image to the colour cover snap and the rear sleeve's be-make-uped rock icon pose. There's little in the way of text, other than an 'In Memoriam' mention for deceased counter culture activist Emmett Grogan.

WHAT THE PAPER'S SAID

"When originally released, 'Street Legal' was greeted with slight disappointment. Neither as personal as 'Blood On The Tracks' or as strange as 'Desire'. But time has been kind, the songs are brilliant and the preoccupation's that fuel them only add to the slightly fevered atmosphere."Danny Kelly, Q on it's re-release

WHAT THE INTERNET SAYS

"For once on a Dylan album, different tracks don't set different moods. Bob himself seems pensive and inert, with his lyrics either rambling and obscure, appallingly crude or baldly straightforward.
DBW, Wilson - Alroy Record Reviews

"There are no real high points here, I can't vouch for the lyrics, and it's truly monotonous, with an early-70's big band sound that emphasises the female chorus, lazy sax, and simple organ. But Dylan's voice, often in a low register, retains some emotional power; and at least there are no disco or pop influences." JA, Wilson - Alroy Record Reviews

WHAT THE WORLD SAYS Only through massive research in second hand record stores across the globe can the presence and reputation of 'Street-Legal' be revealed. It is, without doubt, the most remaindered Bob album with the usual tag at £2.00. Perhaps it was a record label over-fulfilment problem but this is the album that's seemingly Bob's least wanted.

IN A NUTSHELL In context, chronologically following Bob from 'Desire', 'Street Legal' trips down the accessible end of the avenue. Gone is the precise violin, replaced by horns and back-up singers who add a swagger instead of focus to the songs. There's a soulful edge to the songs and some honking sax in places but the plot is lost, it's too indistinct. When the violin does return it's delivered in passing rather than as a power point and, as the whole album does, the music just chugs like an old waltz while Bob rhymes in hand-swaying style. In isolation the album has its own personal identity but the mood is caught in a '70s rock star hyperstate that Bob fails to really make his own.

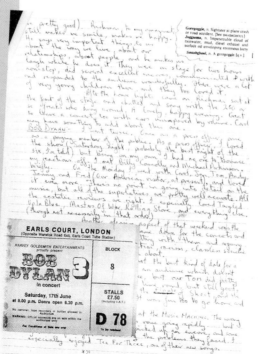

"'Tis madness I tell you. Who in the hours for a Dylan ticket?"

also travelled in time under hypnosis. The European leg of the tour closed in July with sold-out shows at Earl's Court followed by a monumental performance at Blackbushe Aerodrome in England. A quarter of a million people flocked to Fleet for the experience.

ANDY KERSHAW at Earl's Court

"Seeing Dylan live has never really worked for me. I wasn't old enough to have seen him at the peak of his powers in 1965 and '66. Apart from the Isle Of Wight, he didn't come back and play the UK until he played at Earl's Court in 1978. For that show I camped out all night at a record shop in Manchester to get one £5 ticket to sit at the back of the venue to watch him. In fact, it was so far back that it was almost in Northamptonshire.

"I went along hoping to hear what I'd heard on the great bootlegs in the mid-'60s. It was a huge disappointment because he came out with what sounded like a cabaret band. What wounded me deeply was that he was wearing a pair of white flares with a red metallic flash down the leg. Even from all that way back, they looked like they were made of Crimpelene. And the songs were almost unrecognisable. "I was so disappointed because I'd run out of my A Level Economics exam, which I needed to get into university, to see the show. I was at school in Oldham at the time. I'd gone to the exam, hurriedly answered three questions, then jumped into a mate's sporty little run-around and got off down to the station, then on to London.

"I arrived at the venue while he was playing 'Baby Stop Crying', I flopped in my seat at the back of the hall and it was just awful. I came back on the milk train in the middle of the night and it was daylight when I got back to Manchester."

JOHNNY BLACK'S DIARY ENTRIES - *1978*

6.5.78 Looks like the build up to Dylan concerts has started. Tickets go on sale tomorrow at

18.5.78 Continuing the Dylan saga - this ad appeared in Guardian today - Dylan tickets for sale - £25. Makes me a bit sick, but I guess business is business and God only knows how high the price will go on the eve of the shows. Johnny

26.5.78 Latest price for Dylan tickets is £75.00.

19.6.78 We scrambled to our seats just in time as the lights dimmed. A concert that started on time - good start! The band wandered on stage and started the first number, I remember thinking, 'This is it! After all these years!'. They were shit-hot and tight as hell and got better as the concert progressed. I really hope that he keeps this band for a while yet because they're tailor-made for the stuff. Andy

19.6.78 Uh... Bob who? The old fart acquitted himself admirably - he should lose money more often! The entire evening was so fresh, it made me wonder just how long Dylan can go on. Tom

ight mind would queue for 17

10.00am and today at five there were 200 people queuing outside Hammersmith Odeon. We'll just have to get in the queue pdq tomorrow. Johnny

7.5.78 'Tis madness I tell you, Madness! Well, who in their right mind would spend 17 hours queuing for Dylan tickets? Uh... I did. Tom

7.5.78 The Dylan episode has been slightly nuts all the way. There seems to have been lots of people who wanted tickets for the show who won't ever see Dylan. Because of the way the tickets have been pout on sale, ageing Dylan freaks with kids who can't get to the venue for tickets, have no hope. Lots of people also queued all night and didn't get tickets. Seems they could have sold 500,000 tickets easily. I would have thought Dylanmania died years ago, but clearly I would be wrong. Johnny

21.6.78 I went twice. Once as a press officer for CBS. Once as a paying member of the public. As a press officer, I loved the show (Saturday night, probably the best night of the six, I'm told) but being on my own I had no-one to bounce my reactions off. I met Billy Connolly and Michael Parkinson briefly.

"On the Monday I went with my friends and I loved it even more. There's no point in going into details on the music but all the superlatives are accurate.

26.6.78 Bob Dylan was the best concert I've been to for a long time. I adore him - I want to hug him, with his bandy legs and waif face. It contrasts nicely with Mink De Ville - I find him repulsive but compulsive.

Back to Dylan, He means so much to so many people of my generation - yet he managed to play a concert where we sat up and listened as if for the first time.

BOB DYLAN AT BUDOKAN

Tracks: Mr Tambourine Man, Shelter From The Storm, Love Minus Zero/No Limit, Ballad Of A Thin Man, Don't Think Twice, It's Alright, Maggie's Farm, One More Cup Of Coffee, Like A Rolling Stone, I Shall Be Released, Is Your Love In Vain?, Going Going Gone, Blowin' In The Wind, Just Like A Woman, Oh Sister, Simple Twist Of Fate, All Along The Watchtower, I Want You, All I Really Want To Do, Knockin' On Heaven's Door, It's Alright Ma (I'm Only Bleeding), Forever Young, The Times They Are A-Changin'.
Released July (Japan).
Produced by Don Devito.

SLEEVE NOTES *"The more I think about it, the more I realise what I left behind in Japan - my soul, my music and that sweet girl in the geisha house."*

WHAT THE PAPERS SAID *"As with many Dylan live offerings, virtually every cut gets an unfamiliar arrangement, fine when it works, disastrous when it doesn't. A half-good live album, essential only for the terminally smitten."* Johnny Black reviewed on re-issue at Mid-Price in 1993.

IN A NUTSHELL *Whereas previous live albums had either been reasonable facsimiles of studio songs played by bigger bands or a reasonable union between Bob and his contemporaries on new interpretations, 'Live At Budokan' was the first album to openly illustrate Dylan's desire to reshape his past catalogue ad nauseum. The audience clap politely, but 'Mr Tambourine Man' and 'Love Minus Zero' are butchered by flutes early on (not easy) and the rest of the album ends up sounding like an easy-listening back-up orchestra have infiltrated the show. There's a moody four-in-the-morning 'Ballad Of A Thin Man' and 'Blowin' In The Wind', both of which are given a dramatic edge almost sacrilegiously akin to a Springsteen epic but the band are intrusive and every time Bob warbles towards emotion someone cuts in with some heavy plant orchestration.*

BUDOKAN FACTS
The tour of the Far East was preceded by a special Japan only triple set called 'Masterpieces', which included several unreleased tracks, including a song from the Live 1966 recording and a remix of 'Mixed Up Confusion'. The 'Budokan' album was initially set for Japanese release only but no sooner had the die-hard fans shelled out for it, it obtained a domestic release.

SINGLES/EPS/ETC
Baby Stop Crying (45) Changing Of The Guard (45)
Is Your Love In Vain? (45)

MARK ELLEN *on Blackbushe*

"Near where I grew up, Fleet in Hampshire, there's an abandoned airstrip. It's a godforsaken, weed-infested chunk of wasteland circled with gorse bushes whose sole recommendation is that it's flat, hence a crude concrete runway had been pasted in for freight planes towards the end of the Second World War. No-one ever ventured out there it seemed but us, flying our flimsy elastic band-driven aircraft, kicking cans, incinerating small insects with magnifying glasses and doing whatever else it was that small boys did for amusement in the 1960s.

"I will never - ever - forget the shock when the news arrived in the summer of '78 that Bob Dylan, the folk-prophet at whose feet I'd sat mesmerised for the past 15 years, had deigned to add one further fixture to his European tour due to the overwhelming demand for his six nights at Earls Court. And what particular spot in the whole of the United Kingdom had he selected for this historic convention? Blackbushe Aerodrome in Fleet, Hampshire.

DESOLATION ROW: this was the way thousands of Dylan fans spent the weekend, queuing for tickets to see the great Zimmo at agents and box offices around the country. Many waited all day and all night and although there were many complaints about the agonising and inefficient slowness of it all, the crowds were mostly good-natured. London's Hammersmith Odeon generously allowed fans to spend Saturday night inside but the subsequent rush to get in prompted a torrent of four-letter abuse which was heard by delighted listners to the otherwise incurably bland Nicky Horne show on Capital Radio — Horne was doing one of his street-credibility live broadcast walkabouts at the time.
MOST OF the tickets for Dylan's Earls Court concerts next month have been snapped up. Of the 94,000 tickets available 92,000 were sold within eight hours on Sunday, May 7.
The 2,000 remaining tickets are being recalled to London and it will be announced next week how these will be disposed of. Fans started queuing from Thursday morning in some places prior to the 15 box offices opening for business on Sunday at 10am.
Sounds 13/5/78

"It's a Godforsaken chunk of wasteland circled by gorse bushes."

Blackbushe Aerodrome! There were ads in all the music papers - 'The Picnic At Blackbushe Aerodrome', this ropey old patch of scrub somewhat dignified by stylish drawings of striped tents and the suggestion of high pageantry. It was *unbelievable*, as if the cosmic pin had randomly alighted on some secret place apparently known only to myself and Bob Dylan.

  "When the day came I felt a pathetic surge of proprietorial pride. Had I gone to see him or had he come to see me? Here it all was, right here on this godforsaken site of my childhood memories, a great carpet of people, two hundred thousand of them, waving flags and banners, hoisting jugs of cider, roaring their approval, Graham Parker, Joan Armatrading, Eric Clapton, Dylan himself bathed in soft purple lighting and wearing a top hat he'd just borrowed from a hotel porter. And me standing in the middle of it all, possibly a little glassy-eyed at this point, wondering how I'd have felt if I'd ever known back then that, one day, all of this was going to happen.

DAVID LYNN,
slightly stoned of Scotland

"I was dead impressed with him at Blackbushe when I didn't particularly expect to be. In fact, I'd really gone to see Clapton who was absolutely appalling. Aswad kicked it off and were pathetic, Joan Armatrading were superb, Graham Parker was pretty good and then it was on to the huge EC disappointment. When Bob finally came on, I was still punch-drunk with a sense of betrayal, so the fact that his set turned it round for me was quite an achievement. I even forgot to be cynical about people holding up flickering lighters during the set."

TOM PAYNE, *IT Manager*

"I remember seeing him at Blackbushe Aerodrome when he gave some of his old numbers the reggae treatment much to the vocally expressed disgust of the purists. I thought it was great."

CHRIS TAYLOR, *photographer*

"It was the first time he'd played since the Isle Of Wight. We had to queue up in New Bond Street overnight to get tickets and I remember

we were outside of a show shop, with people like Nicky Horne interviewing the crowd at annoying intervals. We went up there at about 4 o'clock the night before the box office opened and we weren't even in the first 20 in the queue. We didn't realise how big Dylan was until then, till we woke up the next morning and saw the queue snaking away behind us."
What was it like when you actually got your ticket?
"It was just incredible. It was a huge rush. All night there'd been rumours that the other box offices had sold the allocation and there wouldn't be any tickets. It was very nerve wracking."
And the gig itself?
"I was desperate to get photos and we were way at the back, Dylan was just a very small dot, so I moved forward, weaving my way through the crowd and taking shots along the way in case I couldn't get any further. When I got to the front, well about 100 yards away, I was just thrilled. I thought I may never see him again so I kept taking pictures and I wrote down every song that he played."

ELIZABETH M THOMSON, *from Conclusions On The Wall*

"As the evening cooled and the moon rose, Dylan turned on the heat. The stage lights glowed and we were all right there with him, swaying with the music, hands held high, 250,000 joining Dylan in song: "How does it feel? How does it feel?"

FOREVER DYLAN

They traipsed across the fields in their tens of thousands, just like they had nine years earlier on the Isle Of Wight. That time it was to see Bob Dylan resurrected from his motorbike smash - or whatever it was that turned him into a recluse for four years.
This time it's to see Dylan coming to terms with his heritage at Blackbushe Aerodrome, 40 miles west of London. His audience are nine years older now, and many of them have brought their children along.
Word of his triumphant London concerts last month has got around, and there are 50,000 people in front of the stage by 11am when the first band appears. Nine hours later, after Graham Parker, Joan Armatrading and Eric Clapton, Dylan strolls on to a gigantic howl of applause and spends the next two and a half hours running through the last 15 years. He reworks old favourites like 'Masters Of War' and 'Ballad Of A Thin Man' into powerful rockers, disco riffing through 'Maggie's Farm', lacing 'One More Cup Of Coffee' with large dollops of Gospel and getting everyone to sing 'Forever Young' as a farewell anthem.
NME, July 1978

Slow Train Coming

AND ON the ninth day, Bob got God, or at least he scanned him from a different angle. Inspired by his girlfriend Mary Alice Artes, Dylan continued his search for a new identity and turned to Christianity. Some of the songs he'd played to Jerry Wexler had hinted at a desire for "understanding" and when he came to record 'Slow Train Coming' with the producer he played music that, according to Dylan, he didn't want to write. "It just came out" he told the police.

In preparation for touring, the bandwagon of belief rolled on to Saturday Night Live, where he premiered some of his new Christian material. When the full set of these new testaments rolled out, the world stood aghast at the transformation, begging for the old Dylan - whatever guise that might have been - to come back. The press, however had mixed feelings, with "Bob Dylan is the greatest singer of our times." countered by "Bob Dylan's God-Awful Gospel". The media was perplexed. Everyone was confused.

ROBERT HILBURN *Los Angeles Times*
"Who would ever have thought in the age of the Sex Pistols and punk rock that the most controversial issue in rock would be religion, and that Bob Dylan would be at the centre of it?"

NEWSWEEK
This time the storm centres not only on Dylan's music, but on his message: the 38-year old former Robert Zimmerman, suddenly resurrected as a born-again Christian, is spouting religious fundamentalism to a rock 'n' roll beat.

GARY HERMAN *from Rock 'n' Roll Babylon*
"If Dylan's Christianity means anything, it is that all the conflicts and struggles that emerged in the Sixties and were embodied in rock 'n' roll have not been resolved. There is, of course, no reason why they should have been after only a

few short years, but Dylan and his Christian cohorts feel the need for such a resolution and, in being 'Born again', they have rendered the life of the spirit itself quite unthreatening to themselves. They have wiped away the sense of risk that gives true rock 'n' roll its edge."

Slow Train Coming

Tracks: *Gotta Serve Somebody, Precious Angel, I Believe In You, Slow Train, Gonna Change My Way Of Thinking, Do Right To Me Baby (Do Unto Others), When You Gonna Wake Up, Man Gave Names To All The Animals, When He Returns.*

Released August.

Produced by Jerry Wexler and Barry Beckett.

SLEEVE NOTES *None as such.*

WHAT THE INTERNET SAYS *"Known as the beginning of his 'born again' period, this was his biggest seller since Desire. Contains the singles 'Gotta Serve Somebody' and 'Man Gave Names To All The Animals'. (Hear that, women?) DBW, Wilson - Alroy Record Reviews.*

WHAT THE WORLD SAYS SINEAD O'CONNOR
"This was really the first album that inspired me to want to be a singer. I was totally inspired by it, especially 'Gotta Serve Somebody', which I like because it's sexy and funky, as well as being religious. "Apparently Bob Dylan feels some sort of shame about the album because he was slagged off a lot for being a Christian, but it's amazing. I was blown away by the fact that a man could be so intimate and I became totally obsessed by him. I used to write his words everywhere, on school copybooks, desks. As far as I was concerned, all of the songs were about me and this album was The Bible."

MARIA MULDUAR
"My daughter's near-fatal car accident in 1979 sparked a profound change. My whole life was severely jolted. It coincided with Bob Dylan's 'Slow Train Coming' album coming out. I heard the words of that album and realised that, no matter how successful your life, without a relationship with God or a higher power, there was something very big missing. It wasn't even a conscious intellectual decision. At that moment, I surrendered to the higher power."

CERYS MATTHEWS
"'I Believe In You' is one of those songs that just makes me cry."

IN A NUTSHELL
Musically there's a carefully-primed but largely over-dramatised power to 'Slow Train Coming'. The gospel-pumped 'Gotta Serve Somebody' sets out Bob's vision early on and whether you appreciate the message or not, the poignancy of the arrangements and the drive of Dylan's delivery is impressive. Side two's 'Gonna Change My Way Of Thinking' rotates with a driving cow bell like some lost rock anthem being played on the road to Heaven. The message is the medium and Dylan's down-home spiritualism adds an underlying reggae-paced click track that allows the vocals and indeed the story to take stage centre throughout.

SINGLES/EPS/ETC
Knockin' On Heaven's Door (45) Lay Lady Lay (45) Forever Young (45) Precious Angel (45) Gotta Serve Somebody (45) Man Gave Us Names To All The Animals (45) When You Gonna Wake Up (45)

ELIZABETH M THOMSON
from Conclusions On The Wall

"It does seem strange that yesterday's angry young man, now approaching 40, should have found religion and found it in such a big way. It was certainly disquieting to find him identifying with Christ. Dylan's suffered artistic crucifixion and resurrection before, now he has chosen to crucify himself on the cross of Christianity."

BOB MARLEY

"If you are an artist like Bob Dylan, you got to make the crowd follow you. I can tell you that it doesn't mean anything to him that people might not like what he's doing."

MARTIN PEARSON
saxophone-playing osteopath

"I was a teenager in the 1970's, going against the grain and even punk rock by listening to Bob Dylan. I was a very active Christian and church goer and 'Slow Train Coming' came out at just the right time for me. I listened to it again and again and again and I knew practically the whole thing off by heart. At the time it was a great re-assurance for me. It re-enforced the faith that I had and by doing that it helped me get through my very turbulent teens.

"It was reassuring that here was this man, Bob Dylan, that I was really into, that I taught myself to play the guitar because of - from the Bob Dylan Songbook - then suddenly here he was announcing that he too was a Christian."

ROBERT SHELTON,
author and writer, from Conclusions On The Wall

"This period of religious zealotry is a good testing-time for his mist dedicated adherents to find out if they really can live the truth with such an explosive existentialist."

PATRICK HUMPHRIES

"I went to see Robert Shelton just after 'Street-Legal' came out. I'd read in the Melody Maker that he lived in Sydenham and I couldn't believe that this legendary Bob biographer lived half a mile from where I grew up. I remember talking to him about classic Dylan lines and I was enthusing about the line "Where you heading, Lincoln County Road or Armageddon", saying that only one person could write a line like that and he said, 'What do you know about Lincoln County Road?' I thought it was just a rhyme in a Dylan song and he explained that Lincoln County Road leads from Jimmy Carter's hometown of Plains, Georgia to Washington.

" And it suddenly dawned on me, all that stuff about Dylan knocking off songs in five minutes was just rubbish. There was obviously a lot of thought that had gone into these songs."

The God question reached ultimate caricatural form in Sounds

"It was reassuring that here was Bob Dylan announcing that he too was a Chrsitian."

AND THAT WAS THE SEVENTIES

BY THE END OF THE '70S I'D PROBABLY drifted further away from Bob. I was in a band who'd toured Leicester - five nights in and around the throbbing city centre - before heading to London to secure fame and fortune. We rehearsed a lot and perfected, eventually, a brace of covers that summed up our musical state. Faust's 'Sad Skinhead', Eno's 'Dead Finks Don't Talk' and a miss-timed attempt at The Chambers Brothers' 'Time Has Come Today' ensured that it would be difficult to secure a Bob Dylan support slot for The Disco Zombies.

In our earliest incarnation, we had unleashed a song called 'I Need You Like I Need VD' but it's subtleties soared over the heads of our fan (!) and it wasn't a match for Bob's 'VD Gunner's Blues'.

In 1979, I was protesting. I was producing a silk-screened fanzine called South London Stinks. I was in poor shape, on the dole and ill from inhaling screen inks, but not as ill as one of my co-conspirators who eventually contracted an ancient form of TB from our ridiculous lifestyle.

Bob was by far richer but, in the post-punk malaise he was in pretty bad shape too. The punk explosion had been wrought to destroy the decade that nurtured rock excess and elevated the likes of Led Zeppelin, Aerosmith and the Stones to megastar status. The shows had got bigger. Tours had become epic and roots and indeed the music fans were left under nourished. The rock dinosaurs roamed the earth with a convoy of artics behind them and Bob followed suit.

As the Dylan legend had been magnified, his early '60s call to arms was well and truly heeded. The punk scene brought politics back to pop and put the old guard, of which Bob was something of a figurehead, on the backfoot. If that weren't enough, then there were the dreaded punk poets - from Patrik Fitzgerald through to John Cooper Clark - who were raiding Bob's back pages in the cause of agit pop.

Certainly, in the early '70s Bob had rekindled his anti-establishment cred by releasing 'George Jackson' and 'Hurricane' but all that good work was marred for the second generation rock fan by double albums recorded at the Budokan, the over-radioed 'Knockin' On Heaven's Door' and his religious rebirth.

As Bob's shares stiffed and his new beliefs became public his sales begin to decline. The real Bob merchandising battle was being fought out on the bootleg circuit and tape trading circles. His live shows still pulled in the punters, even if they were getting older.

A Satisfied Mind

AND THE word was Bob. For he was 'Saved' and in turn he was changed. As part of Dylan's rebirth as a Christian, he began to preach between songs, denouncing his past - "Years ago they used to call me a prophet. Now I come and say, 'Jesus is the answer', and they say, 'Bob Dylan? He's no prophet!'." But his new album was not 'Saved', it was remaindered. The shows were hailed as exciting but fan reaction was highly mixed as they comprised only of his religious songs. In general the crucifixion of Bob was the sport of the day. And even though he scooped a Grammy for 'Gotta Serve Somebody' from 'Slow Train Coming', his new found Faith was the cause of heated debate. By year end, out on the road yet again, some of his older material was beginning to creep back into the set but still people were not convinced and his Grammy acceptance speech confirmed that he knew who his friends were as he opined: "The first person I want to thank is the Lord."

CLIFF WARNKEN, *via internet*
"Dylan's gospel show at Columbus, OH, 5/20/80 was one of the best I've seen/heard him do, it was an all-out rockin', bluesy, gospel show with much of the feel and sound of black gospel groups of the '50s. I think that's the sound he was going for at that point. All the songs he did were from his "Christian" period. The crowd loved it, and nobody booed."

Saved

Tracks: A Satisfied Mind, Saved, Covenant Woman, What Can I Do For You?, SolidRock, Pressing On, In The Garden, Saving Grace, Are You Ready.
Released June.
Produced by Jerry Wexler.

SLEEVE NOTES *"Behold, the days come, saith the Lord, that I will make a new covenant with the house of Israel, and with the house of Judah. Jeremiah Chapter 31."*

WHAT THE INTERNET SAYS *"The comeback marked by 'Slow Train' ended abruptly, with this one failing toeven go gold, much less platinum; Dylan's success with the Top 40 charts also came to a complete halt after 'Serve Somebody'. JA Wilson - Alroy Record Reviews*

WHAT THE WORLD SAYS JERRY WEXLER
"I can't say it's one of his best albums. That's up to Bob and for otherpeople to say. But to me it came off beautifully. In the recording process Bob was always very laid-back, but also very sentient about everything that was going on around him and always focused towards what he wanted to accomplish. The guy is great - a certifiable genius."

WHAT THE PAPERS SAID
"Five years on, 'Saved' sounds like Dylan's most substantial 'Born Again' release, with 'Saving Grace' and 'What Can I Do For You' striking home with a
gentle soulfulness that 'Slow Train Coming' lacked." Record Collector, 1985

IN A NUTSHELL *In as much as 'Street-Legal' presented a different kind of Dylan, 'Saved' moved away from the more obvious invocation of 'Slow Train Coming' and offered a slower, better-paced and more righteous display of Bob's reborn beliefs. Spooner Oldham's piano holds sway on 'What Can I Do For You?' and 'Saving Grace', while the testifying spiritualism of the standard 'Satisfied Mind' gives Bob's vocal more edgy power. The more uptempo 'Solid Rock' throbs along like a Black Crowes' out-take with embarrassing lyrics, losing its potency along the way as the storyline and even Bob's poetic muse fail to keep up. Musically there's a comfortable mid-paced mood that lulls the listener into a false sense of enjoyment. It's only when some of the crass choruses and the*
more hackneyed Biblical visions are rolled out that the proceedings start to get devalued.

SINGLES/EPS/ETC *Gotta Serve Somebody (45) Saved (45)*

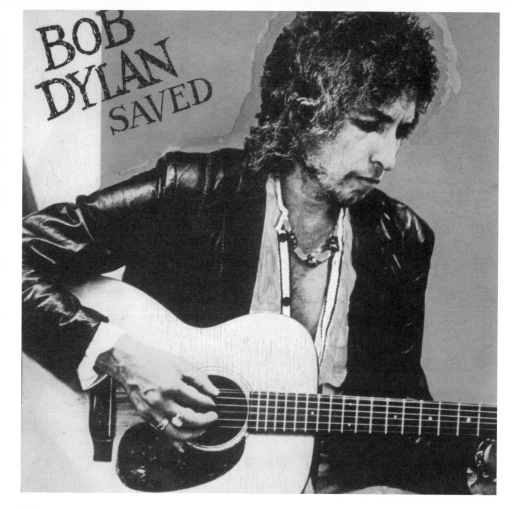

RONNIE HAWKINS *legend*
"He told me he had sold 12 million albums since he became a Christian. I told him to become a Moslem and he might sell 60 million."

MICHAEL FALLON *via internet*
"I recall the shows I attended in 1980 when Bob was doing his gospel show and they were very impressive. Most of the people that came for the old songs were definitely disappointed!!! Some were yelling their opinions quite vociferously (as the tape I still have will attest) There were perceptive opinions like 'Rock and Roll', 'Play some classics', and 'Where ya at?'. Some were no doubt fuelled by not so controlled substances as was the fashion at the time. Many 'fans' retreated to the theatre bar for some libation, especially during the powerful opening set by the female gospel singers.

"Bob's raps disparaged fellow artists who had not found what he had found. He said 'I knew Jim Morrison and I knew Jimi Hendrix and I knew Lowell George (who had just died a few days earlier) and if they knew then what I know now, they'd still be here.' So much for modesty."

> "He told me he'd sold 12 million since he became a Christian. I told him to become a Moslem and he might sell 60 million.?"

1981

Property Of Jesus

AND THE road still snaked, with Dylan covering ground from Illinois through to London's Earls Court. France, Germany, Austria and Switzerland all get the message before he traversed the States and Canada in support of his latest opus 'Shot Of Love'. Sales of his official albums were spiralling down but the merchandising arm, the Bob industry was beginning to flourish. Books, classic Dylan conventions, live bootlegs, nice sweatshirts and the like were all extending the Dylanophile's shopping list. Estranged manager Albert Grossman sued Dylan over royalties and other payments. Bob remained seemingly oblivious to matters arising, claiming that his "rebirth" had made him a new person. The adverse response to his gospel-only perhaps resulted in him revisiting his roots, but he always searched for and exposed 'the message'.

ROBERT SHELTON,
author and writer, from Conclusions On The Wall

"Even if we don't like Dylan's recent albums, we can wait it out. He's got to save himself before he can save his art. He's given us so much more than many other artists, can we really demand "road maps for the soul" once a year?"

DENNIS GREEN, *via internet*
I saw Bobby in October, '81 at the Spectrum in Philly. I went by myself, the night of the concert, to the ticket window and asked for the best seat available: I figured that it wasn't a sell-out. I was correct. I actually got a good floor seat. The most interesting thing about the concert was that Bob had extra security guards who walked around to make sure that NOBODY smoked anything. Pot/tobacco/ hash all was forbidden and really enforced. The first part was gospel (well, anyway this part seemed really looong), well-rehearsed. The audience didn't boo but shouted out requests between songs. Then for around an hour and a half Dylan did a regular concert/greatest hits show. It was really great. People were on their feet. Just as the atmosphere reached a fever pitch - Bob pulled the plug and ended the show. Most people (including myself) were surprised that it wasn't a completely gospel show and left very satisfied."

BRIAN WALKER
"I went to see Bob Dylan at the NEC in Birmingham in 1981. It was OK, well it was a bit gospelly. But, I suppose the thing that struck me was when I looked around was that I realised that there were loads of middle-aged people sitting around having surreptitious joints and I remember I just felt quite old.

"I suppose it wasn't really what I wanted to hear. I would have much preferred him to play some of the songs from the '60s, but that was 20 years earlier."

Shot Of Love

Tracks: Shot Of Love, Heart Of Mine, Property Of Jesus, Lenny Bruce, Watered-Down Love, The Groom's Still Waiting At The Altar, Dead Man, Dead Man, In The Summertime, Trouble, Every Grain Of Sand.

Released August
Produced by Chuck Plotkin and Bob Dylan.

SLEEVE NOTES *"I thank thee, O Father, Lord of Heaven and earth because thou hast hidden these things from the wise and prudent, and hast revealed them unto babes."*

WHAT THE WORLD SAYS
CLINTON HEYLIN, in Behind Close Doors
"'Shot Of Love' failed on its own terms, not because of poor production, or because it was overly concerned with one thematic preoccupation, but largely because the songs that should have been the album's core had already eluded Dylan by the time the sessions began, and their replacements were disappointingly lightweight."

WHAT THE PAPERS SAID
"In the summer of 1985, Dylan released 'Shot Of Love', which he described in contemporary interviews as his best ever album. The cover artwork was less impressive than 'Saved' and the mix even muddier. Much of the songwriting too was unfinished and trite, although 'In The Summertime' and 'Every Grain Of Sand' were amongst his best recent work. The inclusion of several plodding dirges became all the more baffling when it was revealed that he had left remarkable material like 'Caribbean Wind' and 'The Groom's Still Standing At The Alter' off the album." Record Collector

IN A NUTSHELL *More of the same, like 'Saved' part two. There's the by-now traditional revival of the uncomfortable sub-reggae/rock pacing and the a-testifying opening on the title track. In fact, those howling backing singers are on hand for the vital accentuation of the inevitably considerate story-lines and Ringo Starr and Ron Wood drop by for effect on 'Heart Of Mine'. Even so, Bob still seems to struggle with the words. Sure, he's got the message, he's been indoctrinated by the Lord but he just seems like he's having trouble man-handling all those good, good feelings into each song for we the world to understand.*

SINGLES/EPS/ETC *Heart Of Mine (45) Lenny Bruce (45)*
Heart Of Mine (45)

1982

What's The Matter With Me...

RUMOURS ABOUT Bob's re-appraisal of the Christian faith ran riot as he declined to present a Gospel Song Award at a songwriters' ceremony. Around the same time, it was reported that he'd visited Jerusalem and an anticipated return to Judaism was speculated upon. With no product released, sightings of Bob were thin on the ground. However, he performed with Joan Baez for Peace Sunday and mooched around town searching for a producer for his next project. With no profile, the press sweepstakes ran rife and the listed options included Mark Knopfler, Frank Zappa, David Bowie and Elvis Costello.

FRANK ZAPPA

"I'd been getting these messages that Bob Dylan was trying to reach me. I thought it was a joke. Then one night he showed up at the stage gate. I hadn't seen a picture of Bob Dylan for so long I couldn't tell if this guy on the video screen standing down there in the middle of a cold night wearing just a shirt was actually him, so I sent the engineer, who was more pop-aware than I was, to see who it was. It was Bob. He brought him in, we went in the other room and he played some of his tunes on the piano.

"I went through the stuff and made suggestions. We agreed to go ahead, I made suggestions of musicians, got ready to book the studio, then I got a phone call from him saying he couldn't do it right then and that he was going on vacation to the Bahamas. That was the last I heard from him."

1983

License To Kill

Bob Dylan
Hurricane

IN AMERICA THE court is king and lawsuits are everyday. Patty Valentine, a witness in the case of Hurricane Carter, sued Dylan for damages inflicted by the song 'Hurricane'. (She's mentioned in verse one.) The federal judge reviewed the whole song before the case was thrown out of court. Trouble continued when photographer Gary Aloian sued Bob after a scuffle at LAX, but that case was also abandoned. By contrast, Bob's Grossman dispute reached unexpected heights of absurdity when Bob's statement was deemed nonsensical and he was asked to write it again "with paragraphs". Meanwhile, the debate over producers was settled, with Dire Straits' Mark Knopfler stepping in for 'Infidels'. But, the project ran over time and Knopfler was committed to tour with Dire Straits. The album was completed independently of the headbanded guitarist and newspaper reports of an acrimonious split were rolled out. Knopfler eventually added fuel to the fire as he claimed he was unhappy with the end product.

CBS
3878

Infidels

Tracks: Jokerman, Sweetheart Like You, Neighbourhood Bully, License To Kill, Man Of Peace, Union Sundown, I and I, Don,t Fall Apart On Me Tonight.
Produced by Mark Knopfler.

SLEEVE NOTES
There aren't any, just a roll call of the team players, who include ex-Stones' guitarist Mick Taylor and reggae rhythm section Sly Dunbar and Robbie Shakespeare. The information is set on a picture of Bob back in Israel.

WHAT THE WORLD SAYS
MARK KNOPFLER *"He's wild to work with but different people get different results in different ways. You have to be flexible when you're producing and make sure that you respect a person's feelings. The fact is, we can all be proved wrong. "(On Infidels) it was Bob's band, although I did suggest Alan Clark, who I was working with on the soundtrack to Local Hero. Bob came by to say hello and because we were set up I suggested that we just carry on in the same studio and that Alan should do the keyboard stuff. Then Bob brought in Sly and Robbie and Mick Taylor.*

"With Bob all I tried to do was make sure that we were prepared. Bob ran through things at my house and I made sure that we were in 'going' mode when we got to the studios, to make sure that we got at least some kind of recording. "It worked very well on some things, like 'License To Kill' went well on the first take. It was all done live. I learned that from 'Slow Train Coming'. From Barry Beckett. You try and get things down in the first two or three times or Bob will have moved on to something else. I think 'Infidels' would have been a better record if I'd been able to mix the thing, but I had to go on tour in Europe. Bob actually re-sang some of the tracks, which I don't think he should've done and he went ahead and finished it himself."

WHAT THE PAPERS SAID *"'Infidels' was universally treated as a return to form, as much because it didn't sound overtly religious as much as anything."* Record Collector

IN A NUTSHELL *After the cod-reggae and the reggae-paced religious songs, Sly and Robbie were brought in to provide the ultimate skank. The result works admirably on the slower songs, with Sly's drums just that perfect micro-second off the beat to give the backing a unique sound. Both Knopfler and Taylor add their individual guitar rattles to the general ambience, leaving*

Dylan to conjure up a new set of humanitarian but not particularly overtly-religious songs, supported by Alan Clark's melodic keyboard flurries.

SINGLES/EPS/ETC
Union Sundown (45) I And I (45)

THE GROOM'S STILL WAITING AT THE ALTAR

(Previously unreleased recording)
Produced by Chuck Plotkin and Bob Dylan

Photography-Ken Regan
℗ 1981 CBS Inc.
© 1981 CBS Inc.
Manufactured by Columbia Records
CBS Inc./51 W. 52 Street, N.Y./"Columbia,"
and ● are trademarks of CBS Inc./Marcas Reg.
WARNING: All Rights Reserved.
Unauthorized duplication
is a violation of applicable laws.

18 02510

BOB DYLAN

JOHN BERRY

"I've been a fan since about 1987. Bob just changed my life and opened up whole new worlds for me, that's all. Seriously, being a fan of Bob has opened up areas I, a poor kid from Indiana, would have never explored. Poetry, music, books, things that come "recommended" by his Bobness. My epiphany came one spring day during my sophomore year in college. Listening to 'Jokerman' and the entire 'Infidels' album multiple times in one sitting was a life-changing experience."

SID GRIFFIN

"Bob Dylan put out a single, the B-side of it became my favourite Bob Dylan song of all time, 'The Groom's Still Waiting At The Altar'. When I saw a new Bob Dylan single that had a B side that was not on any album, I bought it. "I took it home and I was blasting the song so loud that my room-mates fell in love with it and at the party that Saturday night, I had to play it over and over for people like Dave Alvin of The Blasters, who like me had thought that Bob Dylan's uptempo days were over."

"Listening to 'Infidels' multiple times in one sitting was a life-changing experience."

1984

Real Live

WITH SALES continuing to slide, Dylan reasoned that he shouldn't even bother spending too much time recording. Live shows were his real bag, as he'd proved over the last ten years. To underline this he set off to tour through Europe from May onwards, with former Rolling Stones guitarist Mick Taylor in tow, on a bill that also included Santana. In the UK, at Wembley Stadium, they were joined by UB40 and Nick Lowe for one of the oddest musical evenings imaginable. Meanwhile, a live set imaginatively titled 'Real Live' was released. It was referred to in Q magazine as one of the worst live albums of all time, dismissed as "Unnecessary and oddly unatmospheric", something that couldn't be said for Bob's live appearance on the David Letterman Show. Backed by poorly-dressed post punk outfit The Plugz - later to be renamed Cruzados to hide their shame - they swaggered through three numbers with groove-hustling reverence and unsure direction, typified by Dylan downing guitar and sampling a selection of harmonicas before tooting through 'Jokerman'.

MIKE KAUFMAN *VH-1 head honcho*

"In the summer of 1984 things weren't looking too bad. Even the sun was shining some of the time. And Bob Dylan was coming to town with Mick Taylor and Ian McLagen in his band. That was enough to raise the ante for any lifetime Stones' fans like me and my friend Adrian.
"There weren't too many gigs planned for the summer, so Dylan at Wembley quickly became our focal point and, on the grapevine, we heard that they were looking for stewards. This in our eyes meant not only getting in without paying but, quite possibly, free food and drink at the expense of CBS Records, Bob's label. Surely there was nothing to 'stewarding' and, as upstanding members of the community, we blagged our way into the job and were duly issued with bright orange bibs and even

allowed to stand around near the hospitality area in the build up to the show. This was easy. "As showtime loomed, for reasons I still don't understand, we were hand-picked to stand at the stage front, looking after the crowd who were already in position. What could be better? A fine vantage point. Although, Adrian did point out that a trapped member of the crowd at the Stones show two years ago had pissed over the security guards rather than edge his way backwards to Wembley Stadium's undoubtedly plush toilets. But, we were willing to risk it.
"By mid-afternoon, with Santana already in mid-noodle, it was getting really hot. Too hot for many of the crowd actually who were passing out and having to be carried, shoulder high, to the front where they were then carted off to destinations unknown. We were busy handing out cups of water to the dehydrated and even when we got a minute to have a breather, we were so close to the high stage

"It sounded very much like he was backed by and early Seventies version of The Rolling Stones, which was fine by me."

"Backed by poorly-dressed post punk outfit The Plugz, Bob swaggered through three numbers with groove-hustling reverence and unsure direction"

Bob and Plugz: OK. I'll find the key/capo/harmonica as soon as I can Meanwhile, Letterman skanks on (right)

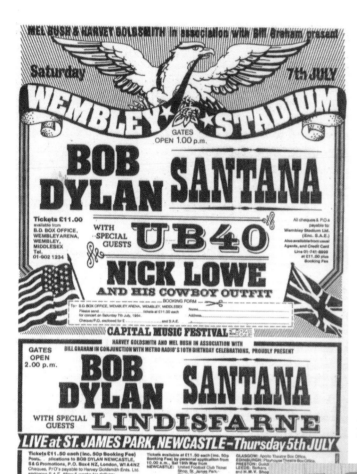

MEL BUSH & HARVEY GOLDSMITH in association with Bill Graham present

Saturday 7th JULY

WEMBLEY ★ STADIUM
GATES OPEN 1.00 p.m.

BOB DYLAN SANTANA

Tickets £11.00
available from
B.D. BOX OFFICE,
WEMBLEY ARENA,
WEMBLEY,
MIDDLESEX
Tel.
01-902 1234

WITH SPECIAL GUESTS **UB40**

All cheques & P.O.s
payable to:
Wembley Stadium Ltd.
(Enc. S.A.E.)
Also available from usual
Agents and Credit Card
Line 01-741-8999
at £11.00 plus
Booking Fee

NICK LOWE
AND HIS COWBOY OUTFIT

BOOKING FORM

To: B.D. BOX OFFICE, WEMBLEY ARENA, WEMBLEY, MIDDLESEX
Please send .... tickets at £11.00 each
for concert on Saturday 7th July, 1984. Name ....
Cheque/P.O. enclosed for £ .... Address ....
.... and S.A.E.

CAPITAL MUSIC FESTIVAL '84

GATES OPEN 2.00 p.m.

HARVEY GOLDSMITH AND MEL BUSH IN ASSOCIATION WITH
BILL GRAHAM IN CONJUNCTION WITH METRO RADIO'S 10TH BIRTHDAY CELEBRATIONS, PROUDLY PRESENT

BOB DYLAN SANTANA

WITH SPECIAL GUESTS

LINDISFARNE

LIVE at ST. JAMES PARK, NEWCASTLE - Thursday 5th JULY

Tickets £11.50 each (inc. 50p Booking Fee)
Post... ...plications to BOB DYLAN NEWCASTLE,
S & G Promotions, P.O. Box4 NZ, London, W1A4NZ
Cheques, P/O's payable to Harvey Goldsmith Ents. Ltd.
enclosing S.A.E. Allow 6 weeks for delivery.

Tickets available at £11.50 each (inc. 50p
Booking Fee) by personal application from
10.00 a.m., Sat 19th May from
NEWCASTLE: United Football Club Ticket
Shop, St. James Park,
and H.M.V. Shop

GLASGOW: Apollo Theatre Box Office.
EDINBURGH: Playhouse Theatre Box Office.
PRESTON: Guild
LEEDS: Barkers
Sunderland, Stock...

"We fought our way through the drunk and departing 72,000 crowd who were less than enthusiastic when confronted by two stretcher juggling fools and eventually found our patient who was lying in the debris of a frenzied rock 'n' roll day surrounding by his pissed-up mates.

"In something close to classic British comedy, we managed to lift the ailing party onto the stretcher but as we took the strain and attempted to rush off, stretcher bearers and stretchered man came a cropper on a mound of half eaten burgers and discoloured chips.

"After we finally delivered our "victim" into the more capable hands of the Red Cross, we looked at each other and realised that even our sartorial fluorescent bibs hadn't prevented us from being smeared with ketchup and "used" beer.

"We eventually made it to the hospitality area and after pinching a complimentary CBS baseball cap from Stevie Winwood, we were able to get into the private label party. Of course, Bob didn't show and even though we were able to finally liberate some free cheese and wine, our soiled demeanour made sure no-one came near us."

front that we couldn't see anything anyway.

"But, we weren't too bothered. We had our important-looking backstage passes and we fully expected that later in the evening we'd be hob-nobbing with Bob. As the night drew on and the crowd cooled Dylan came on and sounded pretty good. It sounded very much like he was backed by an early '70s version of the Stones and the bobbing heads in front of us were certainly into it.

"As the final encore faded, we were ready for some serious drinking but the Head Of Security spotted us and asked the intimate question, "Have you ever done any stretcher work?". Well, it's not something you have on your CV but as we were his only option, he handed us a stretcher and told to get into the stadium where some poor soul, in the midst of the heat and alcohol, had managed to collapse one of his lungs.

EARLS

BOB IN CONCERT DYLAN

REAL LIVE

Tracks: Highway 61 Revisited, Maggie's Farm, I And I, License To Kill, It Ain't Me Babe, Tangled Up In Blue, Masters Of War, Ballad Of A Thin Man, Girl Of The North Country, Tombstone Blues.

Released December.
Produced by Glyn Johns.

sleeve NOTES
Not much copy, some nice pictures of the team, with the info that Carlos Santana crops up on 'Tombstone Blues' and a back cover that repeats the lighter-aloft theme of old. And the people responsible, those credited with "special thanks", they included veteran concert promoter Bill Graham and Marty Feldman (surely not the goggle-eyed comedian of yore).

WHAT THE PAPERS SAID
"(In the absence of e new studio album) CBS filled in time by releasing 'Real Live', a lacklustre souvenir of 1984's European tour, on which only a reworking of 'Tangled Up In Blue' offered anything of value to anyone who didn't attend the concerts."Record Collector

WHAT IAN MCLAGEN SAID
"Dylan had asked me to join the tour and I did it with some trepidation. I'd heard lots of stories about him and I was a bit put out after meeting on the first day. We exchanged pleasantries and then he never spoke to me again for the whole tour which I thought was really unfriendly. Finally, one night I'd had a few beers and I just decided I'd have to have it out with him. It turned out that he couldn't understand my accent and when we met at the start of the tour he thought I'd just slagged him off when all I'd said was hello. Things were a bit better after that."

IN A NUTSHELL
Hard-cut boogie disguises much of this rollicking live show, with Mick Taylor and Bob exchanging licks on top of Ian McLagen's driving keyboards. 'Highway 61 Revisited' and 'Maggie's Farm' are, indeed, whipped off, while 'I And I' gets a squidgey rock-reggae vibe, with some widdling guitar for good measure. Bob unwraps his harmonica for 'Tangled Up In Blue' and the crowd erupts but the mainstay of this "rock-out" frenzy is the guitar duelling that almost engulfs Bob at times. Not for the squeamish.

SINGLES/EPS/ETC
Jokerman (45) Sweetheart Like You (45)

1985

Can You Please Crawl Out Your Window

THINGS WERE getting a touch out of hand. Grossman and Dylan continued to fight it out, Bob had by now counter-claimed and the case was being played out in epic Sergio Leone length proportions. In the midst of those unpleasantness, Planet Rock entered charity time, which resulted in Bob performing alongside Michael Jackson for the single 'We Are The World'. That was swiftly followed by a live and shaky wobble on Live Aid, bolstered by The Rolling Stones' Keith Richards and Ronnie Wood. This inebriated power trio were introduced by the Cuckoo Nest himself Jack Nicholson, who hailed Bob as being simply "transcendent". Dylan acclaimed the plight of the US farmers mid-set for reasons unbeknown to anyone.

PETE SMITH (*World-wide Live Aid co-ordinator*)
"What Irritated Geldof was not the shambolic music, but that Dylan started going on about helping the impoverished American farmers. I think he felt that Dylan was hijacking the show, which was not the spirit of the day."

Dylan's appearance at Live Aid was fraught to say the least. First off there was much debate as to who would do what with whom. "At one point I was set to do a duet with Bob Dylan but it didn't happen." recalls Paul Simon. "It wouldn't have been a problem, I could harmonise with anyone."

With Mick Jagger already committed to sing with Tina Turner, the Stones' guitarists Keith Richards and Ronnie Wood muscled into Dylan's slot and the trio spent a whole evening working out material. So legend has it, just before they were about to go on, Bob announced that they should play 'Hollis Brown', one of the few songs they hadn't worked out.

"I thought it was a cough medicine." claimed Ronnie Wood afterwards. It didn't go well. Publicist Bernard Doherty recalls, "I don't think Geldof could believe how bad Dylan's set was. It really annoyed him."

"I don't think he needed Keith standing with a fag hanging out of his mouth."

ROD STEWART

"I don't think he needed Keith looking like he was doing 'Honky Tonk Women' and standing with a fag hanging out of his mouth. You've got to give the geezer some respect, stand up the back and play acoustic."

KEITH RICHARDS

"I just think Bob should give up playing with bands and do what he does best which is sing his songs with an acoustic guitar, which he is brilliant at."

Twenty-five years on from Gerde's Folk Club, Bob had sold a staggering 35 million albums. To celebrate his career was showcased on the five album box set 'Biograph', which included several unreleased tracks.

SID GRIFFIN

Around 1985, I was in a band called The Long Ryders and we were playing at the Music Machine in Santa Monica with The Three O'Clock. Both bands were doing well as part of what was called The Paisley Underground but that night there was a certain buzz in the air. It

Empire Burlesque

Tracks: Tight Connection To My Heart, Seeing The Real You At Last, I'll Remember You, Clean Cut Kid, Never Gonna Be The Same Again, Trust Yourself, Emotionally Yours, When The Night Comes Falling From The Sky, Something Is Burning, Baby, Dark Eyes.
Released June.
Remixed by Arthur Baker.

SLEEVE NOTES
Lots of lyrics and player information is run around a picture of Bob looking as glam as he can with six days growth of beard.

WHAT THE INTERNET SAYS *"This is a carefully-produced, conventional, and not very exciting record. The uptempo numbers sound like a professionalized white-blues bar band, while the slow numbers are so smooth you hardly notice them. DBW, Wilson - Alroy Record Reviews*

WHAT DAVE PERCIVAL SAYS *After writing The Dust Of Rumour, a book which covered the British press reaction to Dylan from 1964 to 1981, Percival's next book project was Just A Personal Tendency in which Percival explains that 'Empire Burlesque' is in fact one of Dylan's greatest albums which he followed with Some Other Tendencies, which included the press response to the album, both were stacked with in-depth analysis of the album and the subsequent response to it.*

IN A NUTSHELL *And, so, everything you've read about before, well, on Bob's recent albums anyway, comes back again to haunt you. The female gospelisation of the choruses, the reggae rhythms, a few horns and the swaggering rock star Bob. It all makes for another road-weary Revue-styled jamalong that seems to be short of direction. 'Never Gonna Be The Same Again' drifts closer to electric-reggae courtesy of Sly and Robbie, and the Heartbreakers' keyboard player Benmont Tench fills where necessary but it is all goes nowhere fast. By the end of side two the pace has slowed on 'Something's Burning Baby', before Bob sheds the band and takes up his harmonica for the closing 'Dark Eyes', a song of solitude for lost love, which comes as something of a melancholy relief.*

EMPIRE BURLESQUE FACT(ISH) *Scholars of Dylan were impressed to uncover for John Bauldie's Telegraph magazine, that the lines "I'll go along with this charade/Until I can think of my way out" from 'Tight Connection To My Heart' were used in a prehistoric episode of Star Trek when Spock emoted "How long do we have to go along with this charade, Captain?", to which Captain James T Kirk replied "Until we can think our way out, Mr Spock". Talk that this was Dylan repaying a debt to actor William Shatner who plays Kirk and also did a merciless version of 'Mr Tambourine Man', however, remain unsubstantiated.*

Biograph

Tracks: *Lay Lady Lay, Baby, Let Me Follow You Down, If Not For You, I'll Be Your Baby Tonight, I'll Keep It With Mine, The Times They Are A-Changin', Blowin' In The Wind, Masters Of War, Lonesome Death Of Hattie Carroll, Percy's Song, Mixed Up Confusion, Tombstone Blues, Groom's Still Waiting At The Altar, Most Likely You Go Your Way, Like A Rolling Stone, Jet Pilot, Lay Down Your Weary Tune, Subterranean Homesick Blues, I Don't Believe You, Visions Of Johanna, Every Grain Of Sand, Quinn The Eskimo, Mr Tambourine Man, Dear Landlord, It Ain't Me Babe, You Angel You, Million Dollar Bash, To Ramona, You're A Big Girl Now, Abandoned Love, Tangled Up In Blue, It's All Over Now, Baby Blue, Can You Please Crawl Out Your Window?, Positively Fourth Street, Isis, Carribean Wind, Up To Me, Baby I'm In The Mood For You, I Wanna Be Your Lover, I Want You, Heart Of Mine, On A Night Like This, Just Like A Woman, Night In Durango, Senor, Gotta Serve Somebody, I Believe In You, Time Passes Slowly, I Shall Be Released, Knockin' On Heaven's Door, All Along The Watchtower, Solid Rock, Forever Young.*
Released December.

SLEEVE NOTES *Extensive notes from film director Cameron Crowe who gets some chestnuts from the man for a smartly-produced 60-page plus booklet. Intriguingly he has Bob spouting: "I'm not selling breakfast cereal, or razor blades, or whatever. I'm always hearing people saying how 'Dylan should do this and do that, make an album like in the '60s.' How the hell do they know? I could make an album like 'Blonde On Blonde' tomorrow and the same people would say it sounded outdated.*

WHAT THE PAPERS SAID *"Biograph' is only the second collection of its kind to crack the Top Forty. Only 'Elvis Aaron Presley', an eight CD set of Presley,s work has done likewise. Dylan's label, CBS didn't expect the set to sell so fast and had difficulty keeping retailers in stock. Even at Tower Records in downtown New York supply couldn't meet demand as store manager Steve Harman revealed that they sold 2,000 copies in five weeks." New York Times "Chances are that Dylan fans will eventually buy 'Biograph', and they'll enjoy it. The package is luxurious enough to take away any initial doubts. But, there's a less appealing after taste: It sells Dylan short and, in doing so, it sells the fans short too."*

WHAT THE INTERNET SAYS
"A nice place to start with Dylan's career, but you'll want to dig deeper. What makes this collection really worthwhile is the collection of unreleased tunes, alternates and live performances, many of which are magnificent.
DBW, Wilson - Alroy Record Reviews, via the internet

WHAT DYLAN SAID *"I've never really known what this thing is supposed to be. There's some stuff that hasn't been heard before, but most of my stuff has already been bootlegged, so to those in the know, there's nothing that hasn't been heard before." The Herald Examiner*

IN A NUTSHELL

A beautifully-annotated, superbly-illustrated set which features a brief 52-track overview of Dylan's life and times compiled by Jeff Rosen. Included are a host of unreleased tracks or versions of 'I'll Keep It With Mine', 'Percy's Song', 'Lay Down Your Weary Tune', 'Quinn The Eskimo', 'You're A Big Girl Now', 'Abandoned Love', 'Jet Pilot', 'Caribbean Wind', 'Up To Me', 'Baby I'm In The Mood For You', 'I Wanna Be Your Lover' and 'Forever Young'. Live versions of ''I Don't Believe You (She Acts Like We Never Have Met)', 'Visions Of Johanna', 'It's All Over Now Baby Blue', 'Isis', 'Heart Of Mine' and 'Romance In Durango'. The singles 'Mixed-Up Confusion', 'Can You Please Crawl Out Your Window', 'Positively Fourth Street' and the flipside 'Groom's Still Waiting At The Altar'. It's an intriguing collection and a beautiful package that's available for just over 20 quid on three CDs. Essential.

SINGLES/EPS/ETC *Highway 61 Revisited (45)*
Tight Connection To My Heart (45) When The Night Comes Falling From The Sky (45)

was that kind of thing where you knew that there was someone in the audience. In Hollywood it could have been anyone, I guessed it was probably an A&R person or something.

"Anyway, the evening progressed and The Three O'Clock came out and finished the night off with us doing a couple of Easybeats' songs or something. Afterwards, we were packing up the gear and there was a rumour that Bob Dylan was in the house. Bob Dylan being an icon and a pretty distinctive looking guy, we thought we would have spotted him, but nobody had.

"Still, everyone was going that Bob Dylan had been there. We finally got all the gear packed up and I'm standing on the sidewalk with various Long Ryders, Three O'Clock's and

Fiona Flannagan and Bob at the NFT press conference: What on earth were they thinking of?

members of The Rain Parade, Dream Syndicate, Bangles, Green On Red, Blasters and, I think Johnny Doe of X. Y'know, various notables of the then-hip LA scene. All the audience have gone, there's us and couple of waitresses plus the guy locking the club up, it's around 2.30 in the morning and there's a guy, about 15, asking our guitarist Stephen McCarthy and the guitarist from The Rain Parade for some tips.

"With the boy was a smallish guy wearing a hooded parka, with the hood up, on a fairly warm Santa Monica night. The guy's also wearing Aviator glasses and I realised, well, that guy's gotta be somebody, who else would dress like that? The guy in the parka was the boy's dad, who'd come to pick him up after the show.

"Some of our group of people had worked out who the man in the Parka is and one of our female friends is drunk and insisting that she is in fact his cousin, a distant relative through Russian Hebrew connections, she's asking does he recognise her. But the guy is staying pretty quiet and lets her do all the talking.

"As the word gets out to all of us that it is Bob

playing friend, who's now a palaeontologist in California, phones up every one of us and begs us to secrecy. But by then, we'd already told everyone and the word was out."

ANDY KERSHAW

"At the end of 1985, I was coming home from Boston, overnight to London, flipping through a copy of *Spin* magazine and I noticed in the

then the door opens and it's Dave Stewart blinking at me in the light. And I heard myself saying, 'Hi Dave, is Bob in?'

"Dave Stewart said he was and I immediately said 'Can I come in and meet him?' and he said, 'Sure.'.

"We went inside and went to the upstairs of the church which has been converted into a studio and there were lots of Hessian screens on wheels in the middle of which were perspex windows. So I could see this legendary figure shuffling backwards and forwards. And from behind the screen was coming this God-awful clanking and battering, this really tuneless stuff.

"Dave Stewart and I pulled the screens away and there he was, standing in a blue and white leather jacket and cowboy boots and he was actually taller than I expected. All the biographies talk about him being small and wiry. He was certainly thin. But he looked unshaven and unkempt and quite haggard looking.

"When this jamming came to an end, introductions were made. I sat down on the edge of a drum riser and I said, 'I'd like to give

"I could see this legendary figure shuffling, and from behind the screens was coming this Godawful clanking and battering."

Dylan, one of my crowd, who must remain nameless, is so drunk that he starts crying with emotion when he realises it's Bob Dylan. He's a husky American male but he just completely loses it, like a common bar room drunk. He puts his arm around Dylan and starts saying, 'Bob, Bob, you're my hero, you're my hero, man. Let me play lead guitar for you, man, I'll go out for nothing, man.

"Dylan, with a growing smile, under his Aviator shades, says, 'I've already got a band, man. I've got a really good guitar player, it's cool'. But my friend was having none of it and he kept drunkenly touching Bob Dylan and putting his arm round him and repeating, "I'll do it, man, I'll play for nothing, man'.

"So, Dylan went home. He didn't hire my friend and the next morning this guitar-

News In Brief bit, down the side of the page, there was a reference to the fact that Bob Dylan was recording with Dave Stewart. I read this, had a bit of a snooze and woke up and thought, 'Hang on. Bob Dylan is recording at the end of my street'.

"So I got back to where I was living at the time in Crouch End, sat around on the carpet feeling jet-lagged and it seemed absolutely obvious to me that I should go round and see Bob. On the way round I passed a Wholefood Store and I thought a little gift might be in order and the first thing I put my hand on was a jar of Hedgerow Jam.

"I carried on up to the Church Studios, rang the bell and as the entryphone asked who it was, I said, 'Is Bob in?'. The voice said, 'Who is it?', and I said, 'It's Andy Kershaw from Radio 1',

you this as a token of appreciation of all you've done for me' and I handed him the jam. I remember he just sat there and he was turning this jar of jam over and over in his hand like a chimpanzee might do if you'd handed him a mobile phone. There was a look of utter bewilderment on his face. I tried to jolly things along by saying something like, 'Hedgerow Jam, Bob, made with real hedgerows'. And he just said, 'Eeeee' and put it down on the drum riser. For all I know it's probably it's still there.

"What followed was probably the most humiliating experience of my life. When I realised he was up for talking I got a crew from the Whistle Test. It was his first UK interview ever but it was a disaster. He didn't want to say anything and I couldn't form a sentence in my mouth."

1986

Driftin' Too Far From Shore

AND STILL he travelled on. Taking the unwashed hobo spirit to the extreme, Bob took the Heartbreakers from New Zealand and Australia, through Japan, across the States and Canada. It was not a hitchless journey or, initially, a marriage made in Heaven.

BRENT HANSEN *President MTV Europe*
"I remember going with a load of friends to stand outside of Athletic Park in New Zealand and listening to the rehearsals for Bob Dylan with Tom Petty And The Heartbreakers. It was quite clear that they didn't have Bob there at all and it was just the Heartbreakers working their way through some songs.

"The next night the promoter invited a load of people to meet Bob Dylan but he never turned up. The Heartbreakers did and I got talking to the guitarist Mike Campbell. He had the whitest look on his face and I said to him, 'How do you feel?' and he said 'Well, we're here at the bottom of the world, we're about to do a tour with the most famous musician in the world and we have absolutely no idea every time he hits the stage what key he is going to be in'.
"The entire Heartbreakers band took the stage with a complete change of underwear as they had no idea what song he was going to do, what key he was going to be in and, whatever song it was, they had to immediately get into that groove."

DAVID COHEN
Wellington NZ morning daily newspaper
American pop star and erstwhile evangelical Bob Dylan manifested himself in the flesh last night for a poorly-attended Athletic Park concert at The Dominion. Accompanying him were compatriots Tom Petty And The

Heartbreakers.
The 15,000-strong crowd not only testified to an abysmally-promoted event; evidenced also was the breadth of Dylan's fan appeal. Teeny-boppers and breakdancers shuffled uneasily alongside public servants and church youth groups. But that was nothing compared to the sheer incompatibility of Dylan and his backing band. The Heartbreakers were obviously out of sorts with Dylan's material and for the most part they floundered around like a B-grade pub group. During 'In the Garden', they played the entire song in a different key from Dylan's nasal whine. When he could be understood - the man at the helm seemed to be trotting out Bob Dylan's 33 Solid Gold Hits. Surprises of the evening were an unusual amount of gospel material and a

MY SEXY NIGHTS AS A SLAVE TO BOB DYLAN

By MYDRIM JONES

SUPERSTAR folk singer Bob Dylan is heading for London next month—and a reunion with an exotic actress who claims she was once his sex-slave.

Flamboyant Gypsy Fire has told how she danced half-naked for religious-freak Dylan, shared kinky sex sessions—and massaged his feet because she thought he was Christ.

"He might be into religion but he spends more time talking about sex than God," said buxom Gypsy, 40, a well-known Australian actress.

She revealed how she became obsessed with Dylan, 45, in the States and how he finally invited her on stage during a concert in Sydney.

"But his minders brutally dragged me away by my breasts," she said. "Later, at his hotel, I rushed up and complained that I'd been bruised. He asked to see my breasts.

"In a couple of days I was staying in a room next to his. I became his sex-slave. It was really weird. In one erotic scene I danced for him nearly naked."

Gypsy added: "I went

STARRY LOVER

"Bob talks more about sex than God," says Gypsy

MY SEXY NIGHTS AS A SLAVE TO BOB DYLAN

"Superstar folk singer Bob Dylan is heading to London next month and a reunion with an exotic actress who claims she was once his sex slave.

Flamboyant Gypsy Fire has told how she danced half-naked for religious freak Dylan, shared kinky sex sessions - and massaged his feet because she thought he was Christ.

"He might be into religion, but he spends more time talking about sex than God," said buxom Gypsy, 40, a well-known Australian actress. She reveals how she became obsessed with Dylan in the States and how he invited her on stage during a concert in Sydney.

"But his minders brutally dragged me away by my breasts." she said. "Later at his hotel, I rushed up and complained that I'd been bruised. He asked to see my breasts."

---

delightful new song, 'Across the Borderline'. Dylan looked somewhat out of kilter. He didn't even bother with his celebrated harp-solos, and looked grimmer as the evening wore on. Perhaps he was embarrassed about what he was doing to the fans. Perhaps he was cursing the sound guy for not allowing his four funky female back-ups to be heard above the din. Who knows?

Obtuse press calls, the odd recording session and the completion of 'Knocked Out Loaded' were interspersed with preparation, press conferences and the eventual shooting of the film Hearts Of Fire. Dylan played an ageing rock star in a revival/retro band, a role he claimed he knew well.

BILL PRINCE deputy editor GQ magazine

"My main memory of Bob Dylan in those times was when I inveigled my way into the press conference for Hearts Of Fire, a film he was about to shoot in England. He was

---

accompanied by the director Richard Marquand who was on a bit of a roll at the time after Jagged Edge, and no-one could understand why they were involved in this film, a remake of A Star Is Born.

"The press conference took place at the National Film Theatre at 10.00 o'clock on a Sunday morning and it was absolutely packed. I don't think I was aware of it at the time, but here we were about to witness one of the great Bob Dylan shows.

"I do believe that besides his live performance and his recorded work, Bob Dylan's press conferences are extraordinary, there are even three or four of them actually released. Dylan had obviously realised that one-on-one interviews are quite gladiatorial, like a personal battle. With press conferences, Dylan seemed to do them for the enjoyment he got out of them. And, I'm sure this conference was no exception.

"One journalist in particular, Philip Norman, the film critic from The Times, took it upon himself to stand up every minute to remind Bob that he shouldn't be in the film. And, even though there were other questions, Johnson persisted in returning to the same line of questioning, so much so, that he was actually asked to shut up by the director.

"But Norman got up once more and said, 'Mr Dylan, do you have any idea how bored you're going to be making this film?', Dylan waited a split-second, then replied, 'Oh, I don't know, maybe you'll be there'. Of course, the whole place erupts and Bob is once again in charge of the whole event.

PHILIP NORMAN
Sunday Times, extracted from his penetrative interviewing style

"Why are you bothering to be in this film?"
   "Excuse me?"

"Why aren't you writing poetry?"
   "I am, I'm just trying something different."

"I'm sorry to labour this point, but why aren't you doing the things that you're really good at?"
   "I am. I do write poetry. I'm just taking some time off. Trying something different."

"Does that mean you're relaxing. You're not really going to be trying?"
   "Excuse me?"

"Why didn't you write the script yourself?"
   "I couldn't have written it. It's beyond me."

Knocked Out Loaded

Tracks: *You Wanna Ramble, They Killed Him, Driftin' Too Far From Shore, Precious Memories, Maybe Someday, Brownsville Girl, Got My Mind Made Up, Under Your Spell.*
Released July.

Produced by Bob Dylan, Arthur Baker, Dave Stewart and Tom Petty.

SLEEVE NOTES *Not rambling, other than on the sleeve itself, Dylan's follow up to 'Empire Burlesque' featured a cover illustration that looks like a rejected sketch for The African Queen.*

WHAT THE INTERNET SAYS
"Apparently this one is pretty lousy; Dylan even used a bunch of material he hadn't written himself." JA, Wilson - Alroy Record Reviews

WHAT THE PAPERS SAID *"All that big stage fold back is starting to clog up Dylan's ears. He's taken to writing ready-made anthems for stadiums around the world to reverberate to. You can argue that 'Knocked Out Loaded' is a welcome relief from the hellfire and brimstone of a few albums back. But the muddled attempt to go back to early Dylan-rap on 'Brownstone Girl' with its half hearted ambiguity is a bit sad."* Hugh Fielder, Sounds

"'Knocked Out Loaded' is shockingly bad. Barely coherent, it is possibly his worst album to date, which is saying a lot considering how 'Empire Burlesque', 'Shot Of Love' and 'Self Portrait' were really atrocious." Nick Kent, NME

IN A NUTSHELL
Where Bob's head was at in '86 is hard to say. He didn't release another album for two years after 'Knocked Out Loaded' and the assorted musicians - including Al Kooper, T Bone Burnett, Tom Petty, Dave Stewart - struggled to find a formula on several covers (including Kris Kristoferson's over-indulgent 'They Killed Him', which boasted a children's choir), or on a couple of co- written items. There were some indistinct Bob originals too and an unconventional meeting of minds when Reggae met Bluegrass on 'Precious Memories'. Carole Bayer Seger added melodrama on 'Under Your Spell' and four- voiced harmonies fill the middle distance throughout. Only 'Brownsville Girl' stands out as unique. First off it's 11 minutes long but, most importantly, as Bob rolls through the travelogue of his life and various other people's lives, he takes on a screenwriter's role and spins yarns and sub-plots .

SINGLES/EPS/ETC
The Usual (45) Band Of The Hand (45)

"Why are you so modest? Pretending to be inadequate? You're one of the great writers of this age. Why didn't you write the script yourself?"

"I'm just trying something different."

Did you get the chance to ask anything?

"I had one opportunity to ask a question, which I completely failed to do. I'd opted for a two-part question, naively thinking that I was going to entrap the great Bob Dylan. And of course, I only managed to get part one out. The first part was, 'Is it true you said you did a lot of the tours in the Sixties for the money?' and the second part was going to be 'So are you just doing this film for the money?'. I never got the second part out and he didn't even bother to look up as I said, 'Is it true you did a lot of the tours in the Sixties for the money?', he kept his head down and said, 'I did all of them for the money'.

"The conference lasted for 20 minutes then everyone adjourned outside for a photo session in which Bob Dylan was wearing a grotesque cowboy jacket that looked like he had a dead Freesian cow on his shoulders. He was accompanied by co-stars Fiona Flannagan and Rupert Everett and at that point the whole thing evaporated.

"I remember feeling really destroyed that I hadn't made any personal contact with Bob Dylan and also that I hadn't even managed to get my question out. Looking back now I regret not realising what a great experience it was and what a waste of time it was to try and drag it down into some low grade journalistic thing. I should have just enjoyed the game."

CHRIS TAYLOR

"I was at the *Hearts Of Fire* press call on the South Bank. Dylan just stood around with shades on and didn't do anything that the photographers asked him to do, which was really great. It was just what I'd expected him to do. Just what I wanted him to be like. I was proud of him."

In the public eye, on the road and now in a film, Dylan was public property. The British tabloids seized the opportunity to introduce breasts into the equation. Of course, he would never admit to any of this tomfoolery. In fact, as David Hepworth reported in the inaugural issue of Q, Bob Dylan doesn't readily admit to anything.

DAVID HEPWORTH

"There is a stock Dylan posture. During our conversation, he assures me that the collaboration with Petty, the release of 'Biograph', the composition of 'Knocked Out Loaded', his casting in Hearts Of Fire and numerous other ventures were all 'someone else's idea'."

Philip Norman: Probingly intrigued by the plotline of the great movie but not interested in Hearts of Fire at all...

1987

Still down on the farm

Fiona and Bob: "No, you shouldn't have... really.".

ROCK STARDOM was at its peak and none came bigger than Bob. In the early part of 1987, Dylan jammed with George Harrison and Taj Mahal, dueted with Michael Jackson for Elizabeth Taylor's birthday, performed at an all-star gala in honour of composer George Gershwin and guested with U2 in LA. Bono recalled hanging out with Bob: "When we played some of Dylan's songs, I said to him, you know, these songs will live forever. He said, 'Man, I think your songs will live forever too. It's just that no-one will know how to play them'."

Inevitably touring continued. During another epic stint, Bob made a disastrous visit to Jerusalem for two shows. The crowd at the first show were openly hostile. The second night was abandoned due to technical reasons. The by-now controversial-but-universally-slammed *Hearts Of Fire* was premiered in London and shown for a paltry seven days before making its way rather swiftly to video. Dylan didn't attend the premiere.

JOHN BAULDIE, *Q magazine*

"The story is terrible - all the rock cliches you could never wish for any more."

RUPERT EVERETT

"I don't want to talk about it really. I'm sure it will be a complete disaster. I don't know. Really."

FIONA FLANNAGAN

"I don't think the movie's going to be successful."

RUPERT EVERETT

"The film has moments when it's extraordinarily *un*alright."

By now, the first inklings of the precursor the internet were already beginning to host Bob Dylan Bulletin Boards, mirroring the Dylan fanzine scene which aided the insatiable interest that hosts of Bob fans had nurtured since they turned to Bob. The fanzines were there to help, to advise, to inform. Festooned with set lists and contacts, they also boasted incredibly-intense central reference points for Bob stories that appeared around the globe.

THE WICKED MESSENGER 1987

Item 1124 **Some news, some rumour, some pure**

The Bobzine: How much mor could you even begin to want to know?

speculation
a) U2 have a live LP planned, but it may have some additional studio material. This might just include a song co-written with Bob Dylan.
b) Just as 'Clean Cut Kid' came out on 'Empire Burlesque' but is known to date back to 'Infidels', and just as 'Tight Connection To Your Heart' on 'Empire Burlesque' evolved in part out of 'Someone's Gotta Hold Of My Heart' from the 'Infidels' period, so I've now heard rumoured that 'When The Night Comes Falling' is also from the original earlier session.

Item 1127: **New Album**
Basically, there is no news.

Item 1129 **Other News**
The Dead nicknamed Dylan 'Spike' on their last tour as they already had a Bob.

Item 1136 **Snippets Of Info**
The Don't Look Back video is out in Austria... U2 did 'All Along The Watchtower' at a Save The Yuppies Show in the States and 'Maggie's Farm' on the 'Live For Ireland' LP.

Item 1141 **Down In The Groove**
The release of 'Down In The Groove' has been put back - this time to February 1988.

Item 1145 **Barry White and Dylan**
On Hallowe'en when young America takes to the streets to trick or treat those who are older and more gullible, a caller at Barry White's home found Dylan handing out Snickers bars.

Item 1153 **What About Another Tour Here, Then?**
I can barely credit it, but tour rumours abound once more. In Ireland's Sunday Tribune, the one and only BP Fallon reviewed 'Down In The Groove' and said, "if and when he tours Ireland this year..."

Item 1159 **Hearts Of Fire**
News from the States is that, based on European responses, Hearts Of Fire will not go on cinema release at all.

Item 1165 **Very chic**
No wonder our boy seems to have a creative block these days when he is reported in the press to be attending a party at LA's Museum Of Contemporary Art to premiere the Spring / Summer Collection of Georgio Armani.

1988

90 mph

BOB GROUP hopped from his tight touring three-piece, who took the Never Ending Tour out on a winding 71-date American jaunt, to bit-part player in The Travelling Wilburys, a supergroup who were originally pulled together to record a George Harrison B-side. Their ranks groaned under the collected ego's of Tom Petty, Roy Orbison and Jeff Lynne, as well as Harrison and Dylan. But, from one Dylan-garage-recorded song, they went on to record three albums. Sadly Orbison died of a heart attack after the first on the cusp of something of a revival.

Hurricane Carter's release from prison, proved that some good can come from musical intervention, although Carter was quickly in trouble with the authorities again. Dylan was inducted into the Rock 'n' Roll Hall Of Fame, with a keynote speech from Bruce Springsteen setting the tone for the evening.

BRUCE SPRINGSTEEN,
induction speech Hall Of Fame

"The first time I heard Bob Dylan, I was in the car with my mother and we were listening to, I think, WMCA, and on came that snare shot that sounded like somebody'd kicked open the door to your mind - 'Like A Rolling Stone'. And my mother, she was no stiff with rock 'n' roll, she used to like music, she listened. She sat there for a minute and she looked at me and said, 'That guy can't sing.' But I knew she was wrong."

At the ceremony, Dylan took the stage and mumbled a few words before he embarked on 'All Along The Watchtower', backed by the house band from the David Letterman show with George Harrison sitting in. That was followed by an "unusual" reading of 'Like A Rolling Stone' with Arlo Guthrie, Springsteen and Mick Jagger on backing vocals. And, in an unrelated incident...

DYLAN FANS KiLLED BY SOLDiERS

Two drunken Russian soldiers who killed four East German pop fans in a road crash have been executed on the orders of Soviet leader Mikhail Gorbachev.

He ordered the sentence after widespread unrest after the fans died on their way home from a Bob Dylan concert in East Berlin.

The four were burned alive when their small East German Trabant car burst into flames after being hit head on by a Russian military vehicle. The drunken corporal driving it had lost control of the car and fled the scene.

Down In The Groove

Tracks: Let's Stick Together, When Did You Leave Heaven?, Sally Sue Brown, Death Is Not The End, Had A Dream About You, Baby, Ugliest Girl In The World, Silvio, Ninety Miles An Hour (Down A Dead End Street), Shenandoah, Rank Strangers To Me.
Released June.

SLEEVE NOTES *The moody sleeve houses a track-by-track line-up list, including the bizarre mixture of Eric Clapton, Jerry Garcia, Full Force, Paul Simonon, Clydie King, Kip Winger, Mitchell Froom and Steve Jones.*

WHAT THE INTERNET SAYS
"Apparently this one is hardly better than 'Knocked Out Loaded', again including cover tunes. JA, Wilson - Alroy Record Reviews

WHAT THE WORLD SAID CLINTON HEYLIN *"Its release confirmed in many an ex-fan's mind that the man had nothing left to say."*

IN A NUTSHELL
Originally a pot pourri of early Dylan influences from the '50s, including songs by Gene Vincent, Arthur Alexander, Wilbert Harrison, Clyde McPhatter, etc, 'Down In The groove' over a period of numerous sessions was added to and subtracted from constantly. It eventually emerged with two songs featuring lyrics by The Grateful Dead's Robert Hunter one of which is the decidedly poor 'Ugliest Girl In The World'. Interspersed was an out-take from 'Knocked Out Loaded', some of those original '50s muses, an uncomfortable version of the traditional 'Shanandoah' and one of Bob's least incisive tunes in 'Had A Dream About You Baby'. It's messy stuff. With female vocalists whooping and a whole host of musicians pulling it every which way. The cover of 'Ninety Miles An Hour (Down A Dead End Street)' decent enough in itself pretty much sums up the affair.

DOWN IN THE GROOVE FACT
A spokesman for CBS had previously heralded the album with the fateful words, "it sounds a bit like 'Blonde On Blonde'." Advance tapes secured by fans immediately exposed this remark as "twaddle". Instead 'Down In The Groove' was reviled as a thinly disguised collection of 12 bars with much "joyous hootin' and hollerin' on Dylan's part". Some fans were disappointed also to learn that the album comprised of cover versions including John Hiatt's 'The Usual', which was previously aired in the film Hearts Of Fire. Just two tunes were actually penned by Dylan and even they had lyrics supplied by Grateful Dead lyricist Robert Hunter. Q, March, 1988.

SINGLES/EPS/ETC *Silvio (45)*

Caption here to filllCaption here to filllCaption here to filllCaption here to filllCaption here to filll

Everything Is Broken

BOB'S BRIEF sojourn with The Grateful Dead was relived as he teamed up with the group for a show in LA. However, his mind was more focused on a seven-month jaunt that would take him through Europe and across America. Prior to packing his bags he spent time in New Orleans recording with Daniel Lanois for the album 'Oh Mercy' which became his best-received album since 'Blood On The Tracks'.

Adrian Deevoy's relentless efforts to interview Dylan for Q magazine sent him back and forth across the Atlantic over a period of a month before he finally tracked him down. In the pre-chat hiatus, Dylan's office revealed that they have to be incredibly careful vetting people as they had 550 "potentially dangerous" people on computer, who've "generally sent death threats or weird stuff". The office also compiled a list of Dylan Don'ts.

1 Don't treat him like God. It wigs him out.
2 Don't ask who Mr Jones is or about the motor cycle crash, any of that corny Dylanologist stuff.
3 Don't pretend you know about anything you don't. He'll see through you right away.
4 Do not attempt to get the ultimate Dylan interview. Don't dive into his soul, he finds that insulting.
5 Don't ask what specific lyrics mean.
6 Don't use notes.

If Deevoy had problems, spare a thought for the fans and this internet news group contactee from Scotland who admitted his Dylan weakness but still risked hypothermia to meet the man.

UNTOUCHED BY THE HAND OF BOB *via the internet*

Okay, I admit it. I am a fan - have been for more years than I care to mention. Why else would I lurk outside Glasgow's most exclusive hotel in sub-zero temperatures. I'd seen Dylan play Glasgow the year before but decided that a "festival seating" policy at the S.E.C.C. excluded me from shelling out to see him again. Twenty years ago, I didn't mind standing for gigs - but not now.

So, it was down to trying to get a few words with the great man - and - if possible, an autograph. I had a small collection of carefully chosen bits that the addition of a signature would have elevated to holy relic status (1966 tour programme; Isle Of Wight programme; a copy of "Writings and Drawings" and a couple of PR pix). It was one of those incredibly cold, crisp days when your breath billows out as a cloud of steam and for two hours or more, I tried to keep moving just to keep some warmth in my body. God knows what the folks in the hotel thought. I must have been mad - but I was one of only two people there, so I figured I had more of a chance than ever before of getting to Bob.

Eventually, a tour bus pulled up outside the hotel; it was sound-check time - the adrenaline surged. The hotel door was unlocked and out walked ...... the minder. For a few moments, he just stood at the top of the stairs surveying the scene and obviously assessing the risks to his employer. I walked up to him and asked what he thought were the chances of getting an autograph and, surprisingly, he said I could try - so long as I didn't hassle and accepted it gracefully if I was ignored. That was fine. I knew the rules. Now, all I had to do was get Bob to sign something.

After about five minutes, what looked like an

Dylan And The Dead

Tracks: Slow Train, I Want You, Gotta Serve Somebody, Queen Jane Approximately, Joey, All Along The Watchtower, Knockin' On Heaven's Door

sleeve NOTES *Thanks and thanks again to the various road crews for Bob and the Dead are encased in a sleeve illustration by the late psychedelic poster king Rick Griffin.*

WHAT THE PAPERS SAID *"As a backing band the Dead don't roll as Dylan flows, and if Dylan gets knocked out of his vocal stride, they only force him into the mire of lost words and misdirection."* John Bauldie, Q

WHAT THE INTERNET SAYS *"What you see is what you get. If you really think that either Dylan or the Dead had any excitement to offer two full decades after their respective peaks, well, it's your money."* JA, Wilson - Alroy Record Reviews

WHAT THE WORLD SAYS ADAM NORSWORTHY, fan *"You often relate an album to the time that it was released. 1989 was a good time for me and I used to end the day listening to 'Dylan And The Dead' fumbling through some of Dylan's best. For all it's sloppiness, it's such an endearing record. The band so innocent, like they've never heard the songs or played together before. This gives songs like 'Slow Train Coming' and 'Gotta Serve Somebody' a more human and natural groove than they had on the over- produced originals."*

IN A NUTSHELL *The Grateful Dead seem oblivious to Bob Dylan on this seven song release. Jerry Garcia's distinctive guitar style and his interplay with Bob Weir make the arrangements flow like so much stylish psychedelic pop but they could be playing anything. Bob sings on top but there's no real fusion as the Dead don't get the chance to really jam or take off and Dylan sounds almost out of breath at points, trying hard to drive the typical Grateful Dead stoner pace. Having said that Garcia's high, lonesome guitar plays a perfectly passionate 'Queen Jane', it's almost like the lyrics have become superfluous and, as a piece of music, they kind of spoil it when they come in.*

old "bag-man" shuffled out of the hotel wearing at least three jackets, one with its hood pulled over his head. Hands in pockets, he seemed to take an age to walk across to the steps of the bus. It was only then that I knew for certain - It was Bob Dylan. I reached forward with the '66 programme and a pen - he took them both. I had done it!

Reality hit me. It wasn't a blow from the minder or a speeding car - it was DYLAN speaking to ME. My brain snapped into gear, my senses were at fever pitch. "What's this?" he said. "Uh? It's your 1966 tour programme" I replied. His hand moved. The pen moved ever closer to the cover of the programme. I was willing him to do it. His head turned upwards. He looked directly at me. The expression reminded me of a rabbit about to bolt. Bob glanced at the minder and then looking straight into my eyes, he said, "uuhh!"

Panic set in. I had to do something. I was frozen in a moment of incredulity but something made me say, "Could you sign it, please?". His hand moved again but in my mind all I could see was a rabbit racing across a field. It made it to its burrow and I sensed this was the end. The hand stopped. We were both frozen in the same

Oh Mercy

Tracks: Political World, Where Teardrops Fall, Everything Is Broken, Ring Them Bells, Man In The Long Black Coat, Most Of The Time, What Good Am I?, Disease Of Conceit, What Was It You Wanted, Shooting Star.

Released September.
Produced by Daniel Lanois.

sleeve NOTES *Nothing much to write home about here, from the graffiti spray can front cover and Bob's dripping hair on the reverse, there was obviously an image- consultant on hand who probably hadn't heard the music within.*

WHAT THE PAPER'S SAID *"There's an American Gothic atmosphere to the album as a whole, reminiscent in parts of The Band's first couple of albums. It's a stunning return to work after the lacklustre holding actions of Down In The Groove and Dylan And The Dead. Most of the time, for the first time in quite some time, Oh Mercy reminds you of what used to excite people about Dylan."* Andy Gill, Q
"Daniel Lanois accordingly delivered his usual sticky-in-the- heat feel. Dylan did the business with ten superior songs." David Cavanagh, Q magazine, 1993 on the re-issue at Nice Price

WHAT THE INTERNET SAYS *"Saluted as a return to form after unsuccessful Eighties experiments, this Daniel Lanois-produced collection has some excellent blues-rock and bitter/touching failed romance numbers, but also has what rock critics call "heavy handed statements" on 'Disease of Conceit' and 'What Good Am I?'"* DBW, Wilson - Alroy Record Reviews

WHAT THE WORLD SAYS JEFF KRAMER *"On a recent radio interview, a DJ asked, 'Bob, there's a couplet in 'Man In The Long Black Coat' - "People don't live or die/People just float". What exactly do you mean by 'float'?' To which Bob replied, 'I just needed something to rhyme with 'coat'.'"*

IN A NUTSHELL *Daniel Lanois utilises his greatest assets, his echo and reverb, to add a touch of authentic, haunting deep American ambience to Bob. Rolling conga's infiltrate, jangles hum along and Bob sounds likes he's crouched next to you in the back seat of a broken down car. He's leaning in on your shoulder and bending your ear about the wrongs in life and how to get around those problems. About how the world's treated him. Maybe. Dylan's vocal is warm and enveloping and the slow pace adds to the overall mood. It's easy easy listening, that's delivered over an ethereal back- ground rumble.*

SINGLES/EPS/ETC
Everything Is Broken (45)

moment.

I knew he sensed it as he let out a short but oh, so significant, "mmmmmm". I realised I would have to admit defeat but it seemed that it was Bob who surrendered in the way his arms went out, offering me back the programme and pen.

His eyes had gone back into the darkness beneath his hood. He turned and walked on the bus. I had failed."

Even seasoned professional Bobwatchers, like The Telegraph's John Bauldie had trouble actually meeting the man. On a mainland European sojourn trailing the tour through Italy and eventually France, John got very, very close, as he revealed in his excellent magazine The Telegraph. Even in this brief extract of what's a fascinating journey, you get some of the undoubted devotion that surrounds the man.

JOHN BAULDIE
from Diary Of A Bobcat, The Telegraph, 1989

Monday, June 28, somewhere west of Milan
"I see Bob, briefly, backstage in Athens. I'm sitting by myself at a table and he comes out - rare event! - of his dressing room to sniff the air, and the food, and just look around for a few minutes. He walks right behind me and stops... "Oh, look, I don't want to dwell on this gossipy stuff. Funny thing is that I'd almost bought him a little present earlier in the day. I'd seen this book in a shop in Omonia Square. It was a volume of lyrics to Om Kalsoum's songs - Egyptian words, rendered in Greek - but it also had a bunch of scratchy, blurry photos of Om Kalsoum, on stage, off stage, that I thought Bob might like to look at. But for some reason I didn't buy it. Later, I wished I had. There was Bob, standing right next to me, sniffing the warm Greek air. wearing a nice green denim jacket and light brown 1964-style suede boots, and there was I, empty-handed..."

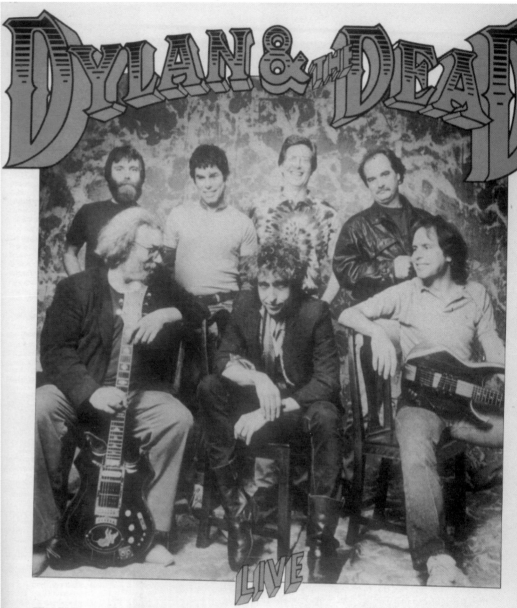

BOB DYLAN WITH THE **GRATEFUL DEAD**

SLOW TRAIN, JOEY, ALL ALONG THE WATCHTOWER, QUEEN JANE APPROXIMATELY, GOTTA SERVE SOMEBODY, I WANT YOU, KNOCKIN' ON HEAVENS DOOR

RECORDED LIVE — SUMMER '87
PRODUCED BY JERRY GARCIA AND JOHN CUTLER

LP · CASSETTE · CD

AND THAT WAS THE EIGHTIES

What was going on in the Eighties? Religion. Testifying. Culture Club. Bob with Zappa. The birth of electronics, rap, hip hop. Arthur Baker with Bob? The canonisation of Mark Knopfler. The arrival of Wet, Wet, Wet and Michael Jackson fever. Live Aid. Charity, charity, charity. Hearts Of Fire. The Never Ending tour. And REM. It was a messy old time where image attempted to replace substance.

Me, I was ensconced at Sounds and witnessing the birth of indie (proper) with C81. Two-Tone with The Specials. Pop music and Smash Hits, with even Paul Weller wearing a touch of rouge. Convening above Covent Garden tube, the daily wrestling match was between heavy metal, punk, Oi! and all of its off-shoots including the first tinkling powerchords of U2.

At Sounds people were harking back to prog rock. Bob was lucky to be slighted in one of the comic strips and only the likes of Sandy Robertson (Kim Fowley, Jim Steinman, Patti Smith) and Hugh Fielder (Queen, Rush, Spingsteen, all points between) had any vague inkling of Bob's fiefdom. Even the emergent REM

were nodding Bobwards but with albums like 'Empire Burlesque' on the racks, no-one was taking the man seriously.

The emergent LA glam scene, spearheaded by the controversial Guns n' Roses were the only people who shone a light towards the old bard and their take on Dylan was strictly theatrical with 'Knockin' On Heaven's Door' in their live set, long before its release and chart status in 1992.

Bob's recorded work had become secondary to his live forays but even they had become too frequent for the existing Bob Mafia. There were even calls for the man to take some time out, to come back later when he'd still be considered an icon and the current crop of copy-book-blotting could be quickly forgotten. Of course, he never did.

Meanwhile, I was dallying in the world of indie labels. I'd met up with Bill Prince, whose obsession with Bob seemed to affect his hair, dress sense and ability to work nine to five. Rumour had it that his desire to go freelance was to give him time to devel-

op his singing, guitaring and harmonica-ing at the same time technique. Not an easy thing. But Bill was committed.

Writing about the indie scene also led me to foolishly think that a career running my own label might not be a bad idea. I strayed into the world of unlistenable industrial noise and put out a handful of albums by unlikely Americans with names like Smegma, Smersh, Corpses As Bedmates and Blistering Moments. They ticked over and demos, as they do, flooded in. It was more of the same - plenty of scary of songs with long titles - apart from a tape by a northern singer/songwriter called Kyle Stewart. He sounded like Gene Clark and those Byrdsian memories led me to eek out a quieter more acoustic life which led me to strummed heartbreakers by the likes of The Raw Herbs among others. This was country folk, by any other name and it wasn't long before I was picking up a copy of 'Nashville Skyline' and dusting off my old Byrds' albums.

As ever, I wasn't in the same hemisphere or timespan as Bob, but his legacy was certainly casting a long shadow.

1990

10,000 Men

Into the '90s and Bob made history! Named as one of the 20th Centuries Most Influential Americans by Time magazine, Dylan celebrated by spending nine months of 1990 living out of a suitcase on the road, only breaking to record a new album with Don and David Was. Unfortunately, the project was ill-starred. After the "return to form" of the Lanois-produced 'Oh Mercy!', the critical response in the UK to 'Under The Red Sky' was initially not great. The album was musically less focused and the sessions included a performance from a bedraggled Slash of Guns n' Roses. Dylan is rumoured to have asked the be-curled and tattooed adonis to play one track in the style of Django Rheinhard.

SLASH

"I did a thing with Bob Dylan. That was terrible. They didn't use what I played. When they took it off, I said to Don Was, the producer, 'What the fuck was all that about?'. And Don said that Bob thought it sounded too much like Guns n' Roses. I'm like, Well that's what I fucking do!

"I grew up with Bob Dylan. But Bob Dylan then is not Bob Dylan now. I met George Harrison there and Kim Basinger. Then I finally met this little guy who looked like an Eskimo. It was a summer day and he's wearing a heavy wool sweater with a hood and a baseball cap underneath. He had big leather gloves and he appeared to be stoned out of his mind. He was really impolite. I didn't really have a good time."

As the inevitable tour arrived in the UK, Bob played a six night residency at London's Hammersmith Odeon, which was suitably scrutinised by all. Q magazine was puzzled. It begged the Dylanquandry, "Exactly how does Dylan select a set from his vast repertoire?"

As attention was focused on the 121 songs he delivered over six nights, a thought was also spared for his dress sense.

ADRIAN DEEVOY

"The widely-celebrated brown spangly suit and bulbous motorbike rig-out made a welcome return," noted Adrian Deevoy, "as did the winning combination of bus conductor trousers, Roman Centurion leather jerkin and billowing white blouse. The only sartorial faux pas was the re-emergence of the hideously embroidered and ill-fitting satin jacket which, on many levels, seems to have been designed for a small child."

BUT WHAT ABOUT THE MUSIC? Having examined the playlists, which are readily available on numerous web sites, I decided to enter into the kind of analysis that I was beginning to encounter

as I tried to understand the man. For example, on the six shows between February the third and eighth, the 68 songs played can be pie-charted as follows.

There was a table topping six appearances for 'Political World' and 'Like A Rolling Stone', five plays for 'Stuck Inside Of Mobile With The Memphis Blues Again' and 'All Along The Watchtower', four for 'What Was It?', 'It Ain't Me Babe', 'Everything Is Broken', 'It

Takes A Lot To Laugh, It Takes A Train To Cry', 'Mr Tambourine Man', 'Man In The Long Black Coat' and 'Highway 61 Revisited', three for 'Tight Connection To My Heart', 'Leopard-skin Pill-Box Hat' and 'Rainy Day Women Nos 12 & 35', two for 'Hattie Carroll', 'In The Garden', 'I Shall Be Released', 'It's All Over Now, Baby Blue', 'Boots Of Spanish Leather', 'It's Alright Ma (I'm Only Bleeding)', 'Seeing The Real You At Last', 'Maggie's Farm' and 'Just Like A Woman', and a paltry single rendition apiece for 'Pretty Peggy-O', 'You're A Big Girl Now', 'Love Minus Zero/No Limit', 'Gates Of Eden', 'Queen Jane Approximately', 'One More Cup Of Coffee', 'My Back Pages', 'Man Of Constant Sorrow', 'What Good Am I?', 'Simple Twist Of Fate', 'Watching The River Flow', 'Don't Think Twice', 'Gates Of Eden', 'One Too Many Mornings', 'Lay Lady Lay', 'Most Likely You Go Your Way And I'll Go Mine', 'I Don't Believe You', 'Hollis Brown', 'Masters Of War', 'Blowin' In The Wind', 'A Hard Rain's A-Gonna Fall', 'Song To Woody', 'Knockin' On Heaven's Door', 'Dark As A Dungeon', 'To Be Alone With You', 'Most Of The Time', 'I'll Be Your Baby Tonight', 'John Brown', 'The Times They Are A-Changin'', 'Mama You Been On My Mind', 'Girl From The North Country', 'Forever Young', 'Tonight, I'll Be Staying Here With You', 'Absolutely Sweet Marie', 'Positively Fourth Street', 'Ballad Of A Thin Man', 'Pledging My Time', 'I Want You', 'You Angel You', 'To Ramona', 'She Belongs To Me', 'Disease Of Conceit', 'I'll Remember You', 'Where Teardrops Fall', 'Every Grain Of Sand' and 'Blue Ridge Mountain Blues'.

He started with 'Stuck Inside Of Mobile' twice and finished with 'Highway 61 Revisited' four times. The last two nights he added more new songs than in the second, third and fourth nights. He did three songs from his debut album but only one from 'Saved'. He did seven from 'Bringing It All Back Home' and just one from 'Planet Waves'. He did eleven that start with the letter 'I' and just one with 'Q'. Then he went to France...

Under The Red Sky

Tracks: Wiggle Wiggle, Under The Red Sky, Unbelievable, Born In Time, TV Talkin' Song, 10,000 Men, 2 x 2, God Knows, Handy Dandy, Cat,s In The Well.

Released September.
Produced by Don and David Was.

SLEEVE NOTES *No messages or meanderings here, only the bizarre twist that has become Bob with his lyrics to the ill-advised 'Wiggle, Wiggle'. Rather than sleeve notes, there's actually an offer where interested parties can secure notes by the author on the songs by writing or phoning Entertainment Connections.*

WHAT THE INTERNET SAYS *"This time, Dylan tossed off a whole album of trivial jingles, recorded with an all-star line-up. Most of the lyrics sound like Mother Goose on Quaaludes."* DBW, Wilson - Alroy Record Reviews

WHAT THE PAPERS SAID *"It only sounds like a great Dylan album from the next room."* Charles Shaar Murray

"'Under The Red Sky' plods along from the moment Dylan tentatively aims a guide vocal at the opening, and dreadful, 'Wiggle, Wiggle' (which features Guns n' Roses' Slash on guitar in the distance), and peters out altogether." David Cavanagh, 1993, on its re-issue at Nice Price.

"There is a unity to the sound and feel of the album which enables the songs to work in accord with each other, each propping the other up. But, Bob is not leading the value-for-money stakes with the album clocking in at 35 minutes." Clinton Heylin

IN A NUTSHELL *Under the guidance of the hip-at-that-time Was brothers, 'Under The Red Sky' boasted a team of players that included Stevie Ray Vaughan, Slash, Bruce Hornsby, George Harrison and Elton John. The album wanders wildly through moods and, if anything, Dylan sounds remotely lost or almost disinterested in places. The title track and 'Born In Time' are decent enough ballads but 'God Knows' is uncomfortable and lacks any kind of religious zeal, the devotion seems to have simply departed him. On 'TV Talkin' Song', Bob sounds a shadow of his former talking blues self and the opening 'Wiggle, Wiggle' and 'Handy Dandy' prove to have as inept lyrics as titles.*

SINGLES/EPS/ETC *Political World (45) Unbelievable (45)*

ORDER OF BOB TO GO

Bob Dylan has been awarded one of France's highest honours, the Commander Of The Order Of Arts And Letters. He received the order from the Culture Minister whilst in Paris on his European tour. During the tour he appeared at the 12-hour Liberty celebrations.

NME, February 1990

Series Of Dreams

1991

O N THE day that original Byrds' member Gene Clark died, Bob turned 50. A natural survivor, of course. More live dates were chiselled in, the 20th Grammy Awards bestowed a Lifetime Achievement gong and Columbia released the 'Bootleg Series Volumes 1-3' to amazing critical response. Included were a host of tracks that had become legend over the years. The set was compiled by Dylan archivist Jeff Rosen and accompanied by liner notes from Dylan scholar and Q regular John Bauldie. The 58-track three-CD box and booklet was as thorough and authoritative a job as the nit-pickingest fan could require. Except there was still a bit of nit-picking...

EOIN O'MALLEY *Intrigued of Dublin*
"All biographies of Bob Dylan give his birthdate as May 24, 1941. But on the back of the sleeve of the recently released Bootleg series there is a photograph which includes his immigration card, with his birthdate as May 11, 1941. Which is right - and why is somebody getting it wrong?"

Q'S QUERY PAGE *London*
"The offending article also claimed that Dylan was Five Feet, 11 inches, so the validity of the whole affair is in question. When contacted for Q magazine to get his insight into the situation, the album's producer Jeff Rosen gave a healthy "No comment". Of course."

DAVID HEPWORTH *Broadcaster*
"I made this trip to America in the early '90s with Mark Cooper from the BBC to interview Bruce Springsteen who was about to put out 'Human Touch' and 'Lucky Town'. We flew to LA, a very long flight, and we got into the hotel and Mark made contact with the film crew and they said, 'You've got to go and see Bob Dylan. He's in town on Hollywood Boulevard, it's a

small theatre and he's just on majestic form. You've got to go'. Now, Mark will go to anything that's live but I'm a little more difficult. Anyway, a combination of him and the camera crew and the jet lag persuaded me to go.

"We got in there and out comes Bob Dylan and he's just terrible. The sound is awful. It's muddy, it's like, 'What's going on?'. Anyway, it goes on and on and getting near to the end of the set, he launches into this tune and Mark and I look at each other and Marks goes, 'It's 'All Along The Watchtower'.' and I go, 'Yeah, yeah'. And we're getting into it, nodding, and then, a few bars later we both look at each other and we realise, 'No! It's 'Don't Think Twice It's Alright'. Which gives you an idea of just how approximate Bob Dylan's renditions of these songs are.

"So, the next day, we do the interview with Bruce Springsteen and the day after I'm sitting at breakfast and Jon Landau, Springsteen's manager, sits down with me and he says, 'Bruce and I went to see Bob Dylan last night', to which I say, 'Really, how was it?' Landau thinks for a minute and then he says, 'Mmm, it was very strange. Do you know what happened? Towards the end of the set, he started this number and we looked at each other and said, 'Hey, it's 'All Along The Watchtower', and we nodded at each other and then we both turned to each other and said, 'No it's not. It's 'Don't Think Twice, It's Alright'!"

The Bootleg Series Vols 1-3

Rare and unreleased 1961-1989 *CD-1 Tracks: Hard Times In New York, He Was A Friend Of Mine, Man On The Street, No More Auction Block, House Carpenter, Talking Bear Mountain Picnic Massacre Blues, Let Me Die In My Footsteps, Ramblin', Gamblin' Willie, Talkin' Hava Nagilah Blues, Quit Your Low Down Ways, Worried Blues, Kingsport Town, Walkin' Down The Line, Walls Of Red Wing, Paths Of Victory, Talkin' John Birch Paranoid Blues, Who Killed Davey Moore?, Only A Hobo, Moonshiner, When The Ship Comes In, The Times They Are A- Changin', Last Thoughts On Woody Guthrie.*

CD-2 Tracks: Seven Curses, Eternal Circle, Suze (the Cough Song), Mama You Been On My Mind, Farewell Angelina, Subterranean Homesick Blues, If You Gotta Go Go Now (Or Else You Gotta Stay All Night), Sitting On A Barbed Wire Fence, Like A Rolling Stone, It Takes A Lot To Laugh, It Takes A Train To Cry, I'll Keep It With Mine, She's Your Lover Now, I Shall Be Released, Santa-Fe, If Not For You, Wallflower, Nobody 'Cept You, Tangled Up In Blue, Call Letter Blues, Idiot Wind.

CD-3 Tracks: If You See Her, Say Hello, Golden Loom, Catfish, Seven Days, Ye Shall Be Changed, Every Grain Of Sand, You Changed My Life, Need A Woman, Angelina, Someone's Got A Hold Of My Heart, Tell Me, Lord Protect My Child, Foot Of Pride, Blind Willie McTell, When The Night Comes Falling From The Sky, Series Of Dreams

Released March.

SLEEVE NOTES *An extensive and deep cover research job from John Bauldie traces the roots, story and execution of every song on this three CD set. The notes are beautifully illustrated by previously unseen pictures of Bob with Suze Rotolo, Dave Van Ronk, in the studio, in the coffee house and, indeed, on the roof.*

WHAT THE PAPERS SAID *"As the best of the many fascinating examples here show, he shot it all back with the conviction of someone who must sing or explode. Dylan is the only artist of his generation whose work never seems to date. Indeed, most of it improves with age."*
David Hepworth, Q

WHAT THE WORLD SAYS J WILSON, fan, Cumbria *"My favourite Bob Dylan track ever is 'Idiot Wind' off the 'Bootleg Series'. I don't know why, but I repeatedly go back to it, usually after a drink. To me, it just beats The Band's 'I Shall Be Released' and The Byrds' 'My Back Pages' when it comes to hitting the heartstrings."*
ELVIS COSTELLO *"I thought that (the waltz version of) 'Like A Rolling Stone' was great. Like 'If You Gotta Make A Fool Of Somebody' in waltz-time. I thought it was terrific. I wouldn't trade it for the version there is, but that's what's interesting about that box set: the original's so good that you can hear a crappy run-through of it and it's still interesting."*
CEDRIC ROSSART, fan, Lyon *"'Series Of Dreams' is Dylan's best single since 1976, from this unbelievable set of unreleased material."*

IN A NUTSHELL *A gift for the collectors which includes album out-takes, songs recorded in hotel rooms, the missing tracks from 'Freewheelin', publishing demos, live cuts, alternate takes and legendary songs that bootleggers and superfans have talked over or just stalked for years. It's an awesome collection that spans numerous periods of Bob and, for anyone who's read Anthony Scaduto's biography, it aurally fills the blanks that complete the story of those fascinating early days, while adding more powerful material left off the electric albums, 'The Basement Tapes', 'Planet Waves', 'Blood On The Tracks' and beyond.*

SINGLES/EPS/ETC *Series Of Dreams (45)*

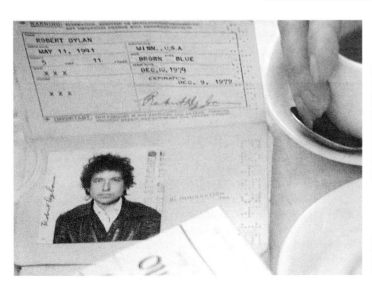

1978. Photo by Morgan Renard

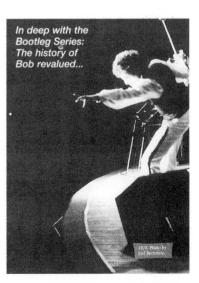

In deep with the Bootleg Series: The history of Bob revalued...

1978. Photo by Joel Bernstein

Sittin' On Top Of The World

TOURING WAS only interrupted by a celebratory, star-studded live show, the Bobfest at Madison Square Garden, which celebrated Dylan's 30 years in the industry. It was nothing short of controversial, thanks to Sinnead O'Connor, who was roundly booed by a hostile audience following her anti-Pope antics on Saturday Night Live the previous week.

EDDIE VEDDER AND MIKE McREADY *Pearl Jam*

"We stayed up drinking until seven in the morning at an Irish bar in New York called Tommy Makem's. Bob had some advice, the biggest piece being, 'Go to Dublin'."

CHRISSIE HYNDE
Singer/songwriter

"He's the man. I think the world is a better place because he's in it. One of the reasons I'm so fond of him personally is that he's very

funny. But even if he wasn't a laugh, he'd still be the one for me because he's such a great songwriter."

ERIC CLAPTON

"Bob's a very sweet man. He's got a heart as big as a house and it's all he can do to keep it under wraps.

101

He said some wonderful things to me in the moments that we had to talk on that night."

SINEAD O'CONNOR
"I think he's beautiful."

Just to confound all and sundry, under the weight of retrospectives and history, Dylan decided to delve further into his back pages. He uncovered a gaggle of original Smithsonian blues songs plus some personal favourites that his early contemporaries had played. The result was his first acoustic album since 1964, the collection 'Good As I Been To You' which included Arthur McBride's 'Hard Times', 'Step Up And Go' (previously recorded by Dylan-mate Paul Brady), 'Tomorrow Night' (culled from Willie Nelson's 'Country Willie' album), 'You're Gonna Quit Me' (a standard of fellow New York coffee house circuiteer The Reverend Gary Davis) and 'Diamond Joe' (a Jerry Garcia tune).

Just to put his 30 years in the business into sharp perspective, Q asked Motorhead's Lemmy what he thought about Bob Dylan. "Nice hair. Good cook." coughed the Lemster. He probably saw him at the Brixton Academy...

JOHN HARRIS
"The first time I saw him live was at the Brixton Academy in 1992. As well as being brilliant it was also hilariously funny. No-one had warned me about what to expect. He was introduced and when he came out he had a harmonica holder on and no guitar and, for the first two songs, he proceeded to dance like Shakin' Stevens, banging his knees together and doing the splits.

It sounded fantastic but it was also just hilarious. I couldn't believe that he could just let himself go to that extent.

"It was amazing and at the very end of the last song, someone had thrown a rose onto the stage and he flicked it up in the air, caught it in his teeth and did a quick flamenco dance off into the wings. I just thought, 'Wow! What a guy.'"

As Good As I Been To You

Tracks: Frankie & Albert, Jim Jones, Blackjack Davey, Canadee-I-O, Sittin' On Top Of The World, Little Maggie, Hard Times, Step It Up And Go, Tomorrow Night, Arthur McBride, You,re Gonna Quit Me, Diamond Joe, Froggie Went A- Courting.
Released November.
Produced by David Bromberg and Debbie Gold.

SLEEVE NOTES *Er, like nothing man. Not even who wrote what on the CD version. In fact, the cover itself looks like one of those tacky re-issues of legendary bluesmen, knocked out in 20 minutes if that.*

WHAT THE INTERNET SAYS
"A collection of little-known folk songs, all solo vocal and acoustic guitar. The track selection is interesting, covering a broad swath from slow blues to love songs, happy and unhappy, to just plain fun."
DBW, Wilson - Alroy Record Reviews

WHAT THE PAPERS SAID *"This back-to-basics acoustic folk record shows that Dylan can concentrate when he puts his mind to it and that the voice can still be an elastic instrument, moving easily between a rasp, a whine and sudden tenderness. Dylan sings with a wise conviction that simply wasn't there when he started out as a folk singer."* from the 50 Best Albums Of The Year review, Q

IN A NUTSHELL
After the inadequacies of 'Under The Red Sky', Bob turned interpreter of classic traditional folk roots, urban and country blues. The result is simply breathtaking. After admiring the back to basics nature of the project itself and his choice of material, you can thrill to his guitar playing! It's simply phenomenal, as he rattles and hammer-fingers across the fretboard, from flat- picking to loose strummage. On top is the lonesome harmonica and Bob in the best vocal nick he's been for some time.

"Someone had thrown a rose onto the stage, he flicked it in the air and caught it in his teeth!"

Ragged And Dirty

THE LEGACY of Folkways and Smithsonian field recordings that had been uncovered by Harry Smith and Alan Lomax had inspired Dylan to revisit the very songs that first set him thinking. Amid stories of a writer's block, a second album of covers, 'World Gone Wrong' was released.

ERIC CLAPTON

"I think those two albums ('As Good As I Been To You' and 'World Gone Wrong') are great, really lovely. And he really can do that stuff. It's possible for him to come in here now with a guitar and tune into himself and entertain for hours. There's no theatre in that, no stance, no profit, it's just spending time on something magnificent for no reason other than that in itself. He's a brilliant guitarist... He's extremely gifted."

Adopting the style of a travelling bluesman, Bob was

again board-treading, with a half a dozen London shows that garnered a variety of comments from the audience.

SUNDAY

"Depressing, even living legends should rehearse sometimes."

MONDAY

"It's just so incredible to be in the same room as Bob Dylan."

TUESDAY

"He isn't so much singing as painting with his voice."

WEDENESDAY

Good things on TV. No show.

THURSDAY

"It wasn't like any other concert I've ever been

to. It was more like being at a weird film."

FRiDAY

"I wasn't crying during Simple Twist Of Fate... I just had something in my eye."

SATURDAY

"You hear people talking about charisma but now I understand what it is."

JIMMY MILLER *London*

"Dylan is not, as critics and audience seem to want, a singing telegram from the Sixties, he's a great performing artist whose studio and stage performances derive their power from spontaneity.

"Dylan's performance on Sunday, February 7 was a masterpiece. He was in a good mood and this was taken up by the band and the very appreciative audience. Yes, he mumbles some of his lyrics - he has done since 1961. Yes, he alters the old songs - sometimes beyond all recognition - but if you want to listen to an old record, then why not stay at home."

BLIND BOY DEREK
AOL co-ordinator, smokin' a cheap cigar in Dublin, Ireland

"I first starting listening to Dylan at the age of 18 when John Byrne gave me a badly recorded tape of 'Biograph'. 'Percy's Song' and 'I'll Be Your Baby Tonight' instantly burned an impression in my mind that would begin ten years of, well I suppose you would call it obsessive listening.

"I saw Bob in '89, '91, '93, '95, '97 and '98. The obsession had kicked in so bad that by 1997 I was travelling to England to catch a show. And, in 1998 one show in Belfast wasn't enough, I also HAD to fly to London to catch another one a week later.

"There's a real sense of community revolving around amateur Dylanologists here in Ireland. I suppose the Mecca for Dylan fans in Dublin is Paul Murphy's bootleg record shop, RPM Records in Dublin's trendy Temple Bar. Not

comes up with an idea. He thinks, 'Maybe Dylan hasn't organised a support act for his European tour' and plots a master stroke that involves him standing in the hallway watching Dylan rehearse, signalling through to The Frames when Dylan stops and ensuring that the break is filled with The Frames playing away. And, play they do, rockin' the house so much so that Bob's manager comes in and invites them to play at the Hammersmith Odeon in London for a series of shows opening for Bob Dylan. Why? Because, as the manager says (I don't know whether it was Rosen, Kramer or somebody else): "Bob likes you guys."

"The Frames / Bob relationship continues and as they're rehearsing, Paul goes to the Coke machine and there's Bob getting himself a drink. Paul thinks to himself, 'I gotta say something, but what?' So he walks up to Bob with an extended hand that Bob takes with a half-ways smile and Paul says, 'Oh man, I dunno what to say, it's probably like when you met Woody or something'. Well, unlike reports

"In 1998 one show in Belfast wasn't enough, I had to fly to London."

that Paul's shop is anything close to trendy.

"Situated above the Regent Barbers in a run down building on Fownes Street, Paul plays host to a countrywide network of Dylanites. Paul, in his early thirties, has been obsessed by Bob for years. He sold sandwiches at Dylan's Slane concert in 1984 and has travelled Europe to see his Bobness in concert. He's even met Bob.

"So the story goes, one afternoon in early 1993 Paul gets a phone call from his long time friend and frontman of Irish rockers, The Frames, Glen Hansard (Glen played Outspan Foster in Alan Parker's The Commitments). Glen frantically tells Paul to shut the shop and head down to The Factory recording studio where The Frames were rehearsing. 'Why?', asks Paul. 'Because Dylan's here!', came the excited reply. And indeed he was. Rehearsing his tour band for two days, he was in the adjoining room to The Frames.

"So Paul, being a shrewd character indeed,

I've heard before where Bob reportedly avoids all contact, he amazingly starts to ramble about the days in the hospital playing to Woody and all the other old village folkies and the conversation goes on for about seven or eight minutes until somebody calls for him."

Bob had become fascinating again. He's become a talking point and interviewees are now regularly asked what they think of him. Alison Moyet quipped "I never think of Bob Dylan."

Pete Townshend gruffly recalled "He is a very poor conversationalist. Give me Joanna Lumley or Mariella Frostrup anyday." The Fall's Mark E Smith questioned his longevity, "You don't have to go on and on like Dylan for eighteen verses, it's not fair on the band. He can't write for toffee." Paul Weller recognised his mercurial spark, "He's a fucking genius and damn all his critics. His last LP was great." And Ray Davies showed concern for his relocation to North London; "If he is moving to Crouch End, I suggest he gets a car alarm."

ANDY KERSHAW

"There was a bizarre period during the summer of 1993 when Bob became a fairly familiar site around London N8. I'd get up and wander down to the newsagent and there'd be Bob gazing into the estate agent window. You'd go into the Indian restaurant and they'd be saying 'Bob Dylan was in here last night'. Rumours were rife that he was going to buy a house there so that he could be "near Dave".

"In fact Dylanologists were setting up birdwatcher's hides along Middle Lane in case Bob decided to look at any of the attractive residences along there. And then there was the incident that I missed of course, in a simple twist of fate, when he walked into my girlfriend's restaurant.

"She has a cafe bar place in Crouch End and on this particular occasion I'd been taken kicking and screaming off to the cinema to see a Jean Renoir film. When we got back, about two hours later the whole restaurant was in a state of trauma. You could see when you walked in that something had happened and I thought, 'Have we been robbed?' or something.

"We went up to the manageress and she said: 'Bob Dylan has just been in.' I couldn't believe it. So, I got her to sit down and tell me the whole story.

"It turned out that the door had opened about half past six. In walked Bob with a man who, from the staff's descriptions I can only guess was his chess roadie Victor Maimudes. They sat down and the waitress looking after their table, a Jamaican girl called Donna, went over and asked them what they wanted.

"Now Donna had no idea who Bob Dylan was and Dylan and Maimudes obviously had no understanding of the British licensing laws in such places, where alcohol can only be served if a meal is bought. So the two of them ordered two whiskies and Donna asks if they're going to be eating and then explains that they can't have alcohol unless they do. Victor and Bob insist that they only want two whiskies and Donna explains the situation again.

"In the end, Maimudes said the most uncool thing that he could have said. He turned to Donna and he said: 'Don't you know who this is?', and Donna, who was wiping the table tops, looked up and said: 'I'm sorry, I don't'."

Dignity

1994

ALTHOUGH, probably wisely, he avoided being part of the original Woodstock festival in 1969, failing to be lured the few miles from his own Woodstock retreat, Bob took the stage on the closing Sunday for Woodstock '94, a 25-year mud-drenched celebration. The, by then, drug-addled crowd preferred his more rambunctious overtures and he climaxed the show with his version of Hendrix's version of his very own 'All Along The Watchtower', before exiting on 'It Ain't Me Babe'. The now-inevitable round of workaday touring continued across America in the guise of The Eternal Tour. When the show stopped off in Rockford, Illinois, a benevolent Bob donated $20,000 to a local trade union to fund a playground for a school for handicapped children. Other more extravagant live shows followed during in the year, none more so than the Great Music Experience in Japan, the first leg of a planned globe-straddling event that was intended to be yearly, culminating in a show at the Forbidden City in Beijing in the year 2000.

DANNY KELLY *Broadcaster and journalist*

"The first rock music that really, really turned my head upside down was Bob Dylan. This was in the early '70s. I can't remember what song it was, it was probably a copy of 'Bringing It All Back Home' that someone had brought into school. I was completely besotted by music but to hear something like this was so different. I remember being really impressed by the voice and the way the words all came out in a tumble, how some of them rhymed and some of them didn't.

"I was lucky because the central library in Islington had 'Freewheelin'', 'Bringing It All Back Home', 'Highway 61 Revisited' and I listened to them all. Even the things that are now discredited, like 'Self Portrait', I listened to over and over again.

"Because I came to him late and because I had other heroes, I never became a Bobcat and I never insisted on hearing every live record

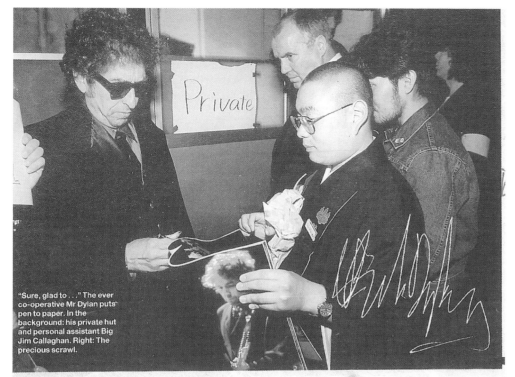

"Sure, glad to . . ." The ever co-operative Mr Dylan puts pen to paper. In the background: his private hut and personal assistant Big Jim Callaghan. Right: The precious scrawl.

Next is the show's low point, a piece of jazz played by ex-Weather Reporter Wayne Shorter and Toshinoro Kondo. You know it's jazz because neither man can seem to remember the tune, as a swirl of accelerated Dr. Who sound effects jitter out. In the good seats, one of the monks looks like he wishes he'd taken a vow of deafness.

The Chieftains, Ry Cooder and an assortment

the discipline of having 60-odd musicians dependent on him, Dylan sings, really opens his lungs and heart and sings, like he's not done for many a year. Kamen's arrangements keep pushing him gently along; it's like watching a creaking old galleon, long becalmed, suddenly setting full sail again, propelled by an irresistible breeze. The only word for it is majestic.

Temple, an ancient wooden building which houses a huge Buddha that fills the whole building. the trick is that people come and have their picture taken in the palm of the Buddha, it's that big, and it's made of brass. It's a very spiritual space, the monks are very young and they were also to be part of the event, doing their chanting.

"The word around the place was that Dylan was actually rehearsing and because he was there, I don't know, I just felt that little bit closer to him.

"On the night before the show I'd decided that I needed to get 'close' to him. This might be my only chance to ever meet him, so I had to do something. At the very worst I wanted to get his autograph and, to speed this along I decided to track down his North-London-Irish bodyguard Callahan. I suspected that even in Japan he'd be searching for a pint of Guinness and I got a cab to take me to a place called Murphy's and there he was. Several Guinness's later I tried to impress on Callahan that I wanted to meet Dylan and through our new found camaraderie I hoped that he might let me do that. He didn't seem that keen.

"On the day, it was a fantastic spectacle, with Kodo drummers bashing away, INXS playing. I began to feel quite excited about the prospect of seeing Dylan. And, just the fact that he was walking around in the backstage area was getting people enthusing about the whole event. Dylan was in his portakabin and,

"Bob's stage shows are unpredictable, or a shambles, depending on how you want to look at it."

ever made. But, when I went to the Great Music Experience in Japan I was amazed at how I felt.

"Let me explain: Bob Dylan usually lives and works several thousand of miles from me. He doesn't know that I exist but I'm very aware that he exists. The people I worked with in the music press always kept me up to date with him. Genuine Bobcats, like John Bauldie or Adrian Deevoy or Bill Prince, would keep me informed of what he was up to. It's fair to say, though, that Bob and I lead pretty separate lives.

"However, when I went to see this gig in Osaka, with people like Joni Mitchell, a

gamelan orchestra, INXS, a full classical orchestra under George Martin, The Chieftains and Dylan all set to play on stage together at one point I was expecting disaster. Bob's stage shows are unpredictable, or a shambles, depending on how you want to look at it. Usually the band don't seem to know what they are supposed to play and he doesn't seem to know what he wants to play. Indeed, Grand pianos remain on stage untouched for several shows. So the prospect of Bob Dylan fitting into this huge ego battle that was about to happen was pretty extraordinary.

"The event itself took place at the Todiji

eventually, I catch sight of him talking to Joni Mitchell and laughing. Now I'd interviewed Joni Mitchell the previous day and I'm fully aware that she's absolutely barking, so the two of them together, well, I've absolutely no idea what they were talking about.

"As night fell, it was Dylan's turn to take the stage and he was great. He actually sang the songs instead of groaning them out. But, the thing that really got to me was when he did 'Ring Them Bells' from 'Oh Mercy'. As he was doing it they opened the giant 12 feet high doors at the top of the temple to reveal the face of the Buddha lit up in the moonlight. I make

THE TELEGRAPH

SUMMER 1994 · 49

an orphanage in Ireland in the last century whose bones had been dug up recently, that lasted 15 minutes. I'm not saying it brought the house down, but it certainly brought me down. But, generally it had all gone well.

"Everyone was slapping each other on the back, but Dylan stood alone with Callahan and his gang of minders surrounding him. You could see that people were desperate to talk to him or to get his autograph but Callahan caught me in the eye and I could tell that now wasn't the time.

"Then Dylan walked along the grass towards Joni Mitchell's portakabin, his head down avoiding eye contact. Suddenly one of the monks who lived at the temple, dressed in a full white cowl, perhaps unaware of the conventions of the west, ran across the grass and stuck a piece of paper in Bob Dylan's hand for him to sign.

"Then, all hell broke loose. Because he couldn't turn down the monk, one after another the monks, all 17, 18 or 19, ran over to get his autograph. The bodyguards were shaking their heads, Joni Mitchell was laughing and people were just generally falling around.

"There were lots of admirers around Dylan, but for some reason we'd stuck about 30 feet away, that seemed to be a suitable exclusion zone. Then me and a photographer moved a bit closer and Callahan stepped in, but all of the drinking the previous night paid off and we took several pictures.

"As far as I could see Dylan was not going to sign any

autographs for westerners, then I had a stroke of personal genius. I'd been with a press officer from one of the companies all weekend and she was a) female and b) black, two of Bob's favourite things when combined. She strode up to him, he turned away but he must have just briefly caught sight of her shapely ankle because he turned and very politely scrawled his name. Boy was I excited.

"Now that was four years ago and the power of that performance and what it made me feel like in that very beautiful, very spiritual and very holy place - and the fact that he didn't at all seem out of place there - meant that when I got back I was pretty obsessed with him. Now, I'm really glad that I got that close to him, that I saw him laughing with Joni Mitchell, that I saw that performance and that the monks proved that even he, whose not short of ego, had to realise that some times people just need your time. Of course, as with all of my great

no excuses, I cried, the tears rolled down my face.

"At that precise moment, for some reason I thought about Frank Sinatra and that when he dies, he was ill at the time, the torch of popular music would pass to Bob Dylan. I felt immense joy at how brilliant he'd been and, I don't know maybe I'm nuts, an intense sadness at the thought of Bob Dylan of all people, given his pretty scatty lifestyle, being responsible for the future of music.

"After the show I went backstage and the mood was very exciting. It had been fantastic. The Kodo Drummers were brilliant, INXS were great, Joni Mitchell - always a laugh - she had decided to unveil a song about pregnant girls sent to

Greatest Hits Vol 3

Tracks: Tangled Up In Blue, Changing Of The Guards, The Groom's Still Waiting At The Altar, Hurricane, Forever Young, Jokerman, Dignity, Silvio, Ring Them Bells, Gotta Serve Somebody, Series Of Dreams, Brownsville Girl, Under The Red Sky, Knockin' On Heaven's Door.

SLEEVE NOTES *The runners, riders, producers and directors listed and compared, plus the information that 'Dignity' is a Daniel Lanois-produced track that's previously unreleased.*

WHAT THE PAPERS SAID

"What Greatest Hits Volume III does for his reputation is hard to say. Dylan's songwriting may have become less sharp and acerbic over the years, but, as this collection shows, he still chases the kind of vision that most of his contemporaries gave up believing in years ago." Charlotte Greig, Mojo

"A haphazard package featuring precious few hits, sequenced in an apparently random order, while ignoring 'Saved', 'Empire Burlesque' and the recent folk albums. It can't decide whether it's for serious Dylan fans or casual consumers." Mark Cooper, Q

IN A NUTSHELL

A strange hybrid of recent times, which threads some semblance of continuity from 'Blood On The Tracks' until just prior to the two covers albums. There's no track culled from any of the live albums and the closing cut harks all the way back to 'Billy The Kid' underlining the dog-leg route that Bob has traversed form near to there. The no direction home tag from his past is all too apt.

Desolation Row (Slight Return)

PEOPLE WERE, yet again, fascinated by Dylan His performance for MTV's Unplugged series was released on CD and video and fans could enter virtual Bobworld with the Highway 61 Interactive CD - a snip at £50. The latter allowed the Bobfan to scan virtual Greenwich Village coffee houses, Columbia Records' recording studios and Madison Square Garden. Rare tracks could be sampled, the working out of 'Like A Rolling Stone' could be witnessed and all the peripheral facts, figures, catalogue numbers and lyrics were on hand.

And, as ever, there were live shows, everywhere from New London in January to Fairfax in Feb, Buenos Aires in March, Nürnberg in May, Rostock in June, Villafranca in July, Adelaide in August, Kahului, Maui in September, Saskatoon in October and Syracuse in November.

The On-Tour routine became an illustrated publication as Drawn Blank (Random House). It included a portfolio of Bob's life drawings reproduced as monochrome plates in a portfolio of work, which acted as Bob's tour diary.

Sue Elliot, writing in Q wasn't particularly aesthetically-impressed: "Unlike his songs, his draughtsmanship fails to seduce."

And, as interest continued to grow, deeper insights into the inner psyche of Bob continued to be delivered in Q magazine's Q&A's. Blues plucker Gary Moore recalled, "I met him once at George Harrison's house. He was very shy and had very small squishy hands.", while Morrissey opined "He would have had much more fun if he'd been in The New York Dolls." Thanks Moz.

MICHAEL EAVIS *Glastonbury Festival*
"A good old mate of mine called Max had worked on the site at Glastonbury for years and years and he had terminal cancer. His brother-in-law asked me if there was any chance that I could get him an autograph of

Unplugged

Tracks: Tombstone Blues, Shooting Star, All Along The Watchtower, The Times They Are A-Changin', John Brown, Desolation Row, Rainy Day Women Nos. 12 & 35, Love Minus Zero/No Limit, Dignity, Knockin' On Heaven's Door, Like A Rolling Stone, With God On Our Side.

Produced by Jeff Kramer and Jeff Rosen.

SLEEVE NOTES *Lotsa lyrics and nice photographs from the vid.*

WHAT MTV SAID

"What an honour. Considering Dylan's performance at Woodstock II and the fact that in recent years he has come full circle back to his earliest folk beginnings, this show seemed like a natural. We taped on two nights and he rose to the occasion, even ushering out 'Desolation Row' for the first time in years. The first night he chose a selection of his most obscure songs. The second night he played the hits. For both evenings, however, he seemed to be reinventing the songs on the spot."

WHAT THE PAPERS SAID

"No-one else, not even Guns n' Roses, would treat Dylan's songs in such a cavalier fashion as he does these days. The shameful dullness of the country-rock arrangements and the yawnsome predictability of the material chosen suggest that, those back pages are being thumbed purely in the service of commercial considerations." Andy Gill, Q

IN A NUTSHELL *There's something very strange on this TV special acousticathon, right from chord one. 'Tombstone Blues' is delivered on the wrong beat, like a rockabilly groove slowed for the hell of it. Later 'All Along The Watchtower' follows the same formula and has little in the way of light and dark. From there on in a steel guitar and dobro fill the air, Dylan sings like he's doing karaoke with a kold and few tracks survive the pacing and arrangements. 'Desolation Row' takes on the ambience of a Ry Cooder song with a cartoon Dylan impersonating a disinterested Sinatra. Even the euphoric 'Like A Rolling Stone' sounds like Bob has brushed up against it, he doesn't really leave an impression. Still, the crowd seem to "bop along".*

SINGLES/EPS/ETC

Dignity (CD single) Knockin' On Heaven's Door (CD single) Like A Rolling Stone (CD single)

Bob Dylan as he was a huge fan.

"I was talking to Bob Dylan's agent about a possible appearance at Glastonbury which never happened and I told him this yarn about a friend of mine who was dying and asked could he possibly get an autograph. The agent said: 'Well, you know what he's like, he's a difficult cuss and he won't respond to something like that'. But I sort of insisted, we'd been working with this agent for about 25 years and I'd never asked him for a favour before.

"So, the agent said he'd ask him but he thought it was really unrealistic. Anyway, he got me to write down a little verse so that Dylan could just sign it. So I scribbled it all down and he took it off to a Dylan concert and after they'd sorted out all the money for the night he asked him if he'd do it for me.

"So I'm told, Dylan said: 'Oh all right, give me a pen,' then he looked at the message and he said he wouldn't sign that twaddle and he wrote down a verse of his own to Max and it came over quite sincere, it showed a lot of sympathy. So the agent rang me and told me he'd done it and I rushed up to London and took it in an envelope back to the train and somehow I left it in the back of the taxi. I phoned the taxi people and they said I'd have to wait six weeks, but I told them that might be too late, so I went up to their office and I was really lucky that it came in to their lost property almost immediately.

"I was so worried by then that I took the train back and drove right to Max's house rather than risk losing it again. Max was so thrilled about it, that it was really worth it."

Recorded across two nights in New York last year 'MTV Unplugged' draws from Bob Dylan's virtually unlimited songbook of classics.

Including ALL ALONG THE WATCHTOWER, RAINY DAY WOMEN # 12 & 35, KNOCKIN' ON HEAVEN'S DOOR, LIKE A ROLLING STONE, JOHN BROWN and a bonus track for the european release only LOVE MINUS Z

"Dylan's Unplugged marked another stage in the creative rehabilitation of rock's most enduring enigma. Now fans get the chance to share in a refreshing reworking of landmark songs from his 33-year-old catalogue". MUSIC WEEK

"It's not without irony, Bob Dylan playing Unplugged. It could argued that the resonant strum of his acou guitar and the plaintive wail of his harp were the original Unplugged". MOJO Magazine

COMPACT DISC · CASSETTE · Double VINYL · Full length VIDEO released in May

BRIXTON ACADEMY

BARRY DICKINS & ROD MACSWEEN FOR ITB present

BOB DYLAN

Friday 31st March 1995

Tickets £20.00 Advance (Subject to Booking Fee)

Doors 6.30p.m. Show Time 8.00p.m.

STALLS STANDING

00118

No More Auction Block

BOB CONTINUED to play live, of course, but it was the mass access of the internet that spread the Bob Dylan dialogue virus pan-globally. On the .net, every Bob show came under scrutiny and every interested party could access reviews, set lists and sometimes sound within hours of a show finishing. And it wasn't purely the domain of the Dylanologist. First timers could put their ten pence in too.

CAZZUAL, *via internet*

"Just come back from the show, April 13 at Madison - some wrinkles to note. Bob sang the first two songs with microphone only - Vegas style - no guitar. Bob was sporting his gold Hall Of Fame shirt. I thought he looked a little heavy."

ROBIN JATKO, *via internet*

"Dylan was wearing that somewhat garish HoF gold satin shirt and loose black pants with a silver stripe down the leg and the ubiquitous black boots.

"There was some incense on stage, but it wasn't overwhelming. I was standing to the right of centre stage and was close enough to see the blue of his eyes - he was no more than 12 feet away (sigh)."

TIMOTHY MICHAEL ELLMORE, *via internet*

"Did anyone catch was apparently an added verse to 'Silvio'? From what I could tell, it had something to do with pride and it seemed well developed and not a spur of the moment lyric change."

KARL ERIK, *via internet*

Bob Dylan in Molde, Norway. Audience: 6,000. Weather: Sunny

"This was my second ever Bob Dylan concert. How can I describe the concert to make you feel you were there?

"The selection of songs was not great, but above average, and the audience and setting must have made Bob feel OK. He said: 'Thank you evr'body' between several of the first songs! He gave us harmonica solos, holding a loose mic with his harp, still keeping the guitar on, and he made great movements. During a couple of songs, he kept the guitar pick in his mouth for minutes, preferring to use his fingers on the guitar. My personal favourite up to then was his performance of 'John Brown', which really got the message through.

"On the way out, Bob gave his harmonica to 10-year-old Odne, who was very touched. Bob seemed to like Molde, called it a 'snappy little town' according to the papers, and went for a walk in the streets around four in the morning (it's not dark at night, even this far south)."

As the fan base grew wider and wider via the internet, taking in more and more diverse views, one of the guiding lights for Dylan enthusiasts died. For followers of the 50-plus issues of *The Telegraph*, there was enormous sadness as writer, guiding light and editor John Bauldie was killed in an air accident, leaving a whole network of fans short of a debating centre and driving wheel.

DEVOTED TO DYLAN AND THE WANDERERS

from: *The Guardian*, Friday October 25, 1996 by Paul Du Noyer
John Bauldie, who was killed, aged 47, in the helicopter crash along with Matthew Harding and three other people, had two passions. One was football and Bolton Wanderers; the other - his defining passion - was Bob Dylan. More than three decades of meticulous research had made John Bauldie into one of the world's foremost authorities on Dylan's music. He wrote several key books on him, ran a superb quarterly fanzine, *The Telegraph*, and was so valued by the Dylan organisation that they enlisted his help in compiling the Bootleg Series, the 1991 CD boxed set which unearthed such lost Dylan gems as 'No More Auction Block' and 'Blind Willie McTell'.

Yet there was nobody less like the stereotyped "anorak" than John Bauldie. A former lecturer in English Literature he was a dapper and cultured man, who brought a well-rounded intelligence to his quest. With his inimitable blend of scholarship and devotion, he elevated the often narrow world of fanzines to a different realm. He was never one to gatecrash Dylan's privacy or to peddle in specious theorising. His vocation was to amass the data and win for his hero the

THE TELEGRAPH

SPRING 1995   51

"The Telegraph?" Bob murmured. "I seen a few issues of that. It's pretty interesting."

serious appraisal due to an outstanding 20th century performer.
Indeed he only met Dylan once, and that was by accident. Following a US tour, he was passing the singer's tour bus when the

reclusive icon sauntered out. The two men held a brief and genial conversation, in the course of which John won a much prized endorsement for his magazine. "The Telegraph?" Bob murmured. "I seen a few issues of that. It's pretty interesting."

PAUL DU NOYER

"John Bauldie probably knew more about Dylan than anyone. Wrote books about him, and everything. I worked with John for five or six years and I loved his love of the music. When he was killed in 1996, it fell to me to write his obituary for The Guardian. So I sat down that day - it was about 24 hours after the news of the accident - and, to focus my thoughts, I played 'The Bootleg Series' whose tracks he had written about so beautifully in the liner notes. About four tracks into the first CD, while I stared bleakly at the computer screen, Dylan launched into 'No More Auction Block'. The shock of a friend's death came tumbling down around me at that instant. For an hour or so I couldn't understand how Dylan music might still be played without John Bauldie around to hear it. I got all the grief out in one go.

"But soon, too, came the sense of consolation that the song carries with it. 'No More Auction Block' is a deeply moving track. The newly liberated slave sings about his freedom, but also mourns the "many thousands gone". Emotionally, the words face both ways at once; they're requiem and celebration. Dylan's voice conveys the pain and dignity of this old folk song, without affection. It's full of quiet strength.

"On that particular day when I struggled to find some words that might do John Bauldie justice, 'No More Auction Block' was a real catharsis (and it was probably Bauldie, a cultured man, who first explained to me what "catharsis" means). It's the sort of music that keeps you company through something dreadful, and you never forget the debt you owe to it."

1997

Million Miles
(Farther Down The Road)

AS WAS Bob, road-rage and general 'No Direction Homeness' continued, only ill health stopped him in his tracks leaving people to re-evaluate his life and times. Reuters in New York reported: "Rock legend Bob Dylan is hospitalised under an assumed name for treatment of an infection producing swelling around his heart, but his life was not considered in danger."

14:59   05-28-97
LONDON (Reuter)
American rock star Bob Dylan called off a European tour after being admitted to a hospital suffering from a potentially life-threatening disease, his publicists said Wednesday.

Media reports here said the 56-year-old singer / songwriter was hospitalised in New York but a spokeswoman for Dylan in New York said her office did not know where he was

being treated or what his condition was. "This past weekend, Bob Dylan was admitted to hospital suffering from severe chest pains. His condition has been diagnosed as histoplasmosis, a potentially fatal infection which creates swelling in the sac which surrounds the heart," Dylan's London publicists said.

Dylan will remain in the hospital until his doctors are confident his condition has improved, they added.

In New York, his publicists said they hoped he would be well enough to go through with a U.S. tour slated for August.

The singer was due to perform in Ireland, Britain and Switzerland during the summer tour. Van Morrison, who was to appear with him in London June 7, said he would still perform.

BLIND BOY DEREK

"I get a phone call at work from a friend of mine in Galway. Dylan had been scheduled to play 'The Homecoming' concert in Cork, and surprise, surprise I had tickets. About two weeks or so before the gig, Tiernan calls me up and says that Van Morrison is playing a small gig in 'The Temple Bar Music Centre' as a special guest of saxophone player, Richie Buckley. Tiernan then tells me that he reckons Dylan's gonna play. He just figures it. No evidence, no rumours, nothing it's just a hunch he has.

"The Temple Bar Music Centre holds about 200-300 people. It's a club, not a concert hall. It's got a bar and it's intimate. It would be like having Bob play in your living room. So, I make a call. I call Paul at headquarters (RPM records) and tell him to go across to HMV and buy as many tickets as he can afford. He goes and buys tickets numbers one to eight.

Time Out of Mind

Tracks: *Love Sick, Dirt Road Blues, Standing In The Doorway, Million Miles, Tryin' To Get To Heaven, Til I Fell In Love With You, Not Dark Yet, Cold Irons Bound, Make You Feel My Love, Can,t Wait, Highlands.*

Produced by DanielLanois.

SLEEVE NOTES

There's little text just two fantastic black and white shots of Dylan. The cover is hauntingly out of focus, while the slight fish-eye on the inside, adds to the eerie ambience.

WHAT THE PAPERS SAID
"When it's good, 'Time Out Of Mind' is a really weird success. It's an album to replay warily but often." Dave Cavanagh, Q

"The likes of 'Lovesick' and 'Cold Irons Bound' surely deserve as lofty a place in the Dylan canon as anything from his far-flung purple period." John Harris, Select

"73 minutes of genius" The Evening Standard

'Dylan at his creative peak." The Guardian

"The original is back." The NME

WHAT THE WORLD SAYS

CHRIS REA *"The production here is simply staggering. I was so surprised when I first heard the sound of it. Made me bang my head against the wall because I'd been thinking along the same lines and I didn't fucking do it. If I wanted to be really bitchy I could say that he's rich enough to take these risks and I'm not. Still, ten out of ten."*

RON SEXSMITH *"'Not Dark Yet' is most people's favourite, but the second song, 'Dirt Road Blues', stood out right away for me; it was like vintage Dylan, even the sound of his voice."*

ELVIS COSTELLO *"I actually think this is the best record he's ever made. The production is very discreet, the recording of his voice is absolutely magnificent. His phrasing is absolutely unbelievable."*

IN A NUTSHELL

Back with Daniel Lanois, the mood is beautifully subdued but devilishly taught. The haunting 'Lovesick' sets a David Lynchian aura of darkened room, smoky haze, etc. You can hear Bob's fingers glide along the strings as he pours the emotion on thick as custard. 'Standing In The Doorway' takes the collapse of a relationship even further as Bob sketches the emptiness of memory. 'Tryin' To Get To Heaven', 'Not Dark Yet' and 'Make You Feel My Love' all follow suit and in between there's smouldering resolution, like on the swampy 'Til I Fell In Love With You' and 'Can't Wait'. And he closes with another lengthy conversation on the state of the world in which he even mentions Erica Jong. Relevant? Bob? You bet.

"Now remember, we've got eight tickets to see Richie Buckley at £13 a pop, and special guest Van Morrison. Sure, who wants to see Van these days? The answer... no-one. Tiernan's hunch better pay off.

"After I finish work I grab a cab in to see Paul and we take a walk over to the Temple Bar Music Centre. We buy a couple of drinks and start to ask vague questions. The barman knows nothing and that's obvious. Then paydirt. A guy Paul knows from the secret Bowie gig he was at a couple of weeks previous shows up. He's a sound engineer, or something, but has a good set of ears and always kinda hears the right things. Paul asks him straight out and he confirms it. "Yeah, Dylan's gonna play here, but keep it to yourself. Okay?".

"Well that was that. I ring Tiernan, who has ticket numbers 16-22, and he does his, 'I told you so' routine, but I can handle it this time. I got tickets to see Bob in the second best Dublin venue (Whelan's would've been just too much to hope for). So, everything is hunky dory until two days before Bob's secret gig in Dublin.

"I get a phone call at noon from Tiernan.

"Did you hear anything about Bob ?" he enquiries.

"No."

" Apparently, he's in a bad way, he had a heart attack and he's not doin' so good, there's all sorts of things floating around. Brain Damage. Nobody knows."

"Where did you get this from?"

" I have a friend at MCD." (MCD are the concert promoters.)

"Fuck."

"I immediately ring a friend of mine in Kerry, Colin Lacey who works for The Examiner newspaper and he's heard nothing... he scurries off to see what he can dig up and all he can get from MCD is that there will be a Press Release at 4.00pm. I can't wait that long, I tell the Boss I'm taking a half-day, grab my telephone numbers and head for the City Centre. Paul closes the shop and we see what we can find out. First port of call is Hot Press magazine, supposedly the eyes and ears of Dublin. Zilch, Niall Stokes the editor, hasn't heard squat.

"We eventually get in touch with a friend of a friend in MCD and he confirms the heart attack (later turns out to be inaccurate, it was as we all know now histoplasmosis), but then we hear from another friend that Bob's in Dublin. He wasn't of course, and this was confirmed by another friend who works for Blackrock Clinic (where Bob was supposed to be). Well the news comes out at four and we hope for Bob's full recovery.

"Fast forward to the Richie Buckley gig. Remember we all have tickets. We stand there in the middle of about a hundred people and Van comes on and does his Jazz thing. I look at the stage, I see how good it is, and I walk out, somehow it just ain't right listening to Van doing his 'Moondance' when it should've been Bob. On my way out I hear the barman talking to a customer, 'You think that's good, we were supposed to have Van and Bob Dylan here tonight'."

06-02-97 SONY MUSIC PRESS RELEASE

Bob Dylan Released From Hospital - Treatment Continues and Full Recovery Expected.

Bob Dylan was released from the hospital this weekend where he had been undergoing medical tests and subsequent treatment for pericarditis brought on by histoplasmosis. He was admitted on May 25. Doctors are continuing to treat him and are confident that Mr. Dylan will make a full recovery in four to six weeks.

When asked about his plans for his recovery period, Mr. Dylan said, "I don't know what I'm going to do. I'm just glad to be feeling better. I really thought I'd be seeing Elvis soon."

While it is unknown exactly how Mr. Dylan contracted histoplasmosis, the fungal condition which resulted in his illness, doctors believe that the severity of his condition was due to the length of time between the onset of symptoms and the eventual diagnosis.

Mr. Dylan was forced to cancel a European concert tour that was to begin June 1 in Cork, Ireland. He plans to fulfil his U.S. concert schedule, and has recently completed work on a new album that will be released this year.

Illness, album releases, Vatican-anointed live shows and recovery topped and tailed the year. On the internet, the 'Bob Dylan Get Well Card' was gathering momentum.

"I hope you get well - U R one terrific person."

CAROL JAMES (Hearts Band) Tue Jun 9
"One day I hear music......words......like never before. It's coming from the living room. It was different yet unique....I liked it. I asked my father "Who sings that?" And who do you think he said??!! THANK-YOU BOB, WITHOUT YOU....LIFE WOULD NOT BE THE SAME!!"

RICHARD J. MARAIA, MD (maraiar@exchange.nih.gov) Mon Jun 15
"Bob. After reading a small portion of the 700 messages to you, I realise how big an influence you have been on so many. The many sweet rhymes in rhythms that you have transferred to me, and now I know to others, have stuck to my insides. You have been my major recording idol since I was a teen, when my cousin first introduced me to the newly released Highway 61, whhheeeeww, that was a trip. I have invested in your music ever since and often still play 'Sad Eyed Lady...' Oh, just thinking about that wonderful swift yet slow blend of vocal music, lyrics and percussions brings about a deep craving for more. It's like that with a lot of your music, a fleeting tune will come up from within in part and I desire more. Quite a pleasurable sensation to be able to satisfy. You have given so much, it would be very nice to give something good back. I hope you receive this message in good spirits. From where I sit, life is good. I can say with sincerity that you have made it better often. Thanks, Rich Maraia.

ANDREW JORGENSEN (lostdog2@aol.com) Fri Jun 19
"Oh man you can take the dark out of the night time. And paint the day time black it has always meant more than the collateral at the bank or the degree in my head or the news on the tube. Time is a jet plane, it moves too fast oh but what a shame that all we've shared can't last I can change I swear ohhh see what you can do I can make it through you can make it too.
"I like talkin ww3 blues good and desire too. you are alright ain't you? You sing older but I love you just the same. I try to turn everyone on to you. You are an inspirational gas tank to me. Add my get well wishes send me a harmonica holder, play me subterranean homesick blues if you can remember"

BARBARA (beslinger@gyral.com) Sat Jun 20
"Bob, you have been my best friend since I was 16 years old. Then, I studied and learned every line of 'Sad Eyed Lady', 'Ballad Of A Thin Man', 'Masters Of War', Blue Eyed Son, and more (it all seemed so much more important than studying). Now, I play 'Hurricane' whenever I clean my house; your words energise me (I am now almost 50, so I need energy). Your new CD is just wonderful. I quote you often and people think I am odd. "It's a chicken" is my screensaver. Saw you in Hartford with the Rolling Thunder Revue. The concert was a birthday surprise from my sister, and I still haven't gotten over it. I am happy you recovered from your illness. I was scared for you. You must take care of yourself because you are not only an earth-wide treasure, but you are, after all, my best friend. I hope you have someone around who makes you good soup."

NATALIE BYRD (Nattyhere@hotmail.com) Wed Jun 24
"I wish I could express my words as you do, however you'll have to settle for plain Kentuckian' talk. One day I was talkin to Jesus and was askin Him some questions and Jeremiah 23:23 popped into my head. It really encouraged me and to know that He KNOWS all that we're goin through and is with us. Also, this might sound silly, plese try and watch some Veggie Tale videos while you rest. THEY are really encouraging in a child like faith. If you ever need an encouraging word or a listening ear, e-mail me your address (p.o. box) and I'll write. Psalms 100

KOLI FYTEN (cooper9834@aol.com) Mon Jun 29
"You have forever left a mark on my life. I am a better person in many ways because of your very existence and your words. I hope you make it through these tough times. I'm praying for you."

TERI LYNN (wtmdc@gte.net) Thu Jul 2
"Get well my 60's Brother. PEACE & LOVE. May your energy return to you full steam ahead I too have H. Capsulatum in my lung. You're in my thoughts and prayers."

ALAN F. ANDERSON (alanderson123@yahoo.com) Mon Jul 6
"Subterranean Homesick Blues..... Bob, stay out of the grave until the time has come. I don't believe your knocking on heavens door as of yet... I sure do hope you stay well."

CENDIE (littlewman@aol.com) Mon Jul 20
"I HOPE YOU GET WELL I THINK U ARE ONE TERRIFIC PERSON> MY PRAYERS AND THOUGHTS ARE WITH YOU MY FRIEND"

KAREN BELL (bell.13@0suedu) Fri Jul 24 10:51:23
"Bob, My God, is it really you I am writing to after all these years? You that tiny frizzy haired figure on stage a million miles away from wherever I was in the audience. My 16-year-old daughter Tess has discovered your old and new

THE BEST OF BOB DYLAN

Tracks: Blowin' In The Wind, The Times They Are A-Changin', Don't Think Twice, It's All Right, Mr Tambourine Man, Like A Rolling Stone, Just Like A Woman, All Along The Watchtower, Lay Lady Lay, I Shall Be Released, If Not For You, Knockin' On Heaven's Door, Forever Young, Tangled Up In Blue, Oh, Sister, Gotta Serve Somebody, Jokerman, Everything Is Broken, Shelter From The Storm.

SLEEVE NOTES *Not that much, just a snatch of type-written, mis-spelt lyric from 'Subterranean Homesick Blues' which isn't included on the album. Initial copies were stickered with the legend '18 Digitally Remastered Classic Songs including 'Lay Lady Lay' and 'Knocking On Heaven's Door' (rather than 'Knockin''). The cover also features a tinted shot of the back page of the booklet from 'Biograph'.*

WHAT THE PAPERS SAID *"The point of this strange compilation remains unfocused. It's a wild selection that seems to have no reason to actually exist."*

IN A NUTSHELL *Bob's Best is simply impossible to collate. The 'Greatest Hits' packages, the 'Biograph' box, the 'Bootleg' series, a host of official albums and a million other less legal ones can't be condensed into 18 songs. Inevitably no-one would agree with the selection. The cover sticker suggests that this was to be a mass-market release and it was TV-advertised for Christmas 1997. Now, imagine waking up with that in your stocking.*

music. Please stick around for us and all of your fans old and new. Elvis can wait. Be well. We love you."

LUKE MULHARE Mon Aug 10
"I would just like to say, I know you hear it a lot now that your not dead, you are my influence of music."

STEVE RUSK (srusk@aol.com) Tue Aug 11 13:56:03
"Do some more work like you did between 'Saved' & 'Empire Burlesque'. Get back to Jesus, He's the "same yesterday, and today, and forever" Hebrews 13:8. Think about it. Much Christian love to you."

JIM WALTON (piper@tesco.net) Wed Sep 16 16:25:39
"I have had the privilege of listening to your music for years. I hope to be able to listen to more of your genius for many years to come. May God bless and keep you always and may your wishes all come true."

Committee formally nominated Bob Dylan to the Nobel Prize of Literature.

Professor Ball writes: "Since the early 1960s Mr Dylan in word and music has created an almost unlimited universe of art which has permeated the globe and in fact changed the history of the world. Though he is of course widely known as a musician, it would be an egregious mistake to neglect his extraordinary achievement in literature. In fact, music and poetry are linked, and Mr Dylan's work has helped very significantly to renew that vital connection.

"The art of poetry is perhaps 15,000 years old, it has survived principally through its oral strengths, not through the rather recent convenience of moveable type. In our modern

USA formally launched Bob Dylan's candidacy. Professor Stephen Scobie, The University of Victoria, Canada, Professor Betzy Bowden, The University of New Jersey, USA and Professor D Karlin, The University College, London UK, have all endorsed Bob Dylan's candidacy for the Nobel Prize in Literature.

Professor Bowden wrote her Ph.D. on Dylan in 1978 at Berkley, published at Indiana University Press in 1982. Professor Scobie is a member of the Royal Society of Canada and has studied Dylan's lyrics for 25 years. Professor Karlin writes to the Nobel Academy: "Even at the most trivial level, he has given more memorable phrases to our language than any comparable figure since Kipling."

"You must take care of yourself because you are not only and earth-wide treasure... I hope you have someone who makes you good soup."

No wonder there'd been no room for Bob to go to the Q Awards. Even if he had been intrigued by such a plan there was an even bigger concept looming. Before John Bauldie's death, he'd been part of a committee whose goal was simply to secure The Nobel Prize for Literature for Dylan.

BOB DYLAN - THE NOBEL PRIZE FOR LITERATURE PRESS RELEASE 1
After years of talk, Bob Dylan has now been formally launched as a candidate for the Nobel prize for literature.

Mr Allen Ginsberg, a member of the American Academy of Arts & Letters, writes: "Dylan is a major American Bard and minstrel of the 20th Century, whose words have influenced many generations throughout the world. He deserves a Nobel Prize in recognition of his mighty and universal powers."

The breakthrough came August 30th when Professor Gordon Ball of the Department of English and Fine Arts, Lexington, West Virginia, USA, on behalf of the Campaign

era Bob Dylan has returned poetry to its primordial transmission by human breath and body, in his musical verse he has revived the traditions of bard, minstrel, and troubadour. His work is widely translated and performed around the world, but it exceeds by far the bounds of 'popular' art (The inclusion of his lyrics in numerous academic textbooks of literature is merely one case in point).

"The extraordinarily inventive symbolism of much of his work deserves comparison with such world-celebrated poets as Arthur Rimbaud and William Butler Yeats, yet in catalysing whole generations of youths, his oeuvre has shown more than any other poets in this century of power of words to alter lives and destinies ..."

BOB DYLAN - THE NOBEL PRIZE FOR LITERATURE PRESS RELEASE 2
Three additional professors endorse Bob Dylan as candidate for the Nobel Prize in Literature.
Professor Gordon Ball of Lexington, Virginia,

Unfortunately the bid failed. And, by year end in a sweet line of juxtaposition, the internet rang to festive carols based on Bob's 'Tangled Up In Blue'. The Nobel Greeting Cards franchise beckoned.

ANITA ROWLAND, *via internet*
Tangled Up in Yule (to the tune of Tangled Up in Blue)

One late December evening
when the family was going to bed
visions of Elmo and Barney
Dancing through the kids' heads
On the tree downstairs the lights were strung
Over the door the mistletoe was hung
Minivan down in the driveway
Cat was looking for mice
And my wife was thinking of all those things
In the Laura Ashley catalogue that looked nice
And me, I just was hoping
that tomorrow I'd receive
a powertool
We were tangled up in Yule
Ouch!

1998

The Ballad Of A Thin Man

BOB WAS ill. Bob was better. But the world still shuddered from the repercussions. My own friends were booking flights to his bedside and the internet was wobbling under the weight of the get well messages. The artfully coded bobdylan.com offered snatches of every track, lyrics and a list of 300-plus rare items, whether they be Bob played on, out-takes, TV appearances or whatever. It joined a virtual black hole of sites dedicated to all things Bob, perpetuating for new generations the world of Dylan. However, the cross-referencing, megabyte information centres played second fiddle the Bobfans who simply wanted to fully express their stress over his mortality.

There was way too much going on in Bob's world for him to come to the Q Awards. His schedule had him in the UK at the end of June for Glastonbury and Columbia were very, very doubtful that he'd come over again. With no product to promote it was unlikely that they'd even ask him.

The event itself already had REM, Blondie and Paul Weller locked in and as the Summer rolled around and the Glastonbury Festival loomed there was even the possibility that Springsteen would attend. It looked like 1998 would not be the year of Dylan, it would have to wait until '99 and the tenth anniversary of the event itself.

Bob's build up to Glastonbury took him through Europe and to the North of England in June and reports were pretty positive even if he didn't play much of his much-touted 'Time Out Of Mind'.

CLIVE PRODUCT *The Big Untidy fanzine*
"The Waldbuhne show saw Bob in good form. Dressed in black and wearing the now almost traditional cowboy hat, he did a 90-minute set that stretched back as far as 'Freewheelin'. To enjoy the Bob experience properly you've really got to save up a bit of cash, take a week off work and follow the shows around. Four days earlier he'd played in Leipzeig and the set was almost completely different, the next day he was in Rostock and there were more changes.

"The gig was over by nine and many people, interviewed by Helmut Neimann for Radio Eins, said that they felt short-changed. There had been no support band and the show started early at 7.30. One guy was even moaning because Bob hadn't played 'Knockin' On Heaven's Door'. In truth, this was more or less business as usual. For the experienced Bobcast of Berlin, the night was still young, with plenty of time to meet later and swap notes, opinions, whatever."

KEITH HUGHES *Get Rhythm magazine*
"Bob Dylan at Newcastle Arena 20.6.98 had an under-stated authority and presence that is hard to define and its as charismatic as any 50s plus person can be. Many of the songs are beefed up, 'Cold Irons Bound' for instance lacking the shimmering subtlety of Daniel Lanois' production. But don't get me wrong it was still great. A roaring 'Highway 61' even

competed in the heads-down boogie stakes with Johnny Winters' blistering version. Bob Dylan in 1998? He rocks!"

And so, to Somerset, the bill finally sorted. The negotiations on the fee finally settled. All that could go wrong now would b that torrential rain would turn the place into a virtual lake. Shit!

JOHN HARRIS
in the Glastonbury Festival programme

"If the stars align correctly, Glastonbury 1998 could well be the equal of his 1997 shows. Whatever, his presence marks one of the dreamlike occasions when a genuine icon crash lands in the festival's midst. Store the memory for your grandchildren."

Discovery and the Limo followed behind and we set off down the hill road to the arena.

"It seemed like there were millions of people. I suppose they'd come from all over the globe to see Bob Dylan. As we moved through the crowd people spotted me and they realised it must be Bob Dylan behind. They'd twigged and I could see in my mirror that his manager had thrown a rug over him.

"He must have been terrified because the crowd were rocking our car and rocking the Limo. It took ages and ages and the only way we could get through was to get a Digger to go in front of us, so that people kept away from us and let the Limo through.

Changin'. I longed to know the real Bob. To find out what was behind the media image - of course, I secretly fancied him and I hoped that he might fancy me. I had long dark hair and I modelled myself on the type of women he seemed to go for. I got the chance to go and see him at a show in Glasgow, fantasising that I might catch his eye, but there were huge crowds and he was just a tiny, lonely-looking figure on a distant stage for about an hour or so.

"After that, real life intruded, his and mine. But the lifeline he'd given me as a young teenager gave me the courage to be myself and make my own life in my own way.

"I longed to know the real Bob. To find out what was behind the media image - of course, I secretly fancied him."

MICHAEL EAVIS

"Dylan had got stuck in the Sunday afternoon traffic and I had to phone the police and ask them for their help to find the Limousine and bring him down. The police agreed but they'd only bring him to the Farmhouse, which is at the top of the basin above the stage.

"So, eventually, the bikes arrived with their flashing lights and Bob Dylan was in the back of the Limo with tinted windows and we had about ten minutes to get to the stage through thousands of people. So I got into my

WALDBÜHNE BERLIN
Radio EINS präsentiert:
BOB DYLAN
LIVE ON STAGE !!!
FAHRAUSWEIS
VBB 03.06.98
DM 58,00
306 3. Jun. 98
19.00 Uhr

"As we got to the front of the main stage, we heard the announcement that Bob Dylan would be on in five minutes but we knew he couldn't be on in five as it was going to take at least 15 minutes for us to reach the stage. When we finally got down there, he scurried off with this blanket over his head like he was some sort of criminal.

"After all the hassle with the fee, getting him there and where he was going to be on the bill, when he finally got on stage he announced that it was all like a dream come true for him. He said it was a big thing for him. I'm told he doesn't normally say anything and he actually volunteered that this was like a dream come true."

MARGARET CHIN

"I'd grown up with Bob Dylan, been liberated with 'The Times They Are A-

MAIN STAGE	
7	7.10 – 8.20 BOB DYLAN
8	8.50 – 10.00 NICK CAVE AND THE BAD SEEDS
9	
10	10.30 – 12.00 PULP

"Then, at Glastonbury, I was suddenly reminded of what he once meant to me. I was plodding through the mud to see him, when I was edged off the path into deepish water by a huge black Limo. 'Poncy git!', I thought, in my usual dismissive of the rich manner. But, as I glanced up and through the leaded windows, I caught sight of a small rigid figure, huddled deep into an oversized hooded top, looking somewhat out of place in this opulent Limousine.

"I immediately recognised the profile. Instinctively, I smiled and waved, hoping to get through, to perhaps send some 'good vibes' through to Bob. The figure inside started and his arm made a gesture as the car passed. To be realistic, it could have been a gesture of surprise or alarm at the looming crowds, but I like to think he waved. Sometimes it's best to stick with the fantasy, it's such a precious part of growing up."

"I went along to see him at Glastonbury and I really wanted to take his photograph, but he'd banned photographers and I stood in the crowd and it was pretty muddy by then and pretty unpleasant. It was late on Sunday and everyone was drowned and wet. But I wanted to stay for Bob Dylan. To be honest I was a bit disappointed but as I walked towards my car, which took some time, he played one of the real oldies, I think it was 'The Times They Are A-Changin'' and I stopped in my tracks and I thought, 'Aaah. this is really nice'. That was the last thing I heard at the Festival last year and then I went home and had a bath."

Live 1966 - The "Royal Albert Hall" Concert

Tracks: She Belongs To Me, Fourth Time Around, Visions Of Johanna, It's All Over Now, Baby Blue, Desolation Row, Just Like A Woman, Mr Tambourine Man, Tell Me, Momma, I Don't Believe You, Baby, Let Me Follow You Down, Just Like Tom Thumb's Blues, Leopard-Skin Pill-Box Hat, One Too Many Mornings, Ballad Of A Thin Man, Like A Rolling Stone.

Produced by Jeff Kramer.

SLEEVE NOTES *These two CDs document one of the great confrontational performances of the 20th century. Bob Dylan, intent on following his own inner vision, wasn't the first artist to not give the audience what they wanted... but he may have been the loudest.*

WHAT THE PAPERS SAID *"It's hard to believe that a country then up to its eyeballs in electric R&B (the Stones, Animals, Pretty Things, Who) was so absurdly parochial about an amplified Dylan. The self-righteous goon who yelled 'Judas!' put the show in the history books. The music is the reason that 'Live 1966' is still epic theatre."* David Fricke, Rolling Stone

WHAT THE WORLD SAYS

CHRIS TAYLOR, fan *"It was an awesome experience hearing the bootleg of the 1966 concert for the first time. That was just mind-blowing. I heard it in the 70s and I just couldn,t believe it. That has to be the best live concert ever."*

NOEL GALLAGHER *"The acoustic side is a bit dull, but the electric side is amazing. The 'Judas' bit is just great."*

ANDY KERSHAW, radio broadcaster

"I still can't believe they've finally put it out. I just keep staring at my copy."

IN A NUTSHELL

Who would have thought that an album over 30 years old could cause such a stir. Whether Bob was souped-up on drugs, high as a kite, or careering in paranoia vibed up on the audience aggression, the performance in both sets is simply stunning. Disc one's acoustic fare-closes with 'Mr Tambourine Man' being spat out like the name of some mutual friend who's fallen from favour and the electric set, with The Band on fine form, explodes with unbridled power. Dylan slurs through the intros, perhaps for effect, as his performance in the songs is simply blistering. 'I Don't Believe You', 'Baby Let Me Follow You Down' and 'Leopard-Skin Pill-Box Hat' are momentous, the closing 'Like A Rolling Stone' is staggering. This was an epic night and, if time travel ever did become possible, you can imagine that a few thousand would be turned away from the door in the days of future past.

SINGLES/EPS/ETC *Not Dark Yet (45) Love Sick (45)*

And that was the nineties

AS WE spin ever-closer to the all night party where everyone applauds the other Minnesota muso Prince, Bob Dylan's '90s have been as demanding as anyones. Unfocussed in the studio, having fun as a Travelling Wilbury, reborn into the faith of American roots music, he celebrated 30 years in the business in the company of The O'Jays, Pearl Jam, Neil Diamond and Kris Kristoferson. What a night. He received the Commander Of The Order of Arts And Letters but didn't get the Nobel Prize For Literature.

In Crouch End he was given a pot of jam and he nearly bought a house. In Japan he was assaulted by monks. At Glastonbury he experienced Michael Eavis's nouvelle driving techniques. He has lived through that and illness too.

We've had Bootlegs 1-5. This time around, when he knew he probably shouldn't, he played at Woodstock. And it was all on the internet and thoroughly pawed over in the excellent Telegraph (thanks to the late John Bauldie).

Me, I got married, rediscovered American roots music too. Met The Dillards, rediscovered The Band,

The Byrds, the Burritos, Gene Clark and fell in love with Uncle Tupelo and their Dylanesque rebirth into back porch playing. Moved to the country, not quite Woodstock, brought up two kids and headed down the trad folk route. Listened to Dylan's compatriots - Ferlinghetti, Spoelstra, Fred Neil, David Blue, Ochs, Baez, Judy Collins. And finally, finally, got round to Bob's back pages. Then Bob's bootlegs.

I was touched by the hand of Bob. From the Whitmark Archives recordings from 1962, through to 'One Too Many Mornings' from the Royal Albert Hall in 1965 and everything from the Isle Of Wight. And I met lots of people...

EVERYONE HAS A STORY about Bob Dylan. From Bobby Vee: "We needed a piano player and he told my brother that he'd played with Conway Twitty.", to guitar technician Joel Bernstein, "He had a beautiful Gibson guitar. One day he played a song and put it down against a chair outside on the veranda and the sun was out, so as guitar caretaker I brought it inside, re-tuned it, and put it back on its stand. A couple of hours later, he came back and said, 'Joel, can you do me a favour', I said, 'Sure.' He said, 'The next time I put a guitar down, could you just leave it where it is? It really confuses me when you move things around'."

People have been inspired to pick up the guitar and write, people have lost their beds for the night. Yes. Everyone has a story…

"I went to Boston in the summer of '64," recalls Joe Boyd, record producer and Rykodisc head man, "I ran into a girl that I'd always fancied but never really got to know. I didn't have a place to stay and she said I could stay with her. She was working as a waitress and going on to see a Dylan show, so she told

But, Bob has that effect on people. They want to gush. Poetry or otherwise. In trailing Bob, in getting close to the heart, without looking too deep into his soul, I'd asked everyone in the world I knew… and lots more I didn't know to help me ink in the sketch of Bob that I'd been left from my youth. The answers, recollections and a bit of verse came back pretty damn quick.

HOWE GELB
singer/songwriter, beatific Giant Sand leader
I've never known a world without Bob Dylan. If that is his real name. I saw that great clip of film several years ago. Where he's in the backseat of a London ride with John Lennon, and Lennon is putting up with just so much, all the while Bob is having a problem with whatever he's ingested. The copy of that clip was so bad, like a copy of a copy of a copy times 32, that it gave off a more ether-like blur dream glow to the entire episode.

rang up her husband and asked him 'Did you invite Bob Dylan to come to our house?' "The husband doesn't know what she's talking about and it comes out that Dylan has got the right number but the wrong street."

A SIMPLE MISUNDERSTANDING? There's nothing simple about Bob Dylan. As I worked my way through the callers of false prophets, the also-rans, the would-bes and the enlightened were knock, knock, knockin' at my door with a range of the brightest and best new anecdotes. It became apparent that his hand had touched more than just people's record collections.

There's an evangelical spirit to Bob. There are even University courses on offer covering his whims and whyfores. In fact, there is a professor at St Mary's, a college in South London, who teaches on the writings of Bob. Dr Allan Simmonds lectures on a regular basis. His ansaphone has 'Highway 61 Revisited' blaring in the background.

"I think Dylan's such an amazing character and when you get into what he's saying, you find he's got something to say about everything."

me to meet her at her apartment later. I was quite pleased by this turn of events, strutting around all evening, knowing that treats were in store, so around 12.30 I roll up at her place.

"I got the key from under the door and there's a note saying, 'I'm afraid there's been a change of plan. You'll never guess who's here'. Her bedroom door was closed, so I slept on the couch and in the morning I had breakfast with her and Dylan. She told me later, 'Joe, I was looking forward to it but, you know, I couldn't turn down the opportunity'."

Wow! Like unrequited love. Young people. Etc! Defeated at the hands of Bob. For some people it's just personal. Like in the front page of a copy of Writings And Drawings I found second-hand, somewhere. Someone had written on the mould-developing front page, "His poems are of love, hate and joy. Explosions in the mind. That give such descriptive verse. Some of them got in my case. The case of love that makes my heart bleed."

I suspect the inscription was not written by Bob himself.

MAYBE THAT blur is the real unreality of Bob. (*Careful, we're getting analytical here.*) It's a circus trick, a sleight of hand. too blurry to let you into the secret. Smoke and mirrors, too quick to be caught out. Bob has a surreal front and, even when he's not being super-real, apocryphal tales of his mishaps just add to the legend. Like the legendary much-told 'Dave Stewart Wrong House' gag.

DAVE STEWART
the man with a case of Eurythmics
"(When we were recording in London several years ago) Dylan arrived at my house an hour late, all flustered. I said, 'What happened?' and he said, 'Well, I rang the doorbell of number seven and this woman comes to the door and I said: 'Is Dave here?' And she said: 'No, he's at work, do you want to wait?'.

"So Dylan waits and thinks: 'That's strange, he told me to come round'. And the woman's thinking: 'This is weird, he looks like Bob Dylan'. She makes him a cup of tea. Then, she

DR ALLAN SIMMONDS
"I teach Literature at St Mary's College in Strawberry Hill, Richmond-on-Thames. I have the ideal job because my hobby is my work. I loved books and literature and it just felt so natural to suggest to my superiors that I could teach a course on Bob Dylan's writing. So, I suggested it. At first they thought I'd come from another planet but I prepared the necessary material for the College boards and bodies and they accepted it.

"The course is designed for students who have done two and a half years of English already and they do a 13 week course with assignments. It amounts to about one twenty-fourth of their year's work.

"I thought at first that there'd be about three people who'd apply to be on it, but we have about 50 people each year. It's quite an interesting examination of Dylan, which involves his films, songs and writing and, for students at that level it looks at musical narrative as opposed to the verbal narrative they might have worked on before.

"I think Dylan's such an amazing character and when you begin to get into what he's saying, you find that he's got something to say on just about everything."

THERE IS A LITERARY VIEW TO BOB. Not just from the fact-hungry, but from the brain-handed. They elevate Bob's work to literary honour status and pontificate on the use of words, the phrasing of syllables and, er, stuff. During my hap-hazard record-buying (all in the course of research, honest), I was beginning to see fanzines and magazines about such stuff and I also happened on an intriguing collection of stories entitled Conclusions On The Wall, which was topped and tailed by Suzanne Macrae. Inside this slimline exposition were analytical and diagrammatic explorations on what chord went where, how the structure of the songs was created, how certain words cropped and and were repeated, indeed there were essays on Bob ending songs without ending them. The scalpels of the incisive tackled the phases of Bobness, his struggle with religion and those puzzling references to, well, the end.

SUZANNE MACRAE
Bob Dylan Is The Weatherman, Conclusions On The Wall
"We find an archetypal plot of death and rebirth in Dylan's first 13 albums, produced between 1962 and 1970, up to and including 'New Morning'. In these albums, Dylan's personal and philosophical development operates through five mythical stages, more or less chronologically distinct: (1) the strident social critic of the first three albums. (2) The apocalyptic visionary of the second through sixth albums. (3) The introspective man epitomised on 'Blonde On Blonde'. (4) The anguished soul in its dark night on 'John Wesley Harding'. (5) And, the reborn man of 'Nashville Skyline' and 'New Morning'."

WILFRID MELLERS
from God, Mode And Meaning In Some Recent Songs Of Bob Dylan, Conclusions On The Wall
"Dylan's verse has been deeply influenced by rural folk ballads, by the poetry of the blues, by The Bible, by Bunyan's *Pilgrim's Progress*, by *Hymns Ancient And Modern*, by children's rhymes and by runic verse of all kinds, including Blake's *Songs Of Innocence And Experience*..."

CHRISTOPHER RICKS
'Can This Really Be The End?', Conclusions On The Wall
"What I want to talk about is the endings of songs and, in particular, how Dylan manages to end them. Two of Dylan's most characteristic lines are "How long must I wait, one more time for that simple twist of fate?" and "Can this really be the end?". In 'Stuck Inside Of Mobile', this is not the end of the verse. The word "end" is repeated again and again and is never really the end. So, the word "final" matters a great deal to Dylan.

"When he was talking about his book (*Tarantula*) in the Studs Terkel interview, Dylan said: "It's about someone who has come to the end of the road and actually knows there's another one but doesn't know exactly where it is. In the end paper of *Writings And Drawings*, we find 'Well it's just around the bend / On a road that's got no end'. Dylan is famously great on endings."

Giant Sand, with Howe Gelb (centre): "Bob's ever present"

DOES BOB BEAR UP under such scrutiny. Such micro-analysis? Are there too many strange revelations? Can an end really mean so much? Ironically, this was just the beginning of a whole heap of Bob rationalisation that I'd come across. Was it all just so much pre-fried psychedelia, that's hoodwinking us into not believing that Bob just does a load of songs, stays up late too much and is encouraged into some embarrassing liaisons, both musical and otherwise from time to time?

Obviously, by now I'd become absolutely fascinated with everything Bob-like and the effect that he had on what seemed to be, on the face of it, quite sane people. And, some of these "sane" people seemed to have tuned into what I was doing, the Arabian drums were pounding. Letters arrived. E-mails were logged. Fanzines were perused.

There were of course some madder than mad people too. Some intriguing people who were a few loaves and fishes short of the traditional full picnic. These people had stories to tell but they couldn't really tell them. They couldn't divulge in fear of... well, that was never quite made clear. But added to the cloak and daggery of it all.

By now, virtually everywhere I turned I started running into Bob artefacts. Bob songs were everywhere. I was dreaming about Bob. Not in a sexual or sensual way, I hasten to add. More like waking up in the middle of the night to lie and idly wonder what the outcome of all this would be. And I was becoming a Bob bore too.

"Ahaaa, yes dear, just one more cup of coffee and, hey, one more for the road."

"What?"

"Nothing."

I was in deep. Too deep to even kid myself that I was trying to get him to some Awards, Q or otherwise. Like any good drama, with a twisting and turning plot, I wanted to pick my way through. I wanted to refile those songs in my brain, I wanted to get over dramatic about it all, get swept away. Somewhere downstream.

In one of my dreams, I was arguing, in a futuristic setting, about songs that Dylan had written and ones that he most certainly had not. There were songs about him. Songs about songs about him. Whatever. It was like a post-karaoke apocalypse, where it was disclosed that he'd had a hand in 'Jingle Bells', obviously the 'Star Spangled Banner' (Hendrix version optional) and lots of show tunes by Liza Minelli.

As part of this odd half-dream there was on one occasion a strange interlude, where Bob was

Dylan: **"I'm not God."**
Interviewer: **"But some people think yo**
Dylan: **"But, I thought that Eric Clapto**

124

"Hey, look... I fucked you up."

revealed as the living hellspawn of Robert Johnson, sold back to the music biz by the devil to repay that old, old debt from the crossroads. It must be true (ish), I pondered the next day when it all flooded back to me, because one of my friends, Phil was in it, smoking a cigar and dressed as Satan. Still, I'd had a few drinks that night.

Around that time I also got a video copy of Bob Dylan being interviewed on the set of Hearts Of Fire. My friend Howard had sent the tape to my office with a cryptic note which described his performance as "disturbing" and claimed my wife was featured in the video. I was intrigued. My wife was less excited.

The interview, for BBC's Omnibus, had taken place after several months of following the entourage of the Hearts Of Fire film around the UK and then Canada. The programme was supposed to be about the film, but the crew were desperate to corner Bob and, after a few close calls between takes, they got their man in his trailer where he agreed to chat.

The usual questions filtered by. To his eternal credit, Bob ignored them and, half-standing, half sitting, he then decided to sketch the interviewer. It was a superb expression of guerrilla tactics. Head down, no eye contact with the camera. Scratching with his pen. Drawing over the interviewer's questions. Bob giggled.

"Why don't you ask this kind of stuff of Roger Daltrey? Or Paul McCartney? Or Peter Townshend?" Bob quizzed.

He laughed to himself. He scribbled on. He laughed again. Disturbingly. Hrrmph.

e."

s God!"

"Are your songs constructed like mini-movies?" enquired the man from *Omnibus*.

"What do you mean?" Bob winked up at the camera. Momentarily.

"Like 'All Along The Watchtower', it's full of tight visual imagery, it almost just has suggestions of sound."

"No." Bob concluded.

The Omnibus man held his cool. Just. He decided confusion was a better option and launched into a long, convoluted statement about Schubert being like a pipe, a conduit even. He briefly went transcendental and mused that people wondered where the inspiration came to Schubert. Who was at the other end of the pipe? Throughout this interlude of utter journalistic madness, Bob was flicking a withering eye past the camera. He sketched on. Watching it, you're just begging that he's going to say, 'So, Bob, who's at the end of your pipe!'. He didn't quite. He just about rallied before, eventually, he rounded on, "So, where do your songs come from?"

Dylan: "I can't tell you. I'm not God."

Interviewer: "Some people think you are."

Dylan: "I thought Eric Clapton was God."

Throughout, Bob scratched away with a biro. He looked edgy, unsure, almost like he didn't understand what was going on. An analyst would probably have a field day with his facial expression and the lack of eye contact. His semi-crouched hunch is just so odd. It's like he's about to leave before anyone can pin him down.

The video continues, of course but by then Bob had lost interest. More questions were assembled. Bob became oblivious. Finally, as a way of drawing the interview to a conclusion, he picked up the drawing and showed it to the camera.

"It was going OK, but I fucked you up." he exclaims. End of story.

JOHN LECKIE
seasoned producer

"I think that the BBC had spent quite a bit of time trying to track Dylan down to do an interview and finally they got into his caravan. Bob spent the whole time sketching the interviewer who was having a hard time getting any answers. Every time he asked something about a song, Bob would reply,'Well, what do you think it's about?'

"Bob has cowboy boots up on the chair and there was a clipping from The Sun in the background. He was being totally Americana

against the Englishness of the BBC and yet he also had that 'man from outer space' look and feel to him."

IN ADDITION TO THE VIDEO, I'd also started receiving some tapes. There was a cool C90 with Dylan songs by such luminaries as James Last, The Cliff Davis Sextet, The Holy Light Singers, Chuck Jackson, Percy Faith, The Johnny Mann Singers, The Village Stompers, Jan & Dean, Buffalo Tom, The Kings Singers, Calliope, Linda Ronstadt, Stanley Turrentine, The Ivy League, The Mike Curb Congregation, The Orson Family, Solomon Burke, The Family Dogg, Buck Owens, The Rotary Connection, Merry Clayton, Frank Marino & Mahogany Rush, Ellis Paul, The Dean Christopher Orchestra, and Orange Bicycle. And then there was a cassette from Simon John, who lived in Milford Haven.

It was a strange package and I was worried from the off because Simon, I assumed, had taken special care to burn a hole in the tape's label with a fag. Being a former music journalist I fast realised this was a warning and put off listening to the tape for some time. But, stuck between Reading and Newbury on an uncommitted train one day I placed it in the Walkman.

The sleeve was sketched, pretty much like the biro epic I'd seen Bob ink on Omnibus and there were lyrics to 'She Was The Mistress' inside. For graphic precision, Simon had cut out an instamatic photo of himself and glued it on the tape's box. He was smoking a fag in the picture. Probably the same one that scarred the tape.

On the spine he'd scrawled 'For Dave Henderson at Bob-Line. Collected music of Simon John 89-97. Bob Dylan very much an influence'.

The cassette hissed like I remembered very old demos on Scotch tape used to in the 70s and there was Bob, or a version of Bob, strumming in a true Bob way. Of course it gave new meaning to the term lo-fi. That method of placing the microphone in a glass in a neighbouring room isn't the done thing anymore, whatever, there was Simon John being Bob. Under the influence. Fully intoxicated. I didn't know what to make of it. Still don't. But, Simon John's desperation to be Bob for eight years - goodness knows he's probably still at it - was the kind of dedication that I'd come to expect and the kind of faith that people put into Dylan.

I remember that old Who track 'The Seeker', where Roger Daltrey, in the middle eight, claims he'd "asked Bobby Dylan, asked The Beatles, asked Timothy Leary but he couldn't help me either". Daltrey's search was along the same lines as Simon John's no doubt, unless, of course, Daltrey had lent one of them 20 quid at a party and he was unsure as to who had his wedge.

Bob seems to have that effect on people. They trust him and find him a very close, personal kind of friend. Take David Bowie's 'Song To Bob Dylan' from 'Hunky Dory', or Ralph McTell's 'Zimmerman Blues', or the role Bob plays as hero and saviour in Don McLean's 'American Pie'. The imagery of Bob is everlasting. He's more than just part of the furniture.

And, like some creepy addictive alien music, it seems that once you're struck by his strange talents then you're hooked. For life.

Let's take a normal working person as a test case. Enter folk singer Joan Baez. She met Dylan. She loved and lost. She recorded lots of his songs. Then, she recorded a whole double album's worth of his tunes.

In 1968, to try and wash that man right out of her hair, Baez submitted 'Any Day Now' to vinyl. Not just one album, but two. An endless stream of Bob, which featured 'Love Minus Zero - No Limit', 'North Country Blues', 'You Ain't Goin' Nowhere', 'Drifter's Escape', 'I Pity The Poor Immigrant', 'Tears Of Rage', 'Sad-

"Enter folk singer **Joan Baez**. She met Dylan. She loved and lost. She recorded lots of his songs."

Eyed Lady Of The Lowlands', 'Love Is Just A Four-Letter Word', 'I Dreamed I Saw St. Augustine', 'The Walls Of Red Wing', 'Dear Landlord', 'One Too Many Mornings', 'I Shall Be Released', 'Boots Of Spanish Leather', 'Walkin' Down The Line' and 'Restless Farewell'.

It's actually a pretty good album. Especially the version of 'Tears Of Rage' which Baez delivers a capella, almost like an embittered plea to someone. Somewhere.

Whatever, Joan Baez's plan was with 'Any Day Now', it didn't cure her of the lonesome Bob Blues. She then took up writing about the man during the '70s and 'To Bobby', 'Diamonds And Rust', 'Winds of the Old Days', 'Time Is Passing Us By' and 'Oh Brother!' all followed.

CHARLIE GILLETT
from The Sound Of The City

"Peter, Paul And Mary played an invaluable role on behalf of the writers whose songs they recorded on their best-selling albums. They opened the doors through which Bob Dylan and others walked, out of the coffee houses and into the limelight."

Entering the UK charts on October 10th 1963, Peter, Paul And Mary's version of 'Blowin' In The Wind' had hung around for 16 weeks and peaked at number 13. Some 35 years later, Steve Gibbons, a former member of West Country also-rans Balls and The Idle Race decided that 15 Dylan songs were better than anything he was currently doing and he released 'The Dylan Project', with Simon Nicol and Dave Pegg

of Fairport Convention. According to the accompanying booklet, Steve discovered Bob in the mid-Sixties and has remained a disciple ever since, even naming one of his children 'Dylan'.

THE OLDEST ALBUM OF COVER VERSIONS is probably Hamilton Camp's 'Paths Of Victory' from 1964, which includes seven Dylan songs in typical Greenwich Village folk style. It was very much the beginning of an artist-by-artist homage that became, in some cases quite incestuous.

Now, I don't for a minute suspect that Bobby had a fling with the man with the 12-string - Roger McGuinn - but, similarly, The Byrds seemed intent on recording a quart of Bob. Certainly, they'd been transported to the top of the charts with 'Mr Tambourine Man' and their following albums, all bore the thumb-print of Bob. Who could blame them for continually returning to the magic cauldron of chart hits for a little touch of that magic dust.

In the end The Byrds did so many Bobsongs that Columbia released 'The Byrds Play Dylan' to cash in on the relationship.

"They never did full justice to Dylan's lyrics - often missing the anger and intellectual tricks - but the combination of McGuinn's lugubrious tones, the endless minor chords and jangly guitars really caught the emotional feel of his music." claimed Q's Colin Shearman, when the album was re-issued on Nice Price a couple of years back. Maybe he's right. The Byrds were a different machine altogether.

PAUL J ROBBINS

Interview, Los Angeles Free Press, in 1965

Robbins: "What do you think of the Byrds? Do you think they're doing something different?"
Dylan: "Yeah, they could. They're doing something really new now. It's like a danceable Bach sound. Like 'Bells Of Rhymney'. They're cutting across all kinds of barriers which most people who sing aren't even hip to. They know it all. If they don't close their minds, they'll come up with something pretty fantastic."

The Byrds' Dylan album was, of course, not alone. The Bob books were brimming with tunes and others quickly recognised that the "talented young songwriter" could knock off a tune or two.

Whole albums of Bob songs became everyday. Hearing Dylan on every station by lots of different performers was nothing new. But some of the people putting these albums of Bobcovers together were a little surprising, starting with the man who created The Wombles, Mike Batt and his Orchestra who lovingly crafted a 'Portrait Of Bob Dylan'. Other music-lite practitioners were less cursory and as soon as the thespians got involved, there was bound to be trouble. Sebastian Cabot's 'Sebastian Cabot, Actor Bob Dylan, Poet' is a challenge to say the least.

But, if Cabot and Batt seemed like unlikely Bob-partners, then Scottish diva Barbara Dickson's 'Don't Think Twice, It's All Right' must seem just plain bizarre.

Add to that the twangmaster general Duane Eddy's 'Does Bob Dylan' and The Fontana Concert Orchestra's 'Portrait Of Bob Dylan' and soon the case for extra racking for your Bob collection becomes a must.

Everybody was doing it. There was The Four Seasons' 'Sing Big Hits Of Bacharach, David & Dylan', not all Bob but well-meaning enough, The Golden Gate Strings' 'Bob Dylan Songbook', The Gotham String Quartet's 'Immortal Songs Of Bob Dylan' and The London Sound & Art Orchestra's 'The Music Of Bob Dylan'.

Then, even if Linda Mason's 'How Many Seas Must A White Dove Sail?' didn't have a Bob song as its title, it had a line on him. And what was loungecore staple Hugo Montenegro doing at the 'Dawn Of Dylan'? Who knows?

Even the hip jazz elite, well The Gene Norman Group, tried a different kind of 'Blowin' on 'Dylan Jazz' and former Bob idol Odetta returned the compliment

Poets: Dylan, Harrison & Simone', Steven Keene's 'Keene On Dylan' (great title Steve), The Silkie's 'Sing The Songs Of Bob Dylan', Steve Gibbons' 'The Dylan Project', The Surfaris' 'It Ain't Me Babe', The Turtles' 'It Ain't Me Babe', Sound Alike Music's 'A Tribute To Bob Dylan', Zuk Milton's 'Hits of Bob Dylan' (let's hear it for Zuk), Julie Felix's 'Blowing In The Wind', The Saxons' 'Love Minus Zero', The Milltown Brothers' EP 'It's All Over Now, Baby Blue', Living Voices' 'Positively 4th Street', Blues & Soda's 'Happy Birthday Mr. Dylan' (shucks), Martin Simpson's EP '61 Highway' (subtle play on words that), The Sports' 'Play Dylan & Donovan', Coulson Dean McGuiness Flint's 'Lo And Behold' (sorta like a version of 'The Basement Tapes' before it came out) or Cher's 'All I Really Want To Do' (only a handful of Bob songs, but worth an ear).

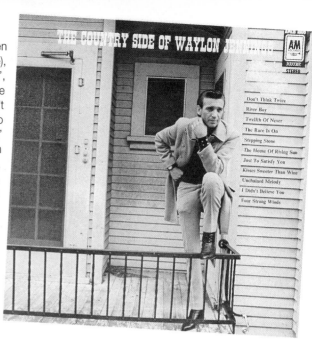

"No wonder I thought that I was seeing Bob's name everywhere and hearing a million Bob-related tunes. They're out there."

with 'Odetta Sings Dylan'. Beyond that, things were getting strange with Danny Roberts' 'Los Exitos de Bob Dylan', The Rockridge Synthesizer Orchestra's 'Plays Classic Bob Dylan Trax', John Schroeder's 'Dylan Vibrations', Strings For Pleasure's 'Plays The Best Of Bob Dylan' and The US Navy Steel Band's 'Blowin' In The Wind' would all be residing in a junk shop nearby, if it weren't for the songs being by Bob. That adds weight and in record-collecting circles the price rockets.

Frankly my dear, that's not the half of it, how could we leave out Country Joe's 'Songs Of Dylan, Donovan And Paxton', Burl Ives' 'Times They Are A-Changing', Waylon Jennings' 'Don't Think Twice', The Metropolitan Pops Orchestra's 'Plays Instrumental Versions of Bob Dylan Favorites' (bet you want to get that one), Strings For Pleasure's 'Plays The Best Of Bob Dylan' (ditto), Judy Collins' 'Sings Dylan ... Just Like A Woman', Keith Gillingham's 'Tribute To Bob Dylan', Richie Havens' 'Sings Beatles & Dylan', Marilyn Michaels' 'Times They Are A-Changin'', Nina Simone's 'Songs Of The

No wonder I thought that I was seeing Bob's name everywhere and hearing a million Bob-related tunes. They're out there. And, not just in cheapo orchestral mode. Each and every Bob album has its wealth of

covers. Like the Bobzombies, they only come out at night.

Pub analogists in my social circle on hearing the news were creating whole Bob albums with versions by other people. The Joan Baez, Byrds and Hollies axis was but a crumb in the fingernail of Bob Dylan's copyright department's everyday fare. With Bob cash-handed for every cover recorded and, indeed, a percentage of the airplay payment for every song that's been covered ever, then its doubles all round.

There used to be a story that Paul McCartney became £600,000 richer every minute that went by simply through radio play of the songs he's written. So, how big is the Bob cheque? Initial research showed that there were, literally thousands of Dylan covers out there. Yes, thousands. I created copious notes and I want to share it with you. To give you some idea, here's a by-album list of just the top five of the best known covers of each track. this is a monster we're dealing with. The players are as diverse as it gets and, amazingly I'd heard one hell of a lot of this frantic checklist.

From the album
Bob Dylan

Song To Woody
Christy Moore
from '*Prosperous*'

From the album
The Freewheelin' Bob Dylan

Blowin' In The Wind
(OK, there's ten versions here of note)
Sam Cooke from 'At The Copa'
Jackie DeShannon from 'In The Wind'
Elvis Presley from 'Platinum, A Life In Music'
Cliff Richard from 'Kinda Latin'
Patrick Sky from 'Patrick Sky'
The Spotnicks
from 'Saturday Night Music'
The Staple Singers from 'Use What You Got'
The Supremes from 'Cream Of The Crop'
Stevie Wonder from 'Up-Tight' ('Everything's Alright')'
Neil Young from 'Weld'

Girl From The North Country
The Clancy Brothers from 'Save The Land'
Joe Cocker from 'Mad Dogs And Englishmen'
Roy Harper (North Country) from 'Valentine'
Boz Scaggs from 'Boz'
Rod Stewart from 'Smiler'

Masters Of War
Mark Arm, single
The Flying Pickets from 'Lost Boys'
Barry McGuire, single
Don McLean from 'Solo'
The Staple Singers from 'Great Day'

A Hard Rain's A-Gonna Fall
Edie Brickell, single
Brian Ferry from 'These Foolish Things'
Melanie from 'Silence Is King'
Nana Mouskouri (Le Ciel Est Noir) from 'A Paris'
The Staple Singers from 'Use What You Got'

Don't Think Twice It's All Right (and ten of these)
Cher from 'All I Really Want To Do'
Bobby Darin from 'Golden Folk Hits'
Nick Drake from 'Tanworth-in-Arden 1967/68'
John Martyn from 'London Conversation'
Melanie from 'As I See It Now'
Peter Paul And Mary from 'In The Wind' and 'Live In Japan'
Elvis Presley
from 'Elvis Presley'
The Shadows from 'Hit Parade'

Patrick Sky from 'Patrick Sky'
Lawrence Welk from 'Wonderful Wonderful'

Bob Dylan's Dream
Peter Paul And Mary from 'Album 1700'
The Silkie from 'You've Got To Hide Your Love Away'

Corrina, Corrina
The Animals, single
Ted Hawkins from 'Corrina, Corrina'
Alexis Korner from 'Bootleg Him'
Mark Spoelstra (Corrina Blues) from 'The Songs Of Mark Spoelstra'

Steppenwolf from 'Early Steppenwolf'

Honey, Just Allow Me One More Chance
Flatt & Scruggs from 'Final Fling'
I Shall Be Free Paul James from 'Acoustic Blues'

From the album
The Times They Are A-Changin'

The Times They Are A-Changin' (ten again)
Beach Boys from 'Beach Boys' Party'
The Byrds from 'Turn! Turn! Turn!'
Spirit from 'Spirit of '76'

Ian Campbell Folk Group, single
Cher from 'With Love'
Billy Joel from 'Kohept'

Simon And Garfunkel from 'Wednesday Morning 3 AM'
Nina Simone from 'To Love Somebody'
James Taylor from 'No Nukes'
Vice Squad from 'No Cause For Concern'

Ballad Of Hollis Brown
Billy Childish, single
Entombed from 'To Ride, Shoot Straight And Speak The Truth!'
Nazareth from 'Loud 'n' Proud'
The Neville Brothers from 'Yellow Moon'
Steven Stills from 'Stills Alone'

With God On Our Side
Manfred Mann EP

The Neville Brothers from 'Yellow Moon'
Wire Train from 'Between Two Worlds'

One Too Many Mornings
The Dillards, single
John Hartford from 'Jud Soundtrack'
Doug Sahm from 'Together After Five'
Patrick Sky, single
Jerry Jeff Walker from 'A Man Must Carry On'

North Country Blues
Frank Tovey from 'Tyranny And The Hired Hand'

Boots Of Spanish Leather
Jeff Beck from 'Beck-Ola'
The Dubliners from '30 Years A-Greying'
Nanci Griffith from 'Other Voices, Other Rooms'
Richie Havens from 'Electric Haven'
Dan McCafferty from 'Dan McCafferty'

When The Ship Comes In
The Clancy Brothers from 'Older But No Wiser'
Arlo Guthrie from 'Hobo's Lullaby'
Chris Hillman from 'Hillmen'
Peter Paul And Mary from 'A Song Will Rise'
The Pogues from 'Pogue Mahone'

The Lonesome Death Of Hattie Carroll
Judy Collins from 'Concert'
Paul Jones from 'Love Me, Love My Friends'
Country Joe McDonald from 'The Early Years'
Phranc from 'Folksinger'

Restless Farewell
Joan Baez from 'Any Day Now'

From the album
Another Side Of Bob Dylan

All I Really Want To Do
The Byrds from 'Mr. Tambourine Man'
Cher from 'All I Really Want To Do'
Joe & Eddie from 'Walkin' Down The Line'

World Party from 'Party Revolution'

Spanish Harlem Incident
The Byrds from 'Mr. Tambourine Man'
Dino Desi And Billy from 'Memories Are Made Of This'
Dion from 'Wonder Where I'm Bound'
The Pozo Seco Singers from 'Shades Of Time'

Chimes Of Freedom
The Byrds from 'Mr. Tambourine Man'
Roger McGuinn, single
Youssou N'Dour from 'The Guide'
West Coast Pop Art Experimental Band
from 'Volume One'
The Textones from 'Midnight Mission'

To Ramona

The Flying Burrito Brothers from 'Flying Burrito Brothers'
Gosdin Brothers, single
Lee Hazelwood from '20th Century Lee'
Sinéad Lohan from 'The Loving Time'

Alan Price from 'Price On His Head'

Motorpsycho Nitemare
Strangelove from the compilation 'Outlaw Blues Volume Two - A Tribute To Bob Dylan'

My Back Pages
The Byrds from 'Younger Than Yesterday'
Dick Gaughan from 'Parallel Lines'
"Sneaky Pete" Kleinow from 'The Legend & Legacy'
The Nice from 'Elegy'
The Ramones from 'Acid Eaters'

I Don't Believe You
Skip Battin, single
Lloyd Cole from 'Jennifer She Said' single
Ian & Sylvia from 'Lovin' Sounds'
Al Stewart from 'Orange'

Ballad In Plain D
Michael Chapman from 'The Man Who Hated Mornings'

It Ain't Me Babe
Bryan Ferry from 'Another Time Another Place'
Joe & Eddie from 'Walkin' Down The Line'
Davy Jones, single
Nancy Sinatra from 'These Boots Are Made For Walking'
Johnny Thunders from 'So Alone'

From the album
Bringing It All Back Home

Subterranean Homesick Blues
Doug Kershaw from 'Louisiana Man'
Harry Nilsson from 'Pussycats'
The Red Hot Chili Peppers from 'The Uplift Mofo Party Plan'
Mitch Ryder from 'Live Talkies'
Dave Stewart & Barbara Gaskin from 'Doin' Dylan'

She Belongs To Me
Bell & Arc from 'Bell & Arc'
The Flying Burrito Brothers from 'Cabin Fever'
Rose Garden from 'The Rose Garden'

Tina Turner (He Belongs To Me)

from 'Tina Turns The Country On'
Tom Tom Club from 'Boom Boom Chi Boom Boom'

Maggie's Farm
The Blues Band from 'Ready' and 'Bye Bye Blues'
Richie Havens from 'Something Else Again'
The Specials, singleThe Walkabouts from 'Death Valley Days'

Love Minus Zero/No Limit
Steve Harley from 'Poetic Justice'
The Leaves from 'The Leaves'
Rick Nelson from 'Rudy The 5th'
Bridget St. John from 'Thank You For ...'
Walker Brothers from 'Introducing The Walker Brothers'

Outlaw Blues
Dave Edmunds from 'Rockpile'
Dream Syndicate from 'Only 39,999,999 Behind "Thriller"'
Grace Slick from 'Conspicuous By Absence'
Richie Havens from 'Electric Havens'
Voices Of East Harlem, single

On The Road Again
Missing Links from 'Missing Links'

Mr Tambourine Man (nine is all I could trim it to)
The Byrds from 'In The Beginning' and 'Mr Tambourine Man'
The Chipmunks from 'Chipmunks Au Go-Go'
Gene Clark from 'Firebyrd'
ConFunkShun single
Crowded House, single
Dino Desi And Billy from 'I'm A Fool'
Melanie from 'Four Sides Of Melanie'
William Shatner from 'The Transformed Man'
Tight Fit, single

Gates Of Eden

Julie Felix from 'Flowers'
Arlo Guthrie from 'The Last Of The Brooklyn Cowboys'

It's Alright, Ma (I'm Only Bleeding)
The Byrds from 'Easy Rider'
Roger McGuinn from 'Easy Rider'
Billy Preston from 'Everybody Likes Some Kind Of Music'
Fairport Convention from 'Fairport Convention'
Tom Petty from 'Let Me Up (I've Had Enough)'

It's All Over Now, Baby Blue (that'll be ten again)
13th Floor Elevators from 'Easter Everywhere'
The Animals from 'Before We Were So Rudely Interrupted'
The Byrds from 'Ballad Of Easy Rider'
The Chocolate Watchband from 'The Inner Mystique'
Marianne Faithfull from 'Rich Kid Blues'
Grateful Dead from 'Vintage Dead'
Hole, single
Manfred Mann from 'Glorified, Magnified'
Them from 'Them' and 'Belfast Gypsies'
Link Wray from 'Bullshot'

From the album
Highway 61 Revisited

Like A Rolling Stone
(there were hundreds)
Cher from 'Sonny Side Of Cher'
The Creation from 'We Are Painter Men'
Dino Desi And Billy from 'I'm A Fool'
Steve Gibbons from 'On The Loose'
Bob Marley And The Wailers from 'The Wailing Wailers At Studio One'
Terry Melcher from 'Terry Melcher'
Paper Lace from 'First Edition'
The Rolling Stones from 'Stripped'
Mick Ronson from 'Heaven And Hull'
Spirit from 'Spirit of '76' and 'Live At La Paloma'

Tombstone Blues
Anastasia Screamed from the compilation 'Outlaw Blues - A Tribute To Bob Dylan'

It Takes A Lot To Laugh, It Takes A Train To Cry
Marianne Faithfull from 'Rich Kid Blues'
Al Kooper from 'Supersession'
Frankie Miller from 'BBC Radio One Live In Concert'
Leon Russell from 'The Shelter People'

The concept of Dylan covers collections started in 1974 with a cut-price European album called 'Hommage To Dylan' on Music For Pleasure. Prior to that several 'Top Of The Pops'-styled collections by unknown artists were released. 'Tribute To Bob Dylan' appeared on the Deacon label - a subsidiary of Beacon - in 1971 and the very same title was used for the 1974 release on the Sound Alike label. However, the albums with 'famous' or in some cases 'infamous' covers of Bob's back catalogue really took off in the '80s with Polystar's 1980 album 'It Ain't Me Babe: Great Artists Sing The Songs Of Bob Dylan', eventually followed by 'The Songs Of Bob Dylan' in 1989. In the '90s, lots of people tuned in and a glut of Bobversions were collated. Scottish label Imaginary released 'Outlaw Blues' in 1992 and asked a host of would-be Bobs to cover tracks. Taken from the indie sector, the selection was nothing short of eclectic. Sonic Youth's Thurston Moore teamed up with Epic Soundtracks for 'Sitting On A Barbed Wire Fence', while fellow Sonic Lee Ranaldo reworked 'Mama You've Been On My Mind'. The Boo Radleys tackled 'One Of Us Must Know (Sooner Or Later)' and Thin White Rope ploughing into the title track. A second volume followed in 1993 and both are pretty rare these days. There are, however, several of these collections currently available and, if you're not too squeamish then they're certainly worth a listen.

THE SONGS OF BOB DYLAN

Start (first released in 1989)

A Hard Rain's A-Gonna Fall (Bryan Ferry), Don't Think Twice It's Alright (Bobby Bare) Tomorrow's A Long Time (Elvis Presley) It Ain't Me Babe (Johnny Cash) Mr Tambourine Man (Byrds) It's All Over Now, Baby Blue (Them) It Takes A Lot To

From A Buick 6
Gary U.S. Bonds from 'Dedication'
Died Pretty from 'Towers Of Strength/From A Buick 6'
Johnny Winter from 'Still Alive And Well'

Ballad Of A Thin Man
The Golden Earring from 'Lovesweat'
The Grass Roots from 'Where Were You When I Needed You'
Uncle Green from 'The Times They Are A-Changin''

Queen Jane Approximately
Daily Flash, single
Lilac Angels from 'I'm Not Afraid To say Yes'

Highway 61 Revisited
Dr. Feelgood from 'Classic'
Bugs Henderson and The Shuffle Kings from 'Four Tens Strike Again'
The Leaves from 'The Leaves'
Terry Reid from 'Move Over For Terry Reid'
Johnny Winter from 'Second Winter'

Just Like Tom Thumb's Blues
Gordon Lightfoot, single
Barry McGuire from 'This Precious Time'
Medicine Head from 'New Bottles Old Medicine'
Doug Sahm from 'Sir Douglas Quintet Live'
Nina Simone from 'To Love Somebody'

Desolation Row
The Rockridge Synthesizer Orchestra from 'Plays Classic Bob Dylan Trax'
Singin' Mike Singer from 'Singin' Mike Singer Sings Good Ol' Folk Songs'

From the album
Blonde On Blonde

Rainy Day Women Nos. 12 & 35
Baroque Inevitable from 'Baroque Inevitable'
The Black Crowes from 'Hempilation'
The Selecter from 'Pucker!'

Pledging My Time
Blues & Soda from 'Happy Birthday Mr. Dylan'

Visions Of Johanna
Marianne Faithfull from 'Rich Kid Blues'
Grateful Dead from 'Fallout From The Phil Zone'
Eric Clapton from 'Backless'

One Of Us Must Know (Sooner Or Later)
The Boo Radleys from the compilation 'Outlaw Blues - A Tribute To Bob Dylan'

I Want You
The Beau Brummels, single
Cher from 'Cher'
Sophie B. Hawkins from 'Tongues And Tails'

Ralph McTell from 'Water Of Dreams'
George Harrison from 'All Things Must Pass'

Stuck Inside Of Mobile With The Memphis Blues Again
The Candymen from 'The Candymen Bring You Candypower'
Steve Colt from 'Paradox'

Leopard-Skin Pillbox Hat
Woody Herman from 'Woody Herman Presents A Great American Evening - Volume 3'
Jimmy LaFave from 'Austin Skyline'

Just Like A Woman (and hundreds again)
The Byrds from 'The Byrds Box'
Joe Cocker from 'With A Little Help From My Friends'
Roberta Flack from 'Chapter Two'
John Lee Hooker from 'Coast To Coast'
Jon Bon Jovi from 'The Great Music Experience'
Manfred Mann, single
Rick Nelson from 'Rudy The 5th'
Doug Sahm from 'The Return Of The Formerly Brothers'
Rod Stewart from 'Tonight I'm Yours'
John Waite from 'When You Were Mine'

Most Likely You'll Go Your Way And I'll Go Mine
Rita Coolidge from 'Nice Feelin''
Davy Jones, single
Patti LaBelle from 'Patti LaBelle'
Todd Rundgren from 'Faith'
The Yardbirds from 'Where The Action Is!'

Absolutely Sweet Marie
Flamin' Groovies from 'Jumpin' In The Night'
George Harrison from 'The 30th Anniversary Concert Celebration'
Jason And The Scorchers from the EP 'Shop It Around'

4th Time Around
Terry Melcher from 'Terry Melcher'

Obviously 5 Believers
Big Foot Chester from 'The Devil In Me'
Toni Price from 'Hey!'

Sad Eyed Lady Of The Lowlands
Bad News Reunion from 'The Easiest Way'
Richie Havens from 'Mixed Bag II'

From the album
John Wesley Harding

John Wesley Harding
Phil Cuneen from 'Australia'

Mckendree Spring from 'Mckendree Spring'

As I Went Out One Morning
Dr. Robert from ''...Other Folk'
The Rainbow Press from 'The Sunday Funnies'

I Dreamed I Saw St Augustine
Julie Felix from 'Lightning'
The Incredible Broadside Brass Bed Band from 'The Great Grizzly Bear Hunt'

All Along The Watchtower (there aer certainly more than a few of these, but here's a selection...)
Elmer Gantry's Velvet Opera from 'Artefacts From The Psychedelic Dungeon'
Giant Sand from 'Ballad Of A Thin Line Man'

Jimi Hendrix from 'Isle Of Wight' and 'Electric Ladyland'
Dave Matthews Band from 'Recently'
Spirit from 'Future Games'
TSOL from 'Scream'
U2 from 'Rattle & Hum'
Bobby Womack from 'Facts Of Life'
XTC from 'White Music'
Neil Young from 'The 30th Anniversary Concert Celebration'

Drifter's Escape
Joan Baez from 'Any Day Now'

Dear Landlord
Joe Cocker from 'Joe Cocker!' and 'Live In LA'
Fairport Convention from 'The Guv'nor'
Janis Joplin from 'Janis'
Dr. Robert from '...Other Folk'
Gavin Friday from 'Each Man Kills The Thing He Loves'

I Am A Lonesome Hobo
Julie Driscoll from 'Jools & Brian'
Triffids from 'Treeless Plain' and 'Stockholm'

I Pity The Poor Immigrant
Judy Collins from Who Knows Where The Time Goes'
Richie Havens from 'Richard P. Havens'
Planxty from 'Words & Music'

The Wicked Messenger

Faces from 'First Step'
Mitch Ryder from 'Live Talkies'
Patti Smith from 'Gone Again'

Down Along The Cove
Georgie Fame, single
Johnny Jenkins from 'Ton Ton Macoute'
West from 'Bridges'

I'll Be Your Baby Tonight
(quite popular with the lazy lovers)
George Baker Selection from 'Little Green Bag'
Rita Coolidge from 'This Lady's Not For Sale'
Bobby Darin, single
Ramblin'' Jack Elliot from 'Bull Durham Sacks'
Marianne Faithfull from 'Faithless' and 'Rich Kid Blues'
Georgie Fame, single
Emmylou Harris from 'Gliding Bird'
Goldie Hawn from 'Goldie'
The Statler Brothers from 'Sing Country Symphonies in E major'
Maureen Tucker from 'Playing Possum'

From the album
Nashville Skyline

Girl From The North Country
(rather popular to say the least)
The Clancy Brothers from 'Save The Land'
Joe Cocker from 'Mad Dogs And Englishmen'
Ramblin'' Jack Elliot from 'Bull Durham Sacks'
Roy Harper (North Country) from 'Valentine'
Ronnie Hawkins from 'Ronnie Hawkins'
Carolyn Hester from '30th Anniversary Concert Madison Square Gardens'
Alan Price from 'Geordie Roots And Branches'
Keith Richards from 'Voodoo Brew'
Boz Scaggs from 'Boz'

Rod Stewart from 'Smiler'

Nashville Skyline Rag
Dixie Flyers from 'Just Pickin''
Earl Scruggs Revue from 'Earl Scruggs, His Family, His Friends'

To Be Alone With You
Steve Gibbons from 'On The Loose'
Catherine Howe from 'Harry'

I Threw It All Away
Aztec Camera, single
Cher from '3614 Jackson Highway'
Scott Walker from 'To Have And To Hold'

Peggy Day
Jim McLaren from 'The New Look Back Basement Tape'

Lay Lady Lay (more romance)
Kevin Ayers from 'Diamond Jack And The Queen Of Pain'
Cher (Lay Baby Lay) from '3614 Jackson Highway'
The Creation from 'We Are Painter Men'
Ramblin' Jack Elliot from 'Bull Durham Sacks'
Mike Harrison from 'Somewhere Over The Rainbow'
The Isley Brothers from 'The Isley's Live'
Ben E. King from 'Rough Edges'
Melanie from 'Garden In The City'
Mike Melvoin from 'The Plastic Cow Goes Mooooooooooooog'
Ministry from 'Filthpig'

Tell Me That It Isn't True
The Fatal Flowers from '2 Meter Sessies - Volume 1'
Robert Forster from 'I Had A New York Girlfriend'

Country Pie
Chet Atkins from 'First Nashville Guitar Quartet'
Lynn Blessing from 'Sunset Painter'
The Nice from 'Five Bridges Suite'

Tonight I'll Be Staying Here With You
Jeff Beck from 'Jeff Beck Group'
Cher from '3614 Jackson Highway' and 'The Beat Goes On'
Tina Turner from 'Tina Turns The Country On'
You Am I, single

From the album
Self Portrait

All The Tired Horses
The Sports from 'Play Dylan & Donovan'

In Search Of Little Sadie
Blue Velvet Band from 'Sweet Moments'

The Mighty Quinn (Quinn The Eskimo)
(You know the story)
1910 Fruitgum Company from 'Red Light'
Ducks Deluxe from 'The Last Night Of A Pub Rock Band'
Ian & Sylvia from 'Nashville'

Ramsey Lewis from 'Maiden Voyage'
Little Angels from 'Sail Away'
Julie London from 'Yummy Yummy'
Lulu from 'It's Lulu'
Manfred Mann, single
Gary Puckett from 'Young Girl'
Leon Russell from 'Leon Live'

Wigwam
Sounds Orchestral from 'Wigwam'
Klaus Wunderlich from 'Hammond Pop 6'

From the album
New Morning

If Not For You
George Harrison from 'All Things Must Pass'
Richie Havens from 'The End Of The Beginning'
George Jones, single
Olivia Newton-John, single
Sarah Vaughan from 'A Time In My Life'

Time Passes Slowly
Judy Collins from 'Whales And Nightingales'
Rachel Faro from 'Refugees'

Winterlude
Manhattan Transfer, single
Jack Parish single

New Morning
Michael Henry Martin from 'Real & Funky'
Nicky Thomas from 'Images Of You'

Sign On The Window
Melanie from 'Good Book'
Jennifer Warnes from 'Shot Thru The Heart'

Father Of Night
Julie Felix from 'Lightning'
Manfred Mann from 'Solar Fire'

From the album
More Bob Dylan Greatest Hits

Watching The River Flow
Joe Cocker from 'Luxury You Can Afford'
Chris Farlowe from 'Lonesome Road'
Steve Gibbons from 'Caught In The Act'
Seatrain from 'Watch'

Tomorrow Is A Long Time
(includes Elvis warning)
Harry Belafonte from 'Sings Bob Dylan' EP
Judy Collins from 'Judy Collin's 5th Album'
Sandy Denny from 'The Attic Years, Volume 3' and 'Sandy'
Chris Hillman from 'Morning Sky'
Magna Carta from 'Pulling It Back Together'
The Pozo Seco Singers from 'Time'
Elvis Presley from 'Spinout'
Rod Stewart from 'Every Picture Tells A Story'
Glen Yarborough from 'For Emily Wherever I May Her'

When I Paint My Masterpiece
Emmylou Harris from 'Portraits'
Mike Whelans from 'When I Paint My Masterpiece'

I Shall Be Released
(it's an anthem)
The Band from 'Music From Big Pink' and 'Live At Watkins Glen'
Joe Cocker from 'With A Little Help From My Friends'
The Flying Burrito Brothers from 'Farther Along'
Jerry Garcia from 'Jerry Garcia Band'
The Long Ryders from 'Metallic B.O'
Bette Midler from 'Divine Madness'

Laugh It Takes A Train To Cry (Stills/ Kooper/ Bloomfield) From A Buick 6 (Gary US Bonds) Absolutely Sweet Marie (Jason & Scorchers) This Wheel's On Fire (Siouxsie & The Banshees) All Along The Watchtower (Jimi Hendrix) Lay Lady Lay (Hoyt Axton) Tonight I'll Be Staying Here With You (Tina Turner) When I Paint My Masterpiece (The Band) Watching The River Flow (Joe Cocker) Knockin' On Heaven's Door (Eric Clapton) Simple Twist Of Fate (Joan Baez) Rita Mae (Jerry Lee Lewis) Abandoned Love (Everly Brothers) Need A Woman (Ry Cooder).

IN A NUTSHELL A mixed bag of 32 versions of Bob Dylan songs featuring the great and the not so great. Country fans are well represented with Johnny Cash, Hoyt Axton, The New Riders Of The Purple Sage and Bobby Bare producing various levels of kitsch. Sam Cooke is represented by a cabaret reading of Blowin' In The Wind. The good and bad you probably already know.

MAY YOUR SONG ALWAYS BE SUNG

BMG (first released in 1991)

All Along The Watchtower (Michael Hedges), Masters Of War (Jose Feliciano), Blowin' In The Wind (Bobby Bare), Chimes Of Freedom (Phil Carmen), Never Can Say Goodbye (Steven Keene), Series Of Dreams (Zimmermen), Memphis Blues Again (Thomas Helmig), When The Night Comes Falling Down From The Sky (The Jeff Healey Band), Seven Days (Jimmy Barnes), Trust Yourself (Carlene Carter), Highway 61 Revisited (Rita Chiarelli), Subterranean Homesick Blues (Nilsson), Ballad Of A Thin Man (The Sports), All I Really Want To Do (The Hooters), Sign On The Window (Jennifer Warnes), I Shall Be Released (The Box Tops), Blind Willie McTell (Dream Syndicate), The Mighty Quinn (Gotthard), Knockin' On Heaven's Door (The Leningrad Cowboys)

IN A NUTSHELL Less than famous covers including Flamenco stylist Jose Feliciano on 'Masters Of War', country veteran Bobby Bare doing 'Blowin' In The Wind', German metalheads Gotthard destroying 'Mighty Quinn', the late great Nilsson attempting 'Subterranean Homesick Blues' and Jennifer Warnes with 'Sign On The Window'.

I SHALL BE UNRELEASED

Rhino (first released in 1991)

Only A Hobo (Rod Stewart), Love Is Just A Four Letter Word (Joan Baez), If You Gotta Go, Go Now (Manfred Mann), Walk Out In The Rain (Eric Clapton), Seven Days (Ron Wood), Wanted Man (Johnny Cash And Carl Perkins), Farewell Angelina (The New Riders Of The Purple Sage), Walkin'

Pearls Before Swine from 'These Things Too'
Elvis Presley from 'Walk A Mile In My Shoes'
Tom Robinson, single
Sting, single
Big Mama Thornton from 'Stronger Than Dirt'
The Tremeloes from 'Greatest Hits'
Delroy Wilson from 'Money'
The Youngbloods from 'Night On A Ridge Top'

You Ain't Goin' Nowhere
The Byrds from 'Sweetheart Of The Rodeo'
Marsha Hunt from 'Desdemona'
Nitty Gritty Dirt Band from 'Live Two Fire' and 'Will The Circle Be Unbroken II'
The Pozo Seco Singers from 'Shades Of Time'
Unit Four Plus Two, single

From the album
Pat Garrett And Billy The Kid

Billy 1
Naked Prey from 'Naked Prey'
Triffids from 'Stockholm'

Knockin' On Heaven's Door
(quite popular - ed)
The Alarm from 'Spirit of '76'
Eric Clapton, single
Kevin Coyne from 'Live In Black And White'
Randy Crawford from 'Randy Crawford The Collection'
Danny & Dusty from 'The Lost Weekend'

Sandy Denny from 'Who Knows Where The Time Goes'
Julie Driscoll from 'The Collection'
Dunblane from 'Throw These Guns Away + Knockin' On Heaven's Door'
Fairport Convention from 'Who Knows Where The Time Goes?'
Jerry Garcia from 'Run For The Roses'
Guns N' Roses from 'Use Your Illusion II'
Beau Jocque and the Zydeco Hi-Rollers

from 'Gonna Take You Downtown'
Roger McGuinn from 'Roger McGuinn & Band'
The Sisters Of Mercy from 'Doctor Jeep' EP
Television from 'The Blow Up'

From the album
Planet Waves

On A Night Like This
Buckwheat Zydeco from 'On A Night Like This'

Going, Going, Gone
Broadways, single
Richard Hell from 'With the Voidoids'

Tough Mama
Jerry Garcia from 'How Sweet It Is...'

Forever Young
(please make sure to check the age of coverees)
The Band from 'High On The Hog'
Harry Belafonte from 'Loving You Is Where I Belong'
Bonnie Bramlett from 'Lady's Choice'
Johnny Cash from 'Red Hot Country'
Fairport Convention from 'A.T.2, The Reunion Concert'
George Hamilton IV from 'Forever Young'
Peter Paul And Mary from 'Reunion'
The Pretenders from 'Last Of The Independents'
Diana Ross from 'Swept Away'
Kitty Wells from 'Forever Young'

Never Say Goodbye
Steven Keene from 'No Alternative'

Wedding Song
Dave Browning from 'Forever Young'

From the album
Blood On The Tracks

Tangled Up In Blue
Hoodoo Rhythm Devils from 'Safe In Their Homes'
Indigo Girls from '1200 Surfews'

Simple Twist Of Fate
Concrete Blonde from 'Doin' Dylan'
Jerry Garcia from 'Jerry Garcia Band'

You're Gonna Make Me Lonesome When You Go
Dave Kelly from 'Making Whoopee - 1979/1982'
Ben Watt from 'North Marine Drive'

Meet Me In The Morning
Freddie King from 'Larger Than Life' and 'Rockin' The Blues Live'
Merl Saunders from 'You Can Leave Your Hat On'

Lily, Rosemary And The Jack Of Hearts
Fairport Convention from 'Fairport

Convention'
Shelter From The Storm
Jimmy LaFave from 'Austin Skyline'
Manfred Mann from 'Soft Vengeance'

You're A Big Girl Now
Jimmy LaFave from 'Austin Skyline'
Lisa Miller from 'Quiet Girl With A Credit Card'

From the album
The Basement Tapes

Odds And Ends
Coulson Dean McGuiness Flint from 'Lo And Behold'

Million Dollar Bash
Fairport Convention from 'Unhalfbricking'
Jonathan King from 'Greatest Hits'
Stone Country, single

Lo And Behold,
Delroy Wilson from 'Money'

Tears Of Rage
The Band from 'Music From Big Pink'
Gene Clark from 'White Light'
Country Fever, single

Jerry Garcia from 'How Sweet It Is...'
Ian & Sylvia from 'Full Circle'

Too Much Of Nothing,
Fotheringay from 'Fotheringay'

Albert Lee from 'Black Crow & Country Fever'
Spooky Tooth from 'It's All About'
Crash On The Levee
Blood Sweat & Tears from 'New Blood'
Sandy Denny from 'North Star Grassmen & The Ravens'
Fairport Convention from 'Live Convention'
Steve Young from 'Seven Bridges Road'

Tiny Montgomery
Coulson Dean McGuiness Flint, single

Nothing Was Delivered
The Byrds from 'Sweetheart Of The Rodeo'
Buddy Emmons from 'Steel Guitar'

Open The Door Homer
Fairport Convention from 'Red And Gold'
Thunderclap Newman from 'Hollywood Dream'

This Wheel's On Fire
The Band from 'Music From Big Pink' and 'Rock Of Ages'
The Byrds from 'Dr Byrds & Mr Hyde'
Julie Driscoll Brian Auger And The Trinity, single
Ian & Sylvia from 'Nashville'
Siouxsie And The Banshees, single

From the album
Desire

Hurricane
The Milltown Brothers from 'It's All Over Now, Baby Blue' EP

One More Cup Of Coffee
Ronnie Hawkins from 'Ronnie Hawkins'
New Deal String Band from 'Blue Grass'
Tony Rice from 'Church Street Blues'

Oh, Sister
Steven Keene from 'Keene On Dylan'

Joey
Johnny Thunders from 'So Alone'

Isis
Popa Chubby from 'Hit The High Hard One'
The Poster Children from the compilation 'Outlaw Blues - A Tribute To Bob Dylan'

From the album
Street Legal

Baby, Stop Crying
Jennifer Kemp, single

Is Your Love in Vain?
Liverpool Express from 'LEX'

Senor(Tales of Yankee Power)
Jerry Garcia from 'Jerry Garcia Band'

We'd Better Talk This Over
Julie Felix from 'Colors In The Rain'

From the album
Slow Train Coming

Gotta Serve Somebody
Casino Steel from 'Casino Steel'
David Allen Coe from 'Castles In The Sand'
Pops Staples from 'Father, Father'

I Believe In You
The Five Blind Boys of Alabama from 'Deep River'
Sinead O'Connor from 'A Very Special Christmas 2'
Shades Of Blue from 'Shades Of Blue'
Phoebe Snow from 'Rock Away'

Man Gave Names To All The Animals
Julie Felix from 'Colors In The Rain'
Townes Van Zandt from 'Roadsongs'

From the album
Shot Of Love

The Groom's Still Waiting At The Altar
Bob Michalzik from 'Look Back Basement Tape'

Dead Man, Dead Man
Steven Keene from 'Keene on Dylan'

From the album
Infidels

Sweetheart Like You
Jimmy LaFave from 'Buffalo Returns to the Plains'
Tony Rice from 'Me and My Guitar'
Rod Stewart from 'A Spanner In The Works'
World Party, single

License to Kill
Richie Havens from 'Sings Beatles & Dylan'
The Replacements from 'Don't Buy Or Sell, It's Crap'

Don't Fall Apart On Me Tonight
Aaron Neville from 'The Grand Tour'

From the album
Empire Burlesque

Tight Connection to My Heart
John Martyn from 'Piece By Piece'

Emotionally Yours
The O'Jays from 'Emotionally Yours'

When the Night Comes Falling from the Sky
Jeff Healey from ''Road House' soundtrack

Dark Eyes.
Judy Collins from 'Sings Dylan ... Just Like A Woman'

Steve Gibbons from 'The Dylan Project'

From the album
Biograph

I'll Keep It With Mine
Fairport Convention from 'What We Did On Our Holidays'
Marianne Faithfull from 'Strange Weather'
Nico from 'Chelsea Girl' and 'Live In Denmark'
Rainy Day from 'Rainy Day'
Richard and Linda Thompson from 'Doom & Gloom From The Tomb'

Percy's Song
Fairport Convention from 'Unhalfbricking'
Arlo Guthrie from 'Washington County'
John Wesley Harding from 'It Happened One Night'

Lay Down Your Weary Tune
13th Floor Elevators from 'The Interpreter'
Albion Band '89 from 'The Guv'nor'
The Byrds from 'Turn! Turn! Turn!'
Fairport Convention from 'A Chronicle Of Sorts 1967-1969'
Steeleye Span from 'The Guv'nor'

You Angel You
Alpha Band from 'Spark In The Dark'
Extremes from 'Driftin''
Manfred Mann from 'Angel Station'
New Riders Of The Purple Sage from 'Brujo'

Abandoned Love
The Everly Brothers from 'Born Yesterday'
Sean Keane from 'Heart No Roses'

Can You Please Crawl Out Your Window?
Wilko Johnson from 'Ice On The Motorway'
Transvision Vamp from 'Transvision Vamp'

Positively Fourth Street
The Byrds from 'Untitled'
John "Speedy" Keen from 'Previous Convictions'
Johnny Rivers from 'Realization'
Lucinda Williams from 'The Bottom Line'

Carribean Wind
Black Sorrows, single
The Revelators from 'Amazing Stories'

Up To Me
Roger McGuinn from 'Cardiff Rose'

I Wanna Be Your Lover
The Blue Aeroplanes from 'Friendloverplane'

Wilko Johnson from 'Call It What You Want'

From the album
Knocked Out Loaded

Silvio
Shane Howard from 'Time Will Tell'

From the album
Oh Mercy

Everything Is Broken
Kenny Wayne Shepherd Band from 'Trouble Is ...'

Ring Them Bells
Gordon Lightfoot from 'Waiting For You'
Heart from 'Desire Walks On'

Man In The Long Black Coat
Diesel Park West from 'God Only Knows' EP
Emerson, Lake & Palmer from 'In The Hot Seat'
Joan Osborne from 'Relish'

Most Of The Time
Lloyd Cole, single

What Was It You Wanted
Chris Smither from 'Up on the lowdown'

From the album
The Bootleg Series:
Vols 1-3

Hard Times In New York
Bob Michalzik from 'The New Look Back Basement Tape'
Tom Ordon from 'Look Back Basement Tape'

He Was A Friend Of Mine
The Byrds from 'Turn! Turn! Turn!'
Ramblin'' Jack Elliot from 'Friends Of Mine'
Dave Van Ronk from 'Folksinger' and 'From ... another time & place'
Eric Von Schmidt from 'The Folk Blues of Eric von Schmidt'

Let Me Die In My Footsteps
Roland from 'Hommage a Bob Dylan

Ramblin', Gamblin' Willie
The Clancy Brothers from 'Older But No Wiser'
Townes Van Zandt (Little Willie The Gambler) from 'Roadsongs'

Quit Your Low Down Ways
Manfred Mann from 'Nightingales & Bombers'
Peter Paul And Mary from 'In The Wind'

Walkin' Down The Line
Skip Battin from 'The Ballad'

Down The Line (Ricky Nelson), Wallflower (Dough Sahm), (If I Had To Do It All Over Again, I'd Do It) All Over You (The Raiders), Dusty Old Fairgrounds (Blue Ash), Ain't No Man Righteous, No Not One (Jah Malla), Quit Your Lowdown Ways (The Hollies), Golden Loom (Roger McGuinn), John Brown (The Staple Singers), Farewell (Dion And The Wanderers), Paths Of Victory (Pete Seeger), Blind Willie McTell (The Dream Syndicate)

IN A NUTSHELL Many of Dylan's own versions of these songs were released on 'The Bootleg Series Volumes 1-3'. Dylan sings them great, but everyone here brought something special to their interpretation. It takes a special kind of songwriter to accommodate the pop whimsy of Manfred Mann one minute and the gospel sound of The Staple Singers the next. Eddie Gorodetsky, from the sleevenotes of the album.

THE BOB DYLAN SONGBOOK

(first released in 1991)

All I Really Want To Do (Cher) Girl From The North Country (Rod Stewart) Si Tu Dois Partir (If You Gotta Go Go Now) (Fairport Convention) You Ain't Going Nowhere (Byrds) Wanted Man (Johnny Cash) Absolutely Sweet Marie (Flamin' Groovies) Outlaw

Blues (Dave Edmunds) To Ramona (Alan Price) I Pity The Poor Immigrant (Judy Collins) Tears Of Rage (The Band) Love Minus Zero/No Limit (Walker Brothers) Blowin' In The Wind (Bobby Darin) Tomorrow Is A Long Time (Rod Stewart) Too Much Of Nothing (Fotheringay) Knockin' On Heaven's Door (Stan Campbell) Wicked Messenger (Faces) Ballad Of Hollis Brown (Nina Simone) You Angel You (Manfred Manns Earth Band) This Wheel's On Fire (Julie Driscoll Brian Auger & Trinity) Mighty Quinn (Gary Puckett & Union Gap) Nothing Was Delivered (Byrds) When The Ship Comes In (Hollies) Highway 61 Revisited (Johnny Winter)

Country Gentlemen from 'The Award Winning'

Jackie DeShannon from 'In The Wind'

The Dillards from 'Live!!! Almost!!!'

Arlo Guthrie from 'Together In Concert' with Pete Seeger

Joe & Eddie from 'Walkin' Down The Line'

Rick Nelson from 'Bright Lights & Country Music'

Rising Sons from 'The Rising Sons'

Glen Yarborough from 'Yarborough Country'

Walls Of Red Wing
Joan Baez from 'Any Day Now'

Ramblin" Jack Elliot from 'FriendsOf Mine'

Paths Of Victory
Hamilton Camp from 'Paths Of Victory'

Anne Murray from 'What About Me'

Pete Seeger from 'Sings Little Boxes And Broadsides'

Talkin' John Birch Paranoid Blues
Pete Seeger from 'We Shall Overcome' and 'Broadside'

Only A Hobo
Jonathan Edwards from 'Blue Ridge'

Heron from 'The Best Of Heron'

Rod Stewart from 'Gasoline Alley'

Seven Curses
Albion Band '89 from 'Saturday Rolling Around'

Larry Barrett from 'Porch Song Singer'

Eternal Circle
Coulson Dean McGuiness Flint from 'Lo And Behold'

Mama You Been On My Mind
Johnny Cash from 'Orange Blossom Special'

Judy Collins (Daddy, You Been On My Mind) from 'Fifth Album'

Dion & The Belmonts from 'Together Again'

Linda Ronstadt from 'Hand Grown ... Home Sown'

Southwind from 'Southwind'

Rod Stewart from 'Never A Dull Moment'

Farewell Angelina
Nana Mouskouri from 'Sieben schwarze Rosen'

Judy Nash from 'The Night They Drove Old Dixie Down'

New Riders Of The Purple Sage from 'Oh What A Mighty Time'

If You Gotta Go Go Now (Or Else You Gotta Stay All Night)
Eric Andersen from 'Party!'

The Cowboy Junkies from 'Black Eyed Man'

Fairport Convention (Si Tu Dois Partir), single

The Flying Burrito Brothers from 'Burrito DeLuxe'

Mae West, single

Sitting On A Barbed Wire Fence
Kim And Thurston from the compilation 'Outlaw Blues - A Tribute To Bob Dylan'

She's Your Lover Now
Luxuria, single

Wallflower
David Bromberg from 'Wanted Dead Or Alive'

Doug Sahm from 'Doug Sahm And Band'

If You See Her, Say Hello
Annie McLoone (If You See Him, Say Hello) from 'Fast Annie'

The Ethel Mertz Experience from 'The Times They Are A-Changin', Volume 1'

Golden Loom
Roger McGuinn from 'Thunderbyrd' and '3 Byrds Land In London'

Catfish
Joe Cocker from 'Stingray'

Kinky Friedman from 'Lasso From El Passo'

Seven Days
Jimmy Barnes from 'Barnstorming'

Joe Cocker from 'Sheffield Steel'

Every Grain Of Sand
Giant Sand from 'Swerve'

Emmylou Harris from 'Wrecking Ball'

George Harrison from 'Far East Man'

Lord Protect My Child,
Lost Dogs from 'Scenic Routes'

Foot Of Pride,
Lou Reed from 'The 30th Anniversary Concert Celebration'

Blind Willie McTell
The Band from 'Jericho'

Dream Syndicate, single

Barrence Whitfield from 'Hillbilly Voodoo'

From the album Unplugged

John Brown
Heron from 'Twice As Nice And Half The Price'

The Staple Singers from 'Pray On'

With God On Our Side
Ramblin" Jack Elliot from 'Bull Durham Sacks'

Manfred Mann EP

The Neville Brothers from 'Yellow Moon'

Wire Train from 'Between Two Worlds'

From Time Out of Mind

Make You Feel My Love
Garth Brooks from 'Hope Floats'

Billy Joel from 'Greatest Hits Volume III'

OR THOSE in need of a complete collection, even tracing these superficial Bobtracks is not easy. In fact, just to hear most of them is more than difficult. There are, or have been, a brace of covers compilations, several of which are still reasonably available. Their merits are, of course variable. Certainly there are some great readings of Bob's songs, but there are some unpleasant live versions and some downright ridiculous interpretations which have been prepared in what seems like all seriousness.

If Dylan's art is engraved in every lyric and within the subliminal arrangement of each and every tune, then the wealth of covers that linger certainly bear testament to the magnificence of his songwriting. Full well knowing Bob's own disregard for some of his tunes, his mad reworkings and the joy of 'Like A Rolling Stone' played as a waltz, it's perhaps surprising that the vast majority of the covers that have been done - and there are thousands - sound so similar to the Dylan original.

Some of them do have their own special majesty. In fact, I've always had a particular soft spot for The Flying Burrito Brothers' reading of 'To Ramona' from their third eponymous album. With Gram Parsons out of the band, the vocals were handled by the silver-tongued Rick Roberts and the song's poignancy isn't lost on the moustachioed soul stirrer.

JOHN LECKIE, *seasoned producer*
"I worked with Andy Partridge on a version of 'All Along The Watchtower' for 'White Music' and there was purposely no guitar on the tracks as Andy, quite rightly, said it would be stupid to have a guitar on it after Hendrix's version. Andy always did it with guitar, harmonica and drums in a dub style."

BRENT HANSEN, *President MTV Europe*
"Bizarrely I quite like Ben Watt's version of 'You're Gonna Make Me Lonesome When You're Gone' from 'North Marine Drive', which I heard before I knew who Ben Watt was."

From my own collection I'd already managed to put together a tape of intriguing and quite entertaining Bobcovers. Now the songs I was listening to, that weren't even played by Bob Dylan were written by him. But, it was all in the name of "art"/"research"/"enjoyment" (delete as appropriate). And with that in mind, here's something to rival the dozen or so Bobilation albums that are still in the shops. Now, I could have gone way out there and sampled the delights of Wilko Johnson, The Five Blind Boys Of Alabama, The 1910 Fruitgum Company, Magna Carta, Joe Cocker and the Pozo Seco Singers - featuring of course Don Williams, but, well, that would have taken a tad longer. Any*who*, try this for size.

Under The Covers

Side One

1 Mr Tambourine Man by WILLIAM SHATNER

2 She Belongs To Me by THE NICE

3 All Along The Watchtower by XTC

4 Can You Please Crawl Out Your Window by TRANSVISION VAMP

5 Don't Think Twice, It's Alright by WAYLON JENNINGS

6 Si Tu Dois Partir by FAIRPORT CONVENTION

7 I'll Keep It With Mine by SUSANNA HOFFS, DAVID ROBACK AND WILL GLENN

8 Tomorrow Is A Long Time by SANDY DENNY

9 Nothing Was Delivered by THE BYRDS

Side Two

1 House Of The Rising Sun by THE ANIMALS

2 Wicked Messenger by THE SMALL FACES

3 Just Like A Woman by RICK NELSON

4 Knockin' On Heaven's Door by RAY DORSET AND MUNGO JERRY

5 To Ramona by THE FLYING BURRITO BROTHERS

6 Maggie's Farm by THE SPECIALS

7 You Ain't Going Nowhere by REM

8 Mama You've Been On My Mind by ROD STEWART

9 Tears Of Rage by IAN AND SYLVIA TYSON

Maggie's Farm (Solomon Burke).

IN A NUTSHELL A 24 track set featuring three chart hits, from Cher, Fairport Convention and Julie Driscoll et al, plus some more obscure items which set the musical boundaries flexing, with Manfred Mann's Earthband proffering their prog rock vision next to the sweet soul of Nina Simone and old crooner Bobby Darin.

30TH ANNIVERSARY CONCERT CELEBRATION

Columbia (first released in 1993)

Like A Rolling Stone, Leopard-Skin Pill-box Hat (John Cougar Mellencamp), Blowin' In The Wind (Stevie Wonder), Foot Of Pride (Lou reed), Master Of War (Edie Vedder/Mike McReady from Pearl Jam), The Times They Are A-Changin' (Tracy Chapman), It Ain't Me Babe (June Carter Cash/Johnny Cash), What Was It You Wanted (Willie Nelson), I'll Be Your Baby Tonight (Kris Kristoferson), Highway 61 Revisited (Johnny Winter), Seven Days (Ron Wood), Just Like A Woman (Richie Havens), When The Ship Comes In (The Clancy Brothers and Robbie O'Connell with Tommy Makem), You Ain't Goin" Nowhere (Mary Chapin Carpenter/Roseanne Cash/Shawn Colvin), Just Like Tom Thumb's Blues and All Along The Watchtower (Neil Young), I Shall Be Released (Chrissie Hynde), Don't Think Twice, It's Alright (Eric Clapton), Emotionally Yours (The O'Jays), When I Paint My Masterpiece (The Band), Absolutely Sweet Marie (George Harrison), License To Kill and Rainy Day Women Nos 12&35 (Tom Petty And The Heartbreakers), Mr Tambourine Man (Roger McGuinn), It's Alright Ma (I'm Only Bleeding) (Bob Dylan), My Back Pages (Dylan, McGuinn, Petty, Young, Clapton, Harrison), Knockin' On Heaven's Door (Everyone), Girl From The North Country (Bob Dylan).

IN A NUTSHELL A celebratory tour de force delivered in big Revue style, with a cast of the famous playing Bob's songs at Madison Square Garden with a whooping crowd and some Hollywood shlock next to some emotive storytelling.

DOIN' DYLAN

Columbia (first released in 1995)

Rainy Day Women Nos 12&35 (The Black Crowes), Simple Twist Of Fate (Concrete Blonde), Seven Days (Jimmy Barnes), Absolutely Sweet Marie (Jason And The Scorchers), Wanted Man (George Thorogood And The Destroyers), A Hard Rain's A-Gonna Fall (Edie Brickell And The New Bohemians), From A Buick 6 (Gary US Bonds), Tight Connection To My Heart (John Martyn), It

Once I'd made that tape, I was more than in the mood. There were a million compilations of Bob-related artefacts that I could now think of. And they weren't just covers or tributes. There was a whole platoon of alleged new Bobs, 'New Dylans' as they were lovingly dubbed. They were out there, having taken the man at face value and donned anything from his cap to his suede jacket with the idea of getting their bootheels wandering.

JOHNNY CASH *on the new Dylans*

"I just don't see any great new song stylists. No Kris Kristoferson. No Bob Dylan. There'll be another Bob Dylan, of course, but I don't see anyone who gets out and does it their own way and damn the torpedoes."

Bob's disregard for convention was pretty apparent by now and it would be very unlikely if there ever was a new version of the wild mercurial sound, the acoustic rebelliousness or even the God-fearing preacher variations on his character. The term is so loose that legend has it that even Marc Bolan was considered to be a 'New Dylan' at one point. He simply pales into the middle distance when compared to these guys..

DAVID ACKLES

Deep American Gothic balladeer who out-worded Bob while storytelling and summoned up the dark brooding underside of folk macabre.

Sounded like a folky Bob with a hangover. Some great albums but no success, (he died as I wrote this).

ERIC ANDERSON

Highly rated Greenwich Villager, expected to take over the mantle of folk hero when Dylan went electric. Opted to re-record his 'Bout Changes And Things' with an electric backing band instead.

DAVID BLUE

Buddy of Bob in the coffee house days as David Cohen, eventually signed to Elektra and unleashed a 'Highway 61'-inspired eponymous debut album before trading his licks for some meaningful melancholy prose.

TIM BUCKLEY

Groomed for the role of Woody Guthrie in the Bound For Glory biopic, but died of an overdose before the camera's rolled. His recorded output fused Dylan's lonesome soul with jazz grooves and emotive etherealness.

DAVID BROMBERG

Folk-based roots player with a hefty back catalogue of session work which led him to play on 'New Morning'. Hardly a Dylan but the association never harmed him.

JOHN COOPER CLARKE

Ridiculously-coiffured (very H61 Dylan) Mancunian punk poet whose political rants drew parallels but lacked strumology. His chew-gum rhetoric and incisive wit was too clever for mass consumption.

JOHN DENVER

Had guitar, did travel from 'LA To Denver' with an unbecoming smile and a tear-sodden story. Too polished and MOR to be really Bob and a bad haircut to boot.

DONOVAN

Lullabied by Dylan in the film Don't Look Back with the ode 'It's All Over Now, Baby Blue'. Donovan claimed it wasn't plagiarism, simply inspiration and he made some good albums too.

PATRIK FITZGERALD

'The new Dylan' in 1979, when punk turned to new wave and Fitzgerald turned his poems into antagonistic strums. Last heard of working in market research.

STEVE FORBERT

"Nobody is the new anybody" claimed the Mississippi-born singer/songwriter when he

Then became the new Dylan but didn't get that together either.

TIM HARDIN

Ex-marine with a drug problem whose bitter-sweet jazz-flavoured folk took from Hank Williams as he penned ''Reason To Believe' and many others. Could have been a contender but the drugs won out.

ROY HARPER

Acclaimed in the press release for his first single, 'Mid-Spring Dithering' with the phrase, 'Is Roy The Man To Succeed Dylan?'. Time has proved he wasn't.

IAN HUNTER

Besotted with Bob, corkscrew of hair, the Mott The Hoople sound was developed from the sleazier end of troubadouring with all the wild abandon of Bob in tow.

"The term 'new Dylan' is so loose that anyone with curly hair, except Brian May and Harpo Marx, can apply."

played Greenwich Village and got a deal in the late '70s. Faced with punk and a disappointing second album his drawl disappeared in clouds of "management problems" only to return in the late '90s as a man of substance.

STEVE GOODMAN

Contemporary of John Prine, who had Dylan play along - as Robert Milkwood Thomas - on one of his early collections of heartfelt folk thoughtful-ness. Mostly too tongue-in-cheek to be really loveable tho'.

DAVID GRAY

Hailed by Joan Baez for writing "the best lyrics since the young Bob Dylan", this Welsh singer/songwriter has since gone on to sound completely un-Bob and far less inspiring.

ARLO GUTHRIE

Son of Woody, tipped to be the new Woody but was too stoned at Woodstock to take advantage.

FRIJID PINK

Detroit quartet who updated The Animals' update of Dylan's arrangement of 'House Of The Rising Sun' by adding extra wattage. Only acclaimed as 'the new Dylans' by mad people.

MARK KNOPFLER

Schoolboy Bob fan turned drawling vocalist with a Dylan shuffle and eventual Bob producer. Sounds like Bob when he's answering the phone in bed but lacks clever wordage.

KRIS KRISTOFERSON

The Bob that could act, with a touch of country credibility. Moulded to be the '70s version of the '60s Bob, but his voice was too gruff to register in the pop world.

GORDON LIGHTFOOT

Canadian singer/songwriter greatly admired and even covered by Bob, who fell short of the vocal

Takes A Lot To Laugh, It Takes A Train To Cry (Chris Wilson), Let's Keep it Between Us (Bonnie Raitt), Catfish (Joe Cocker), Ballad Of A Thin Man (The Sports), Like A Rolling Stone (Ana Christensen), Subterranean Homesick Blues (Dave Stewart And Barbara Gaskin), This Wheel's On Fire (Siouxsie And The Banshees), Farewell, Angelina (The New Riders Of The Purple Sage), Caribbean Wind (The Revelators), Abandoned Love (The Everly Brothers), Boots Of Spanish Leather (Nanci Griffith), I'll Keep It With Mine (Rainy Day), All Along The Watchtower (The Indigo Girls), I'll Remember You (Grayson Hugh), Ring Them Bells (Gordon Lightfoot), Forever Young (Marc Hunter), Girl From The North Country (Rod Stewart), Just Like Tom Thumb's Blues (Nina Simone), With God On Our Side (The Neville Brothers), Need A Woman (Ry Cooder), Golden Loom (Roger McGuinn), Gotta Serve Somebody (David Allen Coe And Lacy J Dalton), I Shall Be Released (Shane Howard), Blind Willie McTell (The Band).
IN A NUTSHELL "It is largely a fairly recent music generation that features on this collection. These are not familiar '60s chart versions of the master's work but rather thoughtful, mature, textured treatments of recordings that range across his 30 year plus professional career." Glenn A Baker

AND THE TIMES THEY WERE A-CHANGIN'

Debutante (first released in 1997)

Mr Tambourine Man (The Byrds), The Mighty Quinn (Manfred Mann), All Along The Watchtower (Jimi Hendrix Experience), It's All Over Now Baby Blue (Them), Only A Hobo (Rod Stewart), Knocking On Heaven's Door (Eric Clapton), A Hard Rain's Gonna Fall (Bryan Ferry), Highway 61 Revisited (Johnny Winter), Absolutely Sweet Marie (Jason And The Scorchers), It Takes A Lot To Laugh, It Takes A Train To Cry (Stills, Kooper, Bloomfield), Tears Of Rage (The Band), Percy's Song (Fairport Convention), Buckets Of Rain (Bette Midler), It Ain't Me Babe (Johnny Cash), Love Is A Four Letter Word (Joan Baez), Chimes Of Freedom (Youssou N'dour), It's Alright Ma, I'm Only Bleeding (Roger McGuinn).
IN A NUTSHELL In many ways it seems you aren't really an artist until you've done your Dylan cover. So Dylan ultrafan Greil Marcus wasn't short of songs to choose from for this 17-song compilation of Those Who Have Paid Homage. The thrust of this idea, it seems, is two-fold. The first is to show how eclectic you can get by taking Dylan's chords and re-inventing them. The second to point out to novices that Dylan wrote some more tunes beside 'Like A Rolling Stone' and 'Blowin' In The Wind'.
HOWARD JOHNSON, Q

range to elevate him to the major league. Got stuck with a MOR tag from his huge hit 'If You Could Read My Mind' and never recovered.

DON McLEAN
Topped the charts in 1971/72 on both sides of the Atlantic with a considered story song about the state of rock, the world and beyond.

BARRY McGUIRE
New Christy Minstrel who penned the kids' fave 'Three Wheels On My Wagon', before sporting a conscience and an agit pop facade for 'Eve Of Destruction' in the wake of Dylan's success.

MOUSE AND THE TRAPS
Wired-period psyche-pop Bob from the mid-'60s courtesy of Chris St John, their Byrdsian take on 'Public Execution' heralded as "Beating Bob Dylan at his own folk-rock game". Allegedly.

ELLIOTT MURPHY
He has an acoustic guitar, writes poignant songs of love and heartache and drinks a lot. (Probably unrelated, maybe.)

PHIL OCHS
Greenwich Village Bob contemporary who wallowed in the protestations of early Dylan and carried the torch for peace with 'I Ain't Marching Anymore' and numerous others.

JOHN PRINE
Kentucky's gravel-voiced country-tinged crooner whose thought-provoking ballads from the early '70s still recall Bob's bittersweet days, with a social docudrama in every verse.

LEON REDBONE
Acclaimed as the man Dylan would record if he ever started a record label, Redbone's coffee house playing the '60s, set him up for rag-time oblivion in the '70s as major acclaim eluded him.

BOB ROBERTS
As played by Tim Robbins in the film of the same name in 1992, Roberts was reactionary folk-singing politician, who offered a response to Dylan with 'The Times They Are A-Changin' Back' before parodying Don't Look Back's cue-card promo for 'Subterranean Homesick Blues'.

PAUL SIMON
Legendarily Art Garfunkel's friend who penned a neat folk rock tune after Columbia electrified their 'Sound Of Silence' in the same experiment that sewed the seeds for Bob's 'Bringing It All Back Home'.

BRUCE SPRINGSTEEN
Hailed as the 'the new Dylan' following his debut album, occasionally reverting to type when not supported by his raucous band. Has written a few successful songs since though.

AL STEWART
Chased the Dylan dream to London, from Glasgow, in 1964, "with a corduroy jacket and a headful of dreams". Shared a flat with Paul Simon in London's East End, argued with him about the merits of Lawrence Ferlinghetti.

LOUDON WAINWRIGHT III
"Dylan was a huge idol of mine" claims the man who wrote 'Talking New Bob Dylan' to commemorate his fiftieth. Wainwright was at first flattered by the comparison but eventually incorporated a comic element to his act to deflect it.

RICH WEBB
Australian singer/songwriter whose 1998 debut album 'The Girl Who Laughed Too Much' belies his obvious Dylan musical influences and came housed with a Dylan-styled folk period cover illustration.

AJ WEBERMAN
Renowned garbologist who stalked Dylan, went through his trash and tried to analyse the great man on his return to New York in the early '70s. At first Dylan was intrigued but after meeting the man, Dylan pronounced "I'm not Dylan, AJ, you are!"

ANDY WHITE
The creator of Rave On Andy White, a mixture of dense lyrics and messy Dylanisms, that earned him critical praise and a 'New Dylan' tag in 1986. "Of course I'm influenced by him."

And then, of course, there was Nick Cave. Not the new Dylan by any stretch of the imagination but inspired nonetheless. Cave, formerly of The Birthday Party and for some time a Bad Seed, is an obsessive Bob fan and, indeed, a lot of his musical make up can be derived from his Dylan fixation and his similarly-motivated quest to plunder the roots of traditional American folk for his own tragic melodies.

In fact, Cave's love of Bob is well known. Way back at the Hearts Of Fire NFT press conference, Nick had begged his Antipodaean buddy, photographer Bleddyn Butcher to take his Dylan albums along in and effort to get them signed. Bleddyn duly tried, trooping up to the great man at the end of the shenanigans but Bob wasn't having any. Nick or no man.

MIKE PEAKE, FHM
You're forever being name-dropped by other musicians. Have you met any of your heroes?
Nick Cave: "No. All the ones I like I haven't yet met. Van Morrison, Bob Dylan - I've never met them and I'm quite happy I haven't, so I can harbour all sorts of romantic illusions about them which I'm sure would be shattered if I ever met them."

Imagine the scene, then at the Glastonbury Festival last year. So the story goes, Bob made a b-line for Cave once he heard he was backstage. Not to finally put pen to vinyl and revalue his collection, but to tell him that he liked his 'Murder Ballads' album. Nick was speechless. Literally he couldn't get a word out.

The Cave connection to Dylan is long and highly detailed. First off, he's covered a number of Dylan songs, including 'Knockin' On Heaven's Door', 'Wanted Man', 'I Threw It All Away' and 'Death Is Not The End'. But beyond that there's a whole hots of other synergistic similarities.

For example, both Nick Cave and Bob Dylan have both covered 'Let It Be Me', 'Wade In The Water', 'Long Time Man', 'Ring Of Fire', 'Jesus Met The Woman At The Well', 'Hey Joe', 'Henry Lee', 'Stagger Lee', 'King Kong Kitchee Kitchee Ki-Mi-O' (Bob Dylan covered it as 'Froggie Went A Courtin'), 'Bottle Up And Go', 'Long Black Veil', 'Blue Suede Shoes', 'Just A Closer Walk With Thee', 'Lost Highway' and 'Fever'. Plus Dylan's reading of John Lee Hooker's 'Tupelo Blues' on 'The Basement Tapes' was the inspiration for Cave's 'Tupelo'. It's like they both key in on personal tragedy and real life storylines, as hard and caustic as they may be...

RICHARD BUTLER
(PSYCHEDELIC FURS) on Bob at college

"I was at Epsom Art College in 1979 and I was listening to Bob Dylan and The Velvet Underground while I worked. I didn't like anything else at all at that time."

PAUL McCARTNEY
on first meetings in 64

"We really admired him. I'd known his stuff as long as I'd known Ray Charles, so he was a big hero of ours."

BRYAN FERRY
on a lack of communication

"I recorded A Hard Rain in 1973 and he still hasn't thanked me for it."

People who do come into contact with him struggle to get a reaction. God. It's Bob Dylan.

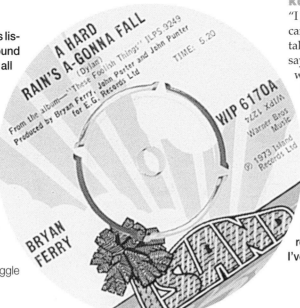

kd Lang *on culinary choice*

"I get very nervous around famous people. I can hardly talk. When I met Dylan, he was talking about songwriting and I didn't want to say something stupid. He said he wanted to write something with me, but that would have just been so hard. Even through I think he's a tremendous songwriter, that would have been like taking two distinct ingredients and putting them together, like curry and chocolate."

NICK CAVE

"I guess (my favourite album) must be 'Slow Train Coming'. That's a great record, full of mean-spirited spirituality. It's a genuinely nasty record, certainly the nastiest Christian album I've ever come across."

Brian Ferry: " I recorded **Hard Rain** in 1973 and he still hasn't thanked me for it"

JERRY GARCIA
The Grateful Dead guitarist on touring with Bob

"We've always loved his music. We do a lot of his songs but as far as what he's like - I can't really tell you what he's like. He's so mercurial that he doesn't give off a 'me' fingerprint at all. He doesn't appear to have a character. He's tough to pin down. I don't think he's much interested in his own performance. And I could understand how he could be burned out on himself. I can see why Dylan might die of boredom. He's not even a musician."

STUART BATSFORD
Catalogue manager, WEA Records

"In 1987 at Wembley, for some reason he'd decided to do a meet and greet. I was a Virgin retail buyer then and I managed to get in with a load of Sony reps to actually meet him. We were all assembled in a room and we were told that he may not turn up, we couldn't take any pictures and that he had a clammy handshake. And he did.
"Eventually he came into the room and he shook hands with the reps who were saying, 'I'm from the North East and I really like your album'. When he came up to my wife and me, I was shaking like a leaf, a complete wreck. I just said, 'How are you? Have you recovered?', because he'd just been ill and he said 'Yeah, man. Thanks for asking'.
"I didn't know what else to say. He's the most important man of the twentieth century."

JOHN LEE HOOKER *on good old times*
"Bob is a beautiful person. A good, good man. Very sweet, very kind. I met him when I was playing in the coffee houses. He wasn't famous then but he came to see me. We played some shows together and he'd come back to my place and we'd stay up all night, playin' and drinkin' wine."

It's true. Everyone has a Bobtale to tell. Whether it be Marlon Brando exclaiming that "The two loudest things I've ever heard are a freight train going by and Bob Dylan and The Band.", or The Jesus And Mary Chain's insistence that "Anything by Bob Dylan before his motorbike crash was brilliant, anything between '64 and '66 is total genius." There's a subtle imprint of Bob that sticks in the mind. Whether it's a lasting influence, a broad admiration or distress that he hasn't been in touch.

SHERYL CROW *on that first date*
"He was very open, intense, really sweet. Beautiful. In fact. I was late for my gig because we talked for so long. All the way through all I could think was, 'Oh my God! I've just been talking to Bob Dylan'!"

BRUCE ROBINSON
on that first handshake
"George Harrison introduced me to him, who has the limpest handshake imaginable, like

shaking hands with a corpse. It inspired a line in one of my films, Jennifer 8, when the cop says, 'He's got a handshake like a partially-excited penis'."

DAVID HEPWORTH

"If you ever get the opportunity to meet Bob Dylan, it's almost like being able to say that you've met James Joyce or Louis Armstrong. What I've found in meeting pop stars is that if you scratch them there is a part of them desperate to be loved but I don't think that Bob Dylan has that at all. I genuinely think that Bob Dylan doesn't give a hoot what anybody thinks about him.

"The source of his artistic energy through the

Madison Square Garden that night and didn't play a single song from that record which is something that nobody else would dream of doing. But that's Bob Dylan.

"Anyway, I was taken into his dressing room to interview him at the show and I was pretty much shaking with nerves. In there was a tall red-haired woman of rather bizarre appearance who I subsequently discovered was his dresser, the woman who was responsible for all those bizarre clothing accidents that he sports live. There was the best stocked bar that I've ever seen anywhere, with rare liquors alongside all manner of scotch. And there in the corner was the legend himself,

value that I just didn't appreciate at the time.

"You go in there with your idea of what Bob Dylan is all about - you think you've worked him out - I'm sure everyone does this. And I remember one thing really clearly, I was talking to him about singers that he admired. And he said Tony Bennett. Now this was 1986, and I thought, 'You're taking the piss', so I didn't put this in the finished interview. Ten years later, Tony Bennett's the hippest thing on the planet and he's regarded as a master interpreter.

"Now, Bob Dylan had that view ten years before anybody else. And that just made me think that Bob Dylan exists outside of the normal chronology of what everyone else is listening to.

"One of the things that I've learned from him in the last few years is that so much of the value of music is going back, not going forward. And,

"I genuinely think that Bob Dylan doesn't give a hoot what anybody thinks about him.

years, the utterly single-minded vision of what he's trying to do has never tried to fit into what anyone expects him to do. It's occasionally let him make appalling judgements and he's been responsible for some of the most shambolic live performances ever witnessed but he's also been responsible for some records that are a work of unique genius.

"I met him twice in one week in New York in 1986. This was the time that Bob Dylan was touring with the Heartbreakers, which was, as far as I could tell, just something that their managers had done. It was acclaimed as a return to the wild mercurial sound of the 'Blonde On Blonde' band but, to anyone with ears, it clearly wasn't.

"He was playing at Madison Square Garden the day that 'Knocked Out Loaded' came out and I'd actually been given a copy at his label that day and I took it down there to get it autographed for a friend and he hadn't seen it. It's a pretty odd thing to be actually acquainting an artist with the artwork for their album.

"In fact, he was sufficiently unconcerned with the whole thing that he went on stage at

strumming a guitar and chain-smoking. I was introduced to him, he didn't get up, he just proffered a hand that felt like you'd shaken hands with a ghost, an image that was increased by the veil of cigarette smoke that was filling the space in front of him.

"I attempted to engage him in conversation and he really didn't make life easy at all. He had absolutely no mercy. Since then I've come not to blame him. After all, this is a man who's been asked to explain himself three times a day since 1963. I'm sure he got rather bored with it all in 1965.

"He twiddled his guitar and occasionally paused to expectorate - at very high volume - right across the room. Everything I tried to talk about he gave short responses to and didn't pursue the conversation. Looking back I think there was a lot of things that he said that had some

in an industry that's obsessed with novelty, with what's the next big thing, you've got to admire Bob Dylan saying, "Go back! Listen to Jimmie Rodgers, 1929, that's interesting'."

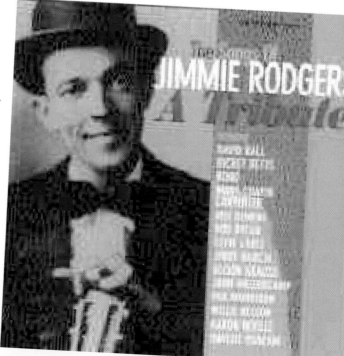

Obviously several believers

I F MEETING Dylan is too hot for the blood, the next best thing is obviously immersing yourself in Dylan "stuff". The stories of his legendary exploits the bootlegs, the books, the badges, the plectrums, the web sites, the fanzines, the albums by other people with Bob appearances on them, the... well, just the facts, figures and the fun of Bob. It's beyond model aircraft building, it covers all media and, when housed in a suitable fashion it has a collectors' tag that's pretty damn enviable.

People smitten by Bob in the '60s still walk this earth quoting from his lyrics and naming their shops after him. Enter Peter Bennion, a Newcastle shop owner who named his ethnic craft shops Freewheelin' and Bringing It All Back Home. OK, so he now runs The Futon Shop (obviously one of Bob's lesser known hard-to-find rare tracks), but he is philosophical about the man.

"He's had his ups and downs but intermittently he's turned out some gems. There were some years in the doldrums but 'Time Out Of Mind' has got to be one of the best albums he's done."

Also housed in Newcastle is surrealist painter Trevor Neal, whose portrait of Bob meeting Salvador Dali was bought by light entertainment personage Michael Barrymore. Evidently Barrymore's not really keen on Bob but ignore that for the sake of the book and continuity.

Trevor: "I've probably been to 25 or 30 of his concerts over the years. He is a guy who is very easy to give up on because of his complete changes in direction, which alienate a lot of fans."

Trevor must be talking about Keith Butler! The Toronoto-residing family man who uttered the immortal put down 'Judas' to Dylan way back in 1966. His infamous remark led to a radio appearance recently with Andy Kershaw who, obsessed with the concert, had prepared a whole documentary on the night. So 'Judas'?

"I was very disappointed, very emotional, and I think my anger just welled up inside me," Butler informed Mojo magazine. "What really sent me over the edge was when he did two songs that I was really fond of, 'Baby Let Me Follow You Down' and 'One Too Many Mornings', in that electric guitar way."

Butler quickly walked out after Bob rebuked him and was picked up on DA Pennebaker's Eat The Document film of the tour exclaiming, "Any bloody pop group could do this rubbish!" ➤

Change is something that the early Bobverts found hard to understand - it's just as well Mr Butler never heard 'Hard Rain', then. The analogists have plenty to say on the changing face of Bob and analysing Bob is a recognised global sport these days.

Way back when, the person who started it all off was undoubtedly AJ Weberman a radical thinker and part-time stoner who saw the light. Or at least a light of sorts. Back in 1965, Weberman was listening to 'Bringing It All Back Home' slightly the worse for wear, and he suddenly flashed that it was a political song

Bob with Tom Petty and The Heartbreakers: "Whose key is it, anyway?"

about capitalism. From there it was a short but radical fall into analysing all of Dylan's lyrics and eventually founding the 'science of Dylanology'. Oh, you know, those kind of things just happen.

Weberman didn't stop at the lyrics. He collected everything he could. He picked up on Bob's every move, he even raided Bob's trash and ended up with an archive to rival any budding museum. At the peak of his collecting powers Weberman encountered Dylan on several occasions and his growing paranoia fuelled numerous analytical pronouncements about Bob's state of mind. Dylan lapped it up at first, Goading Weberman with, "I'm not Dylan - you are." But eventually it got too much and after Weberman stormed Bob's front door, it all ended in tears.

By then, Weberman had even set up the Dylan Liberation Front after he concluded through his research that Bob was in a less than satisfactory mental state due to alleged drug abuse. Beyond that, Weberman had analysed every Dylan word by placing them all on punch cards and running them through various comparative tests.

"I discovered that if you studied Dylan's poetry, word by word and made a complete index of it, you could uncover the secret meaning of all of his songs. You've gotta understand that Dylan is basically a symbolist poet."

Weberman then annotated his findings into what he called a concordance. From that he could analyse each word and uncover new meanings to Dylan's songs. For example, claimed Weberman, "rain stands for violence", so, when you hear the lines, 'Louise hold a handful of rain', 'If not for you, rain would fall' 'Looks like nothing but rain', 'He rolled his body amongst the blood-red rain' or virtually any part of 'A Hard Rain's-A-Gonna Fall', then a whole new focus is applied.

"My method has been used in the Bible for centuries by critics," Weberman enthused, "but people freak out completely when they hear I'm doing it to rock artists."

AJ WEBERMAN
interviewed in 1994 by John Roberts for The Telegraph
Roberts:
How do you feel about the time you put Dylan through?

"He deserved that much. I drove him crazy."

OBVIOUSLY TO be a true Dylan fan you needed time. A theory would also be useful. And money. There was no sign of a friendly fan club providing a monthly A4 newsletter, an autographed picture and a badge back in 1964. The Bob experience took many prisoners and once that pivotal point of interest had given way to early anoracnaphobia it was very unlikely that there would be any turning back. Ever.

STUART BATSFORD
Catalogue manager, WEA Records

"Originally I hated Dylan. I didn,t like his whinging voice. That grating harmonica. I was more interested in sweet pop music, like The Byrds. As far as I was concerned, Bob Dylan couldn,t sing. Then, when I was about 16 or 17 I heard 'Hurricane', and I was really impressed. It had a great story and I felt Dylan was really trying to say something. I bought the album, 'Blood On The Tracks' and when he came to play at Earl's Court I really got caught up in it.

I had to queue for tickets in Birmingham and I was really shocked. There were people I knew but I'd never experienced that kind of peaceful togetherness with people discussing Dylan through the night. There was an incredible atmosphere just in the queue.

"People were playing his songs on the guitar, playing tapes, I really enjoyed it. It was 1978 and there was such a warm feeling, it was so different to punk. The people there were treating it like a second coming, they were all amazed that Bob Dylan was actually going to tour. I'd never experienced that kind of devotion in people for a musician.

"Earl's Court itself is a really cavernous venue and at the show, it just seemed like a

AJ Weberman: "He deserved it!"

normal gig until the fourth number, when he played 'Like A Rolling Stone'. I'll never forget that feeling, the whole audience got up on their feet, there were 20,000 people and they were raised off the ground, it sent shivers down my spine.

"It wasn't a classic gig, but it was his first live indoor show in the UK for 12 years and I'll never forget that moment.

"I still wasn't completely convinced by Dylan and between 1978 and '81 he released what I considered to be the worst records he,d ever done. It's strange because now I really like them.

"I went to see him again in 1981 and I actually walked out. There were lots of people walking out and I really felt that that was it, as far as I was concerned he,d completely lost it. I remember my mate and I moaned all the way home and the next time he played in 1984 I didn't even go. By that time I was into people

"At the time I was working in a record collector's store and I was amazed by all these Scandinavian Dylan fans who came in before the concert. They were talking about the shows in Tel Aviv and the difference between set lists. It really opened my eyes to the fact that Bob Dylan was their reason for living.

"The first night at Wembley was the night of the hurricane which swept over Southern England, I remember it distinctly. There was an odd feeling in the air anyway and the show was just brilliant. It was really moving. I decided I had to go the second night and I ended up paying £50 to a tout. The seat was in the second row and it was the closest I'd ever been to Dylan. I could see that he was just totally into the whole thing. It just really blew me away and I had to go again the next night.

"I paid another £50 for the third night and ended up going on the last night and spending £75. But that was worth it because George

Dylan was like he is and she reckoned he's just in it for the money. But, I can't see that at all.

"For instance, when he toured at the time of 'Time Out Of Mind', he didn,t even play any songs from the album in his set. He played one song in the encore. That doesn't sound like someone who is doing it just for the money."

BILL PRINCE
assistant editor GQ magazine

"My very first exposure to Bob Dylan was from a very serious girl that I went to school with. She was obsessed with Bob Dylan, purely because he was the serious rock star, which I couldn't take seriously. I sort of reacted against that on principal and I avoided Bob Dylan like the plague.

"That was until the early '80s when I was playing in a band and living in London where the singer was rightfully and dutifully obsessed with Bob Dylan.

"I could see that he was just totally into the whole thing. It just really blew me away and I had to go again the next night."

like Green On Red, The Long Ryders and The Rain Parade. I much preferred going to see them in small clubs rather than going through the same thing again with Dylan.

"I didn't really listen to his albums either. I'd heard 'Empire Burlesque' and I thought there were some good songs but it had no lasting effect. Then I heard 'Knocked Out Loaded' and 'Brownsville Girl'. I couldn,t believe how good that track was. It was like watching a Peckinpah film. It had everything. It was *The Gunfighter* with Gregory Peck interspersed with bits from Dylan,s own life. It was so rich in imagery.

"I realised he couldn't be all over and even though the rest of the album sucked, I decided to go and see him on the first night at Wembley when he played with Petty And The Heartbreakers.

Harrison got up and played too.

"After those four nights I just bought everything. All the albums. Then I had my epiphanal experience, I realised that Bob Dylan was just better than anything else. I knew from then on that if Bob Dylan was in town, there was nowhere else that I could be. I would be there. I haven't missed a London show since.

"I've bought more and more Dylan. The albums. Tapes. Books."

So what's your theory about Bob? Why does he keep on doing it?

"I think it's because he likes to play live. That,s the experience for him. He's like an old blues or folk troubadour. I don't think the records matter to him. His life is about touring. I met Joan Baez once and I asked her why she thought

He urged me to go to Record And Tape Exchange and buy every Bob Dylan album I could find. And the conversion was swift. I suppose for about two years I listened to absolutely nothing other than Bob Dylan.

"The first record I got was 'Hard Rain', it must have been the most reduced record there, and I was on my way. But, when I found a suitably reduced copy of 'Blood On The Tracks', things really started to move. Hearing that album was just a huge leap in my understanding and appreciation of Bob Dylan.

"About that time I was working on *Sounds* and it was clear that Dylan was roundly considered to be the slightly dour, cool colossus of rock music.

"However, most people in bands at the time, myself included, failed to notice that he'd already done it all and done it on his own. People just failed to recognise that they weren,t even on the foothills of the Everest of Dylan's talent. That was why I kept listening."

Where have you got most out of Dylan?

"It must certainly be the live shows. They are such a spectacle and so special, whatever happens.

"The first time I saw him was at Wembley Stadium in 1985 and it terms of eras it seemed to me then that it was the end of Bob Dylan's Rock God phase. It was a huge event with that gargantuan early '70s feel, up to and including when his rock star mates came out and joined him.

"Following that there was a rather desultory run of Wembley Arena shows and I remember it was always raining when he played. I was sitting high up on the side and had a fantastic profile of Dylan for one of those nights and I was transfixed with the way he looked. He was leaning into the crowd, his body language was taut and he was actually singing - he was yet to go into his Norman Collier faulty microphone technique where he'd lose syllables or indeed whole lines.

"There was such presence about what he was doing, it was almost like a punk rock set, well as punk as any band playing 'Barbara Allen' could be. He didn't speak, which I learned was his way, he was just vicious. The sound was poor but it was galvanic. It wasn't so much ferocious as a wall of sound and he leant into every song. To be honest it was probably the only one of those arena shows that I really enjoyed.

"During that period, Dylan was playing the UK regularly and I'd have to go because I had no idea how long he'd keep doing that kind of show. I remember there was even talk among the Bobnoscenti that he should perhaps do a Sinatra and take a break for a while, stop playing and come back when we could really appreciate it. I even began to agree with that because it seemed like there was no point in coming over and playing desultory shows, people just thought he'd lost it.

"Little did I know that, at that point he was gearing up to come every year for six or seven years. And when he announced that he was playing at Hammersmith Odeon I couldn't believe it. I couldn't believe that an artist of his stature would not play arena shows and would come in to do six nights at the Hammersmith Odeon.

"I think I got tickets for two of the nights and the shows were spellbinding.

The shows were great and he seemed to enjoy the intimacy of them. It was really something special to be that close to him.

"After those shows I always made a habit of seeing two or three shows every time he played here."

Obviously you'd reached a comfortable level with Dylan, accepting whatever shortcomings there might be and virtually signing up for yearly prescriptions. Did you ever feel that you had to take it to the next level?

"Three years ago I decided I had to see him abroad, to go on tour. So a friend and I went to Brussels, Paris and London. There I met Dylan's chosen coach driver, Dougie, a trucker from the Midlands who usually drove the likes of Terrorvision and Pulp around but who was always requested when Bob came to Europe.

"And, through meeting him, my friend James and I learnt more about Bob's ways on

the road than reading any articles or anything else.

"For me, it re-inforced the idea that he's a working musician, it suits his purpose in what he does. He shuns celebrity and, as a musician, he believes his job is to work. For him to work is to tour and the only comfort he gets is the comfort he gets on the road, the quality of his bus, the timekeeping of his bus driver and the fact that he's relatively unbothered when he's touring.

Touring is such a regimented lifestyle that it's easier for him to protect his privacy on the road, ironically in front of 20,000 people, than it is for him when he's back home in LA."

DOUGIE HAMNETT *tour bus driver*

"Sometimes he'd sit on the bus without saying

a word for two whole days. And he likes European Motorway Services. In the middle of the night he'd ask to stop at one and go off and walk in the fields behind them for an hour.

"He'd stop there too because he collects kitsch, tacky stuff like little windmills. I saw him buy 64 pairs of wooden clogs once. Scandinavian drivers wear them a lot and for some reason Bob had taken a fancy to them. He bought this service station's entire stock. Apparently, there's a whole floor of his house where he stores all his junk."

BILL PRINCE

Why did you decide to do three nights in Europe? Was it a pilgrimage?

"Yes it was. We were well into double figures for seeing Bob at that time but we'd not seen him on his own turf or seen him in front of a

foreign audience.

"That kind of legitimised it to our girlfriends but really we wanted to spend three days talking, thinking and drinking Bob.

"We got tickets for Brussels and Paris and headed off by Eurostar. The first show was actually outside of Brussels and he played the same set he'd done earlier that year in London. No speaking, but it was really good. Well, it was an OK show.

"When the show ended we were kind of stuck four miles from the centre of town with no real means of getting back. We saw a couple, the guy was dressed in early-infatuation mock-'60s-style Bob garb. We realised he must have been a recent convert and thought he must be from the city, so we chased after them and asked for a lift back to town.

"They spoke really good English and we

en roue libre...

BOB DYLAN

BLOWIN' IN THE WIND
(Ecoute dans le vent)
GIRL FROM THE NORTH COUNTRY
MASTERS OF WAR
DOWN THE HIGHWAY
BOB DYLAN'S BLUES
A HARD RAIN'S A-GONNA FALL

DON'T THINK TWICE, IT'S ALL RIGHT
(N'y pense plus, tout est bien)
BOB DYLAN'S DREAM
OXFORD TOWN
TALKING WORLD WAR III BLUES
CORRINA, CORRINA
HONEY, JUST ALLOW ME ONE MORE CHANCE
I SHALL BE FREE

ended up spending a really great night with them, touring the bars of Brussels and talking about Bob. Eventually they dropped us off at the station so that we could get the milk train to Paris. I remember saying to James as we left them that there really is a brotherhood between Bob Dylan fans. There's a kind of openness that, in a way, makes up for our hero's lack of openness.

"In Paris Elvis Costello was supporting and in a way we'd have preferred it to have been a young Parisienne band because it made us realise that our road trip was nearly over and we were edging back towards the UK. It was good nonetheless but our rock 'n' roll odyssey was slightly shattered when we were mugged by half a dozen 12-year-olds after we left a night-club at four in the morning.

"Back in London, with our ego's bruised and

BUT SOME people just can't slow down. When I started to amass information for this book, my first port of call was my friend Chris, who I knew to be an obsessive Dylan fan. Years of Bob-ing had left him still as keen as mustard.

He had the ticket stubs, the old *Melody Maker* reviews stuffed inside his album sleeves, he had the bootlegs too. When I first met Chris, years ago, he'd just ended a relationship that was built on the rock of Bob. His girlfriend Caroline and he had, at the end, been united on one thing, Bob was still God. But they had to split up the albums.

Chris' devotion to Bob was unequalled in my eyes. Sure, he was eccentric anyway, but going every night to a series of Bobshows, keeping all the reviews for the albums neatly pressed inside the album sleeves, learning all the songs and even becoming vaguely proficient on the harmonica?

embarrassing, getting up in front of some girl you fancied and playing 'Don't Think Twice, It's Alright'."

How did you get into Bob?
"I think it was just my age. In the early '70s there was nothing going on and by the time punk happened I was just completely into Dylan.

"My biggest Dylan phase was in 1974 when 'Blood On The Tracks' came out. That was just the most amazing, personal thing with 'Idiot Wind', 'Tangled Up In Blue'. It was just fantastic. It,s just such a moving record. It's just beautiful and it summed up the break up of a relationship. That was an amazing feeling, it was like a knock-on effect and I know a lot of people who felt that."

"I really like 'Time Out Of Mind' but it

"I think Dylan just runs through every emotion possible, which I think can be a great help or even a hindrance to things."

no wallets, we could have given up, but we carried on for the next night's show in Brighton where he played what was, by common consent, the best show of the year. It was quite amazing as well because at the end he actually spoke. It was like a call to arms, he announced that 'We gotta go now, we got things to do, places to be'. It was such a relief after such a monosyllabic few years, it really re-engaged my interest in Bob Dylan."

So, is this a craving that's ever-present, something that sits with you like a tousled-haired tattoo?
"I would have to say that Bob Dylan is a dish too rich for me. I go through long periods of just not listening to him, maybe for six months. Then there'll be an overwhelming urge to go back to it and I get into it big time. I listen to it constantly and intently, then I find myself getting wrapped up in it too much and it's taking over a bit. Affecting my attitude to life, people, the future. Then I have to go onto lighter fare. It's not a conscious effort to stop, I just have to slow down."

CHRIS TAYLOR photographer
"I used to busk Bob's back catalogue from this book, *Writings And Drawings*.

"I'd play anything by Bob. All the early ones, everything from 'All Over You, 'Love Minus Zero', you name it. I was a student and I needed money, so I worked my way through Dylan's repertoire, then I'd end up playing at parties.

People would say, go on, you're good at the guitar, play us some Dylan songs. It was really

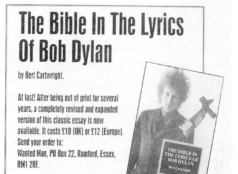

The Bible In The Lyrics Of Bob Dylan

by Bert Cartwright.

At last! After being out of print for several years, a completely revised and expanded version of this classic essay is now available. It costs £10 (UK) or £12 (Europe). Send your order to:
Wanted Man, PO Box 22, Romford, Essex, RM1 2RF.

doesn't have the same qualities as 'Blood On The Tracks'. Maybe it's an age thing and what I was going through when 'Blood On The Tracks' came out. Back then, for me, it was like a first hand experience. The first time his music really moved me and you don,t get another first time around. I met my girlfriend Caroline at college at LCP, it was like a duel sadness. Our relationship was built on the rock of Dylan. If anything she's worse than me.

"Caroline and I met in 1979 and we lived together for ten years. The first time we met, I was standing by a jukebox at college and a Dylan song came on and she was amazed that I knew all the words. We met through that.

"We then moved in together and lived together and it was fantastic. I had a stupid little beard and I'd wander around singing Bob Dylan songs. It was great."

Were you getting guidance for your relationship from Bob Dylan's songs?
"Sadly... yes. I think Dylan just runs through every emotion possible, which I think can be a great help or even a hindrance to things."

So, when you split up was there a Dylan hangover?
"Oh yes. There were tracks that you'd listen to and there were new meanings in every single song. It's the same as when you hear the 'Albert Hall' bootleg in 1966 and Dylan doesn't waste any words. He gives every song a different meaning from what you'd understood on the album. Those sort of things that you get when you listen to something can transcend the meaning of the song and somehow it feels like it was just written for you."

Was there one song that summed up the split for you?
"There were loads of songs. But something like 'Mama You've Been On My Mind'. That was fantastically poignant. It summed it up really."

Can you listen to it now?
"Yeah. But you can still feel the pain and sorrow that he's feeling."

CAROLINE GRIMSHAW

"When I first met Chris I was really taken aback. Here was a man who invited me to his flat, where he sat and sang and played the whole of the 'Desire' album. I'd never experienced anything like that before.

"Our relationship was quite odd. We listened to Dylan constantly and I remember, after a while, that I was looking to his songs to tell me what to do. At one time I had a job interview for a magazine called The Hit and I couldn't decide if I should do it or not. I looked at the front cover of the magazine with Paul Weller on it, wearing boxing gloves around his neck, and I just thought, 'No! Bob Dylan wouldn't do that'. Bob would despise this magazine. I didn't take the job.

"When Chris and I split up, I didn't have too much time to feel what was going on because I moved straight into a relationship with Adrian Deevoy and, at the time he was trying desperately to interview Dylan for Q in the States. I was getting letters from Adrian telling me about what was going on and I felt like I was getting closer to Dylan rather than moving away from him. And, after Adrian had done the interview, I could listen to Dylan talking on a tape and see the faxes he was sending to Adrian. I'd moved from liking Dylan to almost being in the same room as him."

Bob's penchant for marriage guidance almost took off in the UK student community

Everything that the budding Dylanologist needs. Explained. Pontificated over and reviewed...

IF THE Dylan fan seems eccentric, a bit obsessive and slightly prone to talking about Bob Dylan quite a bit, then that's fine, if you've got the feeling and you're still searching for the perfect place to tap into the fountain of Bob, you will always come across people who are more mad keen than you. At least there's always someone there to talk to.

Yes. There are those who are plugged in on full power. Insiders, without being accepted, into the intuitive meaning of the bard. These people aren't interested in 'Wiggle, Wiggle', well who is, they are the analysts that failed biology, the academics who construe Bob themselves. They are the disciples. It's like a release for them. I'm sure you've met some of them on your travels.

BARRY O'BRIEN
Dylan-scarred sufferer from Reading

"When I was at college, 'Live At Budokan' was pivotal but the only album that did it for me was the first 'Greatest Hits', which I always heard when I went to my cousins' house. They were all older than me, three, four and five years and their influence got me into a few tracks. I think I actually bought it because I began to feel guilty because I didn't have anything by Dylan in my collection. I suppose, my Dylan fixation just failed to materialise.

"And my inadequacy with Bob became even more apparent as I went through life. I was certainly primed by my cousins but when I found myself surrounded by Dylanologists it was hard to take.

"There was even one guy who I worked with who successfully brow-beat his parents into going to see Bob with him. I couldn't understand his level of devotion, it all seemed a touch unconvincing to me."

PARENTS AT gigs? Surely he's gone too far. What the hell does that achieve? These are sick people. People who lurk beneath the subculture and think that the original fanzines - *The Telegraph, Isis, Wicked Messenger, Diginty* et al - are too tame. Too mainstream. They probably think that the only fair point of view is one that's immediately counter-claimed. Polar opposites attract and if a word can be spelt or interpreted in different ways, it stands to reason that there'll be two Dylan fans arguing the toss of which way the toss should be tossed.

RUTH FARRAR,
The Case Against Sad Eyed Lady Of The Lowlands, greatly abridged from Dignity 16

"It's about four hours long. Every time I hear it, it's longer. The tune is a serious weakness in a seriously weak song. The words are utter rubbish.

"What the hell is 'A sad-eyed lady of the lowlands, a streetcar vision, a geranium kiss, a warehouse eye, a face like glass, a cowboy mouth...'?"

NICOLA MENICACCI,
Sad-Eyed Lady Of The Lowlands, Symbolism And Poetry, greatly abridged from Dignity 16

"Like Shakespeare's dark lady, Dylan's sad-eyed one is a great source of inspiration. From the first line the song reveals its deep symbolism. The lady has eyes like smoke and her prayers are rhymes, the cross is made of silver the lady's voice is like chimes, all of these lines are highly symbolic. The poetic structure owes much to Walt Whitman in the way the stanzas are structured in long sentences, lines beginning with prepositions, the verb at the end of the sentence."

THE CHURCH Of Dylanology is based two blocks away from Desolation Row. And Dylanologists are now able to do degrees in their chosen subject. And strangely enough, these are the people who weren't expelled for writing a poem on their maths paper.

To give this some balance, I must take a second to note my father's great input into my career in music journalism, record producing, label running, gig promoting and failed pop-starring. While worrying over my spots and listening to Neil Young bellowing from the lathe-like mono record player in my bedroom my dad would often stride into my room, sending the arm of the record player skipping across my copy of 'Everybody Knows This Is Nowhere'. Inevitably he'd ask me to turn it down, but he'd always conclude the conversation, after I'd quipped that it's so hard to hear it in Braille, that I'd "never get anywhere by listening to music'." (Of course, he was absolutely right, I'm still in the bedroom with the stereo on.)

If he'd have known that one of the "blokes with hair" that I was listening to was up for the Nobel Prize, that doctorates of Literature were written about him, indeed that degrees could be spun out on his lyrics, then it might have been a different story. But, then again...

DAVID ROBINSON,
Conclusions On The Wall, from his degree dissertation reprinted in Dignity 16.

"'Ballad Of A Thin Man' is not the only song that could be interpreted as having a homosexual undercurrent. One only has to look at the amount of his songs that mention the word 'Queens': 'Queen Jane, Queen Mary, the Queen Of Spades, 'ye gifted Kings and Queens' and of course, 'The motorcycle black madonna two-wheeled gypsy-Queen' from 'Gates Of Eden'. 'Temporary Like Achilles' from 'Blonde On Blonde' contains the lines "He's pointing at the sky, An' he's hungry like a man in drag". The phallic insinuations of "He's pointing at the sky" are accentuated by the refrain in the chorus, "Honey, why are you so hard?" Transvestites or cross-dressers also appear in 'Bob Dylan's 115th Dream'. "The waitress he was handsome, He wore a powder blue cape'.

"Michael Gray makes the rather dubious claim that 'Just Like A Woman' is Dylan's "most homosexual statement" as "none of the description of 'woman' in the song is about real femininity". He goes on to claim that if the song were about a woman it would be an "uncharacteristically bad song from Dylan". Here though, I think Gray's tenuous interpretation stretches the boundaries of credibility a little too far, and misses the true irony of the lyric."

SO, WHAT does Dylan think about all this pontification? This star adoration. Let the ultimate Dylanologist, AJ Weberman explain as he deconstructs 'Desolation Row' to illustrate just how much Bob likes being a star.

JOHN ROBERTS/AJ WEBERMAN
from Roping Off The Madman's Corner This is how Dylan ends 'Desolation Row', by addressing his fans who live there...

"Yes, I received your letter yesterday
(Dylan confirms the arrival of their fan mail)

About the time the doorknob broke
(And puts down its trivial content)

When you asked how I was doing Was that some kind of joke?
(If his fans had been digging his pessimistic lyrics they wouldn't have to ask if he was happy)

All these people that you mention Yes, I know

them, they're quite lame
(He goes on to explain that he sees the inhabitants of Desolation Row as greedy, revolting squares...)

**I had to re-arrange their faces
And give them all another name**
(...And because of this he had to represent them all symbolically in his poetry)

**Right now, I can't read so good Don't send me no letters, no Not unless you mail them
From Desolation Row**
(Dylan ends by telling his fans that they ought to cool the letters until they see America the way that he sees it)

IT'S ALL got a little hi-brow. My 'O' Level English Language and Literature and the inevitable Art degree are out of kilter in such rich surroundings and hey, haven't we just got some way away from the thing that got me involved in this in the first place? The music?

There's too much reading between the lines already and not enough, 'Hey! Wow! Did you hear that song by The Mississippi Sheiks? Or that cool New Lost City Ramblers' compilation? If the fans and the infatuated turned the fanzine world into a centre for advanced study, then the ever-multiplying internet generation simply enlarged the classes.

Out there in space, no-one can hear you scream. There's an analytical insight into Bob that's unmatched up there. There are web sites that explain every character in every song. There are web sites that list all the albums, all the set lists, just all that stuff.

There's even a site that lists every Dylan song and when it was last played live. It's fascinating stuff, the tote love it. The numerical graphology of it all may look like a form sheet, but you can't help but it's pretty intriguing.

You can't help but peruse and say, 'Ooooh', or even 'Aaaah.' You've just got to analyse it in your own way.

The intriguing thing for me was a per album perm of songs that had never been played live. Were these the real stinkers? Just the fillers? Or maybe they were too difficult. Knowing Bob's reputation for dropping his band in it at the drop of a wink, it's maybe only a

matter of time before some of them actually do get an airing. But, as 1999 rolls on, let's look at the contenders and remember, we have to make allowances for 'Ballad In Plain D', which was possibly played once in 64 but no tapes can corroborate this and 'Lily, Rosemary And The Jack Of Hearts' from 'Blood On The Tracks' which might possibly have been knocked out once in '76. And the same goes for 'Black Diamond Bay' from 'Desire' which is a maybe again, from '76. Obviously. So, by album...

BOB DYLAN
She's No Good
THE FREEWHEELIN' BOB DYLAN
Down The Highway, Bob Dylan's Blues, I Shall Be Free
ANOTHER SIDE OF BOB DYLAN
Black Crow Blues, I Shall Be Free No 10, Motorpsycho Nitemare
BRINGING IT ALL BACK HOME
Outlaw Blues, On The Road Again
BLONDE ON BLONDE
Temporary Like Achilles, Sad-Eyed Lady Of The Lowlands
JOHN WESLEY HARDING
John Wesley Harding, I Am A Lonesome Hobo, Down Along The Cove
NASHVILLE SKYLINE
Nashville Skyline Rag, Peggy Day, Tell Me That It Isn't True, Country Pie
NEW MORNING
Time Passes Slowly, Went To See The Gypsy, Winterlude, If Dogs Run Free, Sign On The Window, One More Weekend, Three Angels, Father Of Night
PAT GARRETT & BILLY THE KID
nothing played live at all, except for 'Watching The River Flow'
PLANET WAVES
On A Night Like This, Dirge, Never Say Goodbye
BLOOD ON THE TRACKS
Meet Me In The Morning
STREET-LEGAL
New Pony, No Time To Think
SHOT OF LOVE
Property Of Jesus
INFIDELS
Sweetheart Like You, Neighbourhood Bully, Don't Fall Apart On Me Tonight
EMPIRE BURLESQUE
Something's Burning, Baby
KNOCKED OUT LOADED
You Wanna Ramble, They Killed Him, Maybe Someday,

Under Your Spell
DOWN IN THE GROOVE
Let's Stick Together, Ugliest Girl In The World, Ninety Miles An Hour
UNDER THE RED SKY
10,000 Men, Handy Dandy
TIME OUT OF MIND
Dirt Road Blues, Standing in the Doorway, Tryin to Get to Heaven, Highlands

WHAT CAN we deduce from that? 'New Morning' - shit album? Too painful to work into the set. Too verbose for his throat these days? Written in a haze of post-motorcycle fumes? Who knows?

The internet is rife with this stuff and, the more you read about Bob the more you become accustomed to his list-value - whether it be the collectible price of 'En Roue Libre... Bob Dylan', that's French for 'Freewheelin', or just the finite details of the songs that mention Bob Dylan which, quite plainly someone has spent many a late night finding, then writing down, then launching into virtual Bobspace. It's just fascinating stuff. Where else could you discover that

BEFORE THE floating mothership became all-consuming and information-heavy there were just fanzines and the network of people who ran them nurtured debate, desire and incisive information about Bob. They were in some cases rather heavy-going, suitably under-inked when being printed and designed by people who were short of a good ruler.

The Telegraph, which launched in 1981 was quite different. For one thing it was designed by the same person who "did" *Q*, *Empire*, *Mojo* and, believe it or not, *Trout Fisherman*. Andy Cowles had met up with *The Telegraph*'s John Bauldie when they both worked on Q magazine and Bauldie's influence on all around him at the magazine and the clarity of his thinking on Dylan was nothing short of impressive. No-one at *Q* could remain unaffected.

ANDREW COLLINS *former editor of Q*
"I had a pet rabbit called Dylan when I was a kid. I'd dearly love to tell you that it was named after Bob, but in fact it was named after Dylan the rabbit off *The Magic Roundabout*. The

Northampton Goth like myself, introduced me to the delights of The Byrds. I taped 'Mr Tambourine Man' off him. While working for the *NME* in the late '80s and early '90s, a place not especially big on Dylan during the Acid House years, I was sent to interview indie janglers The Sundays, and, charmed by their bun-haired singer Harriet Wheeler, felt compelled to seek out the Dylan track 'Corrina, Corrina' which, she revealed, her father used to sing to her as a kid. For research, I bought the CD of 'Freewheelin'. I had finally entered the world of Bob Dylan, albeit in a roundabout way. A magic roundabout way.

"But it was no great epiphany. 'Corrina, Corrina' was sweet, and I discovered that I already knew 'The Times They Are A-Changin' (blimey, hadn't my Emerson Lake & Palmer-digging schoolfriend Matthew Allen played it on an acoustic at some lower sixth form concert?), but my kaleidoscopic journey into the heart of Bobness stalled right there. So

" I became very taken with a comic rendition of 'Subterranean Homesick Blues' by Jools Holland, but made no effort to seek out the original. "

The Animals' 'The Story Of Bo Diddley' featured the immortal lines "So he pulled his hat down over his eyes, and headed out for those western skies, I think Bob Dylan said that", or that Pete Atkin's 'Uncle Sea-Bird' fondly summed up Dylan as "a snot nosed kid called Zimmerman was looking for a new surname to scan Uncle Sea-Bird filled his lungs with hash, and Weberman he muttered in a flash."

Maybe we all recall The Beastie Boys' immortal "I'm just chillin', like Bob Dylan." from Three Minute Rule' but who would spare a thought for Bob Doldrum's 'I Am The Way' as he hollers "I changed my name to Zimmerman just to fool the cops."?

Obviously, you'd suspect that Donovan would be there with a Bobline and on 'The Trip' he doesn't disappoint with "Bob Dylan he sat as the mad hatter broken hour glass in his hand.", while the real music fan can certainly identify with (and here's that Marc Bolan connection in full, I suspect) T Rex's 'Telegram Sam' and its enthusiastic croon "Bobby's all right, Bobby's all right, he's a natural born poet, he's just outasight!"

fact that Dylan the rabbit off *The Magic Roundabout* was named after Bob Dylan meant nothing to me as a child, and this perfectly illustrates my lifelong relationship with the great man. We've always been one step apart.

"In my pre-teens I loved *The Magic Roundabout*, and the guitar-playing rabbit who said "man". In my teens I loved ' Song For Bob Dylan' on David Bowie's ' Hunky Dory' album, a pretty unequivocal tribute but nevertheless as close as I got to Dylan's music. As an analy-retentive 18-year-old during home video's first wave, I recorded every episode of BBC2's The Young Ones onto Betamax tapes and labelled them carefully. On repeated viewings I became very taken with a semi-comic rendition of 'Subterranean Homesick Blues' by Jools Holland. I knew it was a Bob Dylan song, but made no effort to seek out the original. At college, a new mate called Rob, who had far more catholic musical tastes than a

where's all this going? Two words: John Bauldie.

"There can be few Dylan fans who don't know John's name, even cherish it for all the words he's written in the name of the common cause of Bob, be they in book, magazine, newspaper or *The Telegraph*.

"When I started work at *Q* magazine in October 1993 as features editor, I knew John Bauldie only as an office legend whose steadfast, no-nonsense reputation and unbeatable "Bobcat" credentials preceded him. After a few months it became clear that he exerted a presence and influence at *Q* that far exceeded his job description (a freelance, he quietly sub-edited under the jurisdiction of the production editor and edited the Systems hardware section). To a non-Dylan touchee like me, John Bauldie *was* Bob's earthly representative nothing less, and one Bob should've been proud of. John was so steeped in Dylan, he seemed to have no time for any

Bob circa Don't Look Back: Setting the format for rock movies and fully educational in how to handle departing girl-friends and intrusive press

other musician except maybe Bert Jansch and Tim Hardin (well, there was an awful lot of Dylan to get steeped in, and unlike other relics from the '60s and '70s beloved of the greyer *Q* staff, he was ongoing). Through my relationship with John, at first professional, but as time passed, something jollier than that, I grew closer to the previously elusive Bob Dylan. Know Bauldie, know Dylan.

"The rummage sale of weatherbeaten CDs that ingloriously formed the *Q* office collection contained one Dylan album, 'Nashville Skyline' and I even stuck it on a few times. Out of choice. John would ritually hand round the new issue of *The Telegraph* when it was done to his staff colleagues, humbly placing one on our desks, and we would each ritually cry, "Who's on the cover, John?" It got a smile every time. Unlike Bob, John was not as grumpy as he liked to make out.

"The rest of us would secretly marvel at the fact that John and his girlfriend Penny had two flats, one to live in and one for his Dylan archive. True love.

"We would relish displays of John's barely-concealed contempt for other prominent Dylanologists (especially Americans): a stoically Northern 'tut' identical to his reaction when some crazy modern beatbox sounds blared from the *Q* hi-fi, at which without fail the disapproving Bauldie would make some crack about something coming through on the fax machine.

"It was John Bauldie's quiet self-assurance that he and he alone knew what made Bob Dylan tick, and his coach-booking Dylan's Travel Agent zeal, that endeared him to the lot of us as we gently mocked (and secretly respected) his obsession. He made your own devotion to a band or singer seem frivolous and half-hearted. The darkest of rumours went around that it was Bauldie who, from the sub's desk, had deliberately sabotaged Adrian Deevoy's fine Dylan exclusive for *Q*, piqued that his own finest hour had passed him by. It was both hard to believe of a man so gentle, and easy. Let's hope the hipsters who are gradually re-manning *Q* for the 21st century have also heard of "the great Bauldini", one or two actually will remember the shockwaves wrought by his cruel, premature death, and, more light-heartedly, still refer to the heretic office practice of making a single cup of tea for

yourself as "doing a Bauldie", but I doubt they have The Dylan Conundrum in the office any more.

"The question "Would we spike a cover story to make way for Bob Dylan if he died?" hung over our every editorial move in those far-off days of the late mid-'90s. But Dylan keeps going, as does John Bauldie's memory, itself on a never-ending tour of our heads.

"I once had a professional exterminator round to see to a wasp's nest in our loft, and after just 20 minutes in the company of a man in *Ghostbusters* overalls who clearly loved bees and wasps' I came away with not only a greater understanding of our buzzing brethren, but an immovable sense of respect. I was fortunate enough to spend almost four working years with John Bauldie, and am proud to say that if I had a rabbit now, I'd name it Dylan after Dylan, and not Dylan. John Bauldie did that."

IN 1981, the first issue of *The Telegraph* had been published with a front-page illustrated by a hand-written letter from Nigel Hinton, which divulged - "...that's the odd thing about Dylan: he reduces me almost to the level of screaming groupie, anxious for details about what he eats for breakfast and for the latest photograph of him and, at the same time, inspires me to a contemplation of the most crucial questions about Life and Art."

And it's that kind of fan enthusiasm that the magazine encouraged with its many in-depth interviews with the people who'd spent their time in and around the world of Bob. Bauldie let the magazine and the writers run with it and the result was more often than not completely captivating. Just a scan at the Letters pages showed the devotion and concerns of the average Bobfan. Only here could they ask and get an answer to those "difficult" questions...

DEAR TELEGRAPH
I just heard about 'The Times They Are A-Changin' being used in a television advert for accountants...

DEAR TELEGRAPH
In reply to Paul Emma's letter in the last Telegraph, I fear that Paul is suffering from Dylanic Bulima...

DEAR TELEGRAPH
I read with interest John Way's article on the origins of the 'World Gone Wrong' songs...

DEAR TELEGRAPH
You describe Dylan fans as "mainly solitary rather than social creatures" and give a rather pathetic scenario of us "all alone with our tapes"...

DEAR TELEGRAPH
I don't know where Bob stands spiritually and don't presume to, that doesn't mean that I don't care though...

DEAR TELEGRAPH
Can I be the umpteenth to point out that 'Blowin' In The Wind' on the Baez box set is from Fort Collins 1976, not Forest Hills 1963...

DEAR TELEGRAPH
As a guitar player, I find it hard to suss out what chords, tunings and keys Dylan has used in the past...

DEAR TELEGRAPH
Dylan has surprised us all, particularly over the last six or seven years by playing live songs we never thought he would...

DEAR TELEGRAPH
I believe that everyone has the right to their own opinion and as such I am not a frequent writer to The Telegraph, but...

DEAR TELEGRAPH
Regarding the suede jacket that Dylan wears on the cover of 'Freewheelin' that was "lost somewhere along the line"...

OUTSIDE OF the jurisdiction of analysis and sheer fandom, there are other elements co-existing in Bob's world. People feel that Bob is more than human beyond normal rules and the everyday confines of life. He may be able to touch the Bob-afflicted but has he also, in turn, been touched by a spirit even bigger than him?

SEAN CASTEEL
Taken from Bob Dylan And A Possible UFO Connection, via the internet

There have been innumerable attempts in the past to see past the artistic guise of Bob Dylan, I am here to suggest an explanation that has, to my knowledge, never been previously offered - UFO contact. I base this on a fairly rigorous study of UFO interaction with humans and a listeners fascination with Bob Dylan that I began as a 12-year-old in 1970.

When I first heard the song '1,000 Men' from the 'Under The Red Sky' album, I was struck by the appropriateness of the line '1,000 women in my room Spilling my buttermilk, Sweeping it up with a broom'. Using 'Buttermilk' as a euphemism, Dylan gives us a straightforward account of a sperm sample being taken. Even the female nature of his alien attending physicians squares with many other UFO abduction accounts in which human subjects are matched with aliens of the opposite sex.

One of the most important aspects of Dylan's body of work is obviously his social conscience, his concern for all human beings and their right to various personal and political freedoms as well as a very healthy dose of the fear of God-like and Old Testament prophet's sense of reverent social criticism. Here again Dylan has very much in common with a UFO "experiencer", as they are now sometimes called.

Abductees are often shown a holographic image of the world on fire which imprints on them permanently an apocalyptic sense of the immediate future that tends to manifest itself in increased spirituality and implants the notion of unselfish devotion to their fellow man.

Is this a possible explanation for Dylan's extremely moralistic social and political stance and his dire warnings of doom through decadence and unrestrained wickedness?

"The farmers and the business men, they all did decide, To show you where the dead angels are that they used to hide..."

Although that line dates from 1966, 'Sad Eyed Lady Of The Lowlands', it seems a fairly good summation of the now famous Roswell Incident, in which a New Mexico farmer reported finding a crashed disk with the bodies of dead aliens strewn nearby. The "dead angels" were subsequently covered up by the military and the whole incident was said to consist of nothing more than a downed weather balloon.

Dylan's subconscious mind was somehow directed to write a neat little summary of the incident in rhyme nearly 13 years before the public knew anything about it.

The experience that Dylan had in his house in 1978 or 79 in which he was alone and experienced a 'presence' that was rattling his windows and trying o communicate was also a possible incidence of UFO contact. Dylan interpreted what happened as a message from Jesus Christ that he should convert officially to Christianity, which Dylan did.

So, did Dylan ever comment directly on UFO's? In Robert Shelton's biography on Dylan, No Direction Home, Dylan is quoted as saying, "The '60s were like a UFO landing. A lot of people heard about it, but very few actually saw it'. His reference is made in passing as an intended joke, but it may yet prove to be the tip of an iceberg buried deeply in the nearly infinitely complex unconscious memory of Dylan.

If it is true that the aliens behind the UFO phenomenon are here on earth seeking a "chosen few", who could begrudge them their choice of Bob Dylan as a human specimen deserving of their special care and attention?

Pat Kahnke
Taken from What Would Jesus Say to Bob Dylan?, via the internet

A Message given at Hope Community Church, Minneapolis. For His Glory and our joy!

So there I was about eleven years ago. I had just heard the best news of my life: The "Man Himself," Bob Dylan, was coming to town!

Jane walked in the room just after I heard it on the radio and found me sprawled out on my knees looking up into the sky with my arms thrashing around in delight. "Yes! Yes! Yessssss! He's commmmmiiiiiiiiiiiiiiiinnnnng! Yessssssssss!!!!!"

I don't remember being quite that excited about anything before or since, but this was special. I had worshipped Bob Dylan for years, and I was finally going to get to see him in the flesh. Maybe I would get close enough to see him grimace as he tore into 'It's Alright Ma, I'm Only Bleeding' or maybe get sprinkled with some of his sweat as he ripped through 'All Along The Watchtower'. I mean, this was big. The "Man Himself!"

Bob Dylan has been, for myself when I was younger and for many others, an object of worship - and that's not a good thing. I need to worship someone.

Hear that, please: I need to worship someone. That's how I've been created and that's how you've been created. Unfortunately for myself, Bob Dylan fulfilled that need for a time. I propped him on his wobbly pedestal and worshipped him, because I needed someone to worship.

Unfortunately for Bob, many people have used him in this manner. I found a recent quote from Mark Knopfler in which he said, "I've always felt protective of Bob. The first time I met him I felt like putting my arm around his shoulders because...I think he's always had a difficult life, being deified virtually since he was a kid."

It's not easy being God. People expect you to do the God thing their way, and if you try to change at all, you get ripped to pieces. "You can't change. You're my God! If you change, where am I supposed to go?" That's happened

"**I need to worship someone. Unfortunately for myself, Bob Dylan fulfilled that need for a time...**"

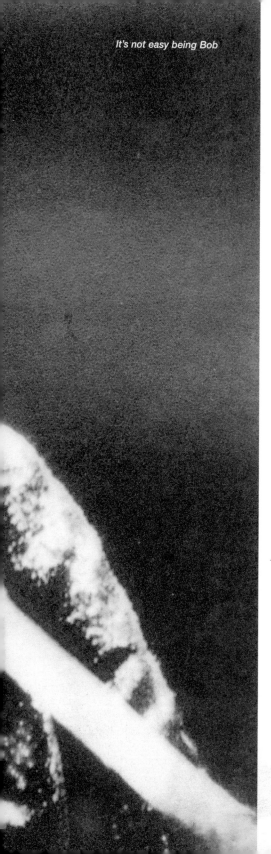

to Bob Dylan his whole life. I read an interview with him recently where the questioner, Ellen Futterman, asked him if he's comfortable after three decades of being a living legend. His response was, "I try to be an illuminated person. Nobody should put anyone on a pedestal - it really can damage a person's mentality and lead to ignorance. At that point, a person ceases to be a person." Now, that's not entirely comprehensible, but I think you get the point that he's been dealing with this issue for a long time.

I have only within the past few years begun to give to scripture the same respect that I gave to the words of Bob Dylan. But let me tell you this: God in His mercy, has made it easier for us to get to know Him.

I should tell you what I think Jesus would say to Bob Dylan. I don't claim to know this with any authority but I can take a stab at it.

for me, as I sat and watched one of my false gods being tossed off the flimsy pedestal I had constructed, the way was being cleared for me to more fully worship the true God, through His Son, Jesus Christ.

WHATEVER YOUR VIEW ON BOB Dylan. Whether you believe he's at the heart of matters or still rebelling against the system, his powers of persuasion are as potent today as they were back in the '60s and '70s. Yes, even after the dubious albums, the lacklustre live shows, the crazy dancing, the re-release of Hearts Of Fire on video, he still commands high regard and spans the generations with his ability to provide a "difference" for emerging revolutionaries to be angry against or about. Nothing's changed. There are kids locked in their bedrooms now attempting to be anarchistic in their musical tastes, much in the same way that people who first encountered 'Highway 61 Revisited' were. That experience is timeless...

> ## "I have only within the past few years begun to give to scripture the same respect that I gave to the words of **Bob Dylan.**"

First, I think he'd say, "Bob, I've gotta tell you, man. I really loved 'Gotta Serve Somebody'.

Then maybe he'd say "Bob, we've known each other a long time now. I know your hurts, your disappointments, your sin. I know every time you've fallen short and I know every time you've called upon me to help you through. Please know this: I, for one, don't expect you to be God. My relationship with you is not based upon how well you perform or how well you fill my emptiness, because I have no emptiness. In fact, I'm overflowing. Worship Me."

I still like Bob Dylan, obviously, but it's different now. I don't look to him for my salvation or for the source of meaning in my life. I like him for what he is, a human being whom, for some reason, I can relate to on a level that resonates within me in a meaningful way. I don't know what Bob was thinking that night on stage - I hope that he was worshipping God in the best way that he knows how, but I do know this. As painful as that experience was

JOHN HARRIS

"My whole formative musical experience centre around the records I borrowed from Wilmslow Library. I was about 11-years old and obviously records are prohibitively expensive then. At the time, libraries seemed to be well-funded and they were staffed by ex-hippies who bought racks and racks of records to cheat the system.

"Bob Dylan was in fact pretty normal by comparison to most of the stuff at Wilmslow - the racks were breaking with stuff by people like Quicksilver Messenger Service, Captain Cody and there was lots of Santana. That was where I first heard all the Beatles, Stones and Bob Dylan records. "Also in the library they had a load of sheet music and I used to get stuff out and teach myself on the guitar which I was learning at secondary school.

"By then I had a Bob Dylan fixation, I thought he was the next thing on from The

157

Beatles. I thought he made me even more of a beatnik than being a Beatles fan did. I thought liking Bob Dylan was sailing close to the intellectual edge. I'd also borrowed a book of Rolling Stone articles on Dylan called *Knockin' On Dylan's Door*, which must have made absolutely no sense to me at all. I remember thinking that he wasn't that good because the book said that he was into astrology. But the book looked cool just to carry around.

"So, anyway, I borrowed the sheet music for 'Highway 61 Revisited'. The next challenge was to build some kind of harmonica holder to wrap around my head so that I could look authentically Dylan in the small folk club that was, in fact, my bedroom. I went to my parent's bedroom and got a coat hanger and untwined the hook wrapped it around my neck, bent it up to make two struts and miracle, on miracles,

"Even as a punk growing up in Middle England in the mid-'70s I was aware of Bob Dylan. He'd come back from the brink. He'd delivered the pain of 'Blood On The Tracks' and the glorious 'Desire'. Posters of him adorned elder brothers' bedrooms wherever I went. And those elder brothers told me about him at length, while explaining that punk was little more than a flash in the pan and not really music. It seemed older people at parties or in the local needed little encouragement before breaking into 'Blowin' In The Wind'. Slow dances at the village disco were inevitably conducted to 'Lay Lady Lay', perfect if only for innuendo alone. I was dismissive of the man. If only I'd realised he was the first real punk.

"Natural selection dictated that I was steered away from subsequent punk movements, finding solace in the dark sounds of Joy Division. Amazingly, I still had a steady

dumbfounded by Bob,s decline into religion the gospel backing singers and his lack of cool. But the pre-God Bob provided much excitement and, albums bought, I soon succumbed to reading all the books.

"Over the next 15 years musical genres came and went with alarming regularity.

Being young and naive I fell for most of them, neglecting Bob in the process.

Ska, Two Tone, Acid House, New Romanticism, Cowpunk, Roots Rock (American) Electro, Hip Hop, Baggy, Madchester, Shoegazing, Britpop, it all seemed perfectly right at the time. They took up all my time and, apart from a brief relationship with 'Infidels', I was praying at the church of the inconsequential. I sincerely lacked salvation.

"I'm sure my life as a fashion victim had no bearing on Bob,s decision to make a relevant record again, but from where I was sitting the

"'Like A Rolling Stone', which was the one song that I learnt, was gloriously easy. All it is is C, D minor, F and G, which are very rudimentary guitar chords... they don't even hurt your fingers."

it actually fitted onto the £1.50 Chinese harmonica that I'd bought from the local shop.

"From there it was just plain sailing because 'Like A Rolling Stone', which was the one song that I learnt was gloriously easy. All it is is C, D minor, F and G, which are very rudimentary guitar chords... they don't even hurt your fingers. And I played the harmonica as well, not in any kind of tune, but he didn't seem to be in tune either. I suppose it must have been a bit like hearing 'Like A Rolling Stone' played by a tramp with Jimmy Somerville on vocals."

THE BLUE Peter-styled reshaping of a coat hanger deserves a badge though. Meanwhile, Bob's world-view continues to travel on to a new generation. Does it all still have the same meaning? Perhaps the greatest challenge to Bob's unique stature came in the late '70s punk boom, but Bob rode it out...

SIMON F MORGAN *music fan*

girlfriend who was keen on Bob and indeed his former squeeze Joan Baez. In those days girls were like that.

"In the early days of our relationship 'Street Legal' was a big record for us and, needless to say 'Diamonds And Rust' still brings a tear to the eye today. Unfortunately for Bob and both us Christianity was around the corner and as we crawled into the '80s the last thing a loving couple needed was a belly full of God. So, with the whiff of religion in the air, we did what any self respecting twentysomethings would do, we completely blanked him.

"About that time I was chasing a copy of The Clash's 'Capital Radio' EP and met a guy called Dave Jones who was selling a copy. Bob Dylan was his punk rock, circa '65 to '69 and as our music-based relationship developed I found myself drawn into Bob,s late '60s cool persona.

"Dave taught me well. He too was

coincidence was spooky. As soon as I heard the first seconds of 'Lovesick' I knew it had all finally fallen into place. 'Time Out Of Mind' provided all the answers and the critics even liked it. You could almost hear the credibility rolling back all the way to Hibbing, Minnesota. Bob was back and the irony of his brush with death made his return all the more valuable.

"Bob flooded back into my world and musical maturity soon followed. 'The Basement Tapes' were re-issued in a single duel case, Anthony Scaduto's biography was republished, it all seemed like one masterplan. CP Lee,s small town view of the 1966 tour was touching and real, *Don't Look Back* was stuck in my video for months and I traded appalling Dylan licks and growls with my 16-year old nephew whenever we met up. Weddings, parties, anywhere."

WHILE WRITING THIS BOOK, the most valued opinion on Bob has, quite obviously come from my son Lewis who insists that Bob Dylan is a "cowboy with a guitar".

In a way, after Hank Williams and Woody Guthrie, I guess that's all he ever wanted or possibly intended to be anyway. And, if teenagers are picking up guitars and playing the tunes of Bob with such romanticism (Lewis is only five, mind you) then that can't be a bad thing.

PATRICK *fan from Chicago*

"I have a family reunion every year in upstate New York and every year my Uncle Louie sings songs around the campfire. When I was younger (around 10) he would often pay the song 'I Shall be Free #10' which I thought was absolutely hilarious. I went to the record store with my mom, a Dylan fan in the '60s that kind of lost interest in the '80s, and bought the album she was oh so familiar with, 'Another Side Of Bob Dylan'. From there I collected his first seven albums, up to the big motorcycle crash, and for some reason had a bias against any later music.

"I eventually got past that and started collecting post-crash albums, which was helped by my dad already having many of them. My interest rekindled his and together we have collected all of his official albums and twenty some bootlegs. We both play the guitar and he plays

piano and harmonica and it is a rare occurrence that a little Dylan isn't either being played by one of us or on the CD player around the house. We are complete Dylan junkies, it's a little obsessive but hey, it's music, and more importantly, it's Dylan.

"I am absolutely entranced by Dylan's music. I listen to it constantly, every era from the folk stuff in '61 to his Christian stuff to 'Time Out Of Mind'. I've been to three of his concerts as well.

"I do a lot of boot trading over the internet and have a pretty substantial and wide variety of his studio stuff and concerts. I also have the 'Highway 61' computer game, his book Tarantula, a couple of biographies, and a lot of merchandise; but most importantly... his music. I am also not too shabby on the guitar and like to experiment with his songs.

"Dylan is truly a genius and I can really feel his music. It's not a matter of understanding or analysing with Dylan, its feel. His music has nearly brought me to tears from its beauty. I can feel the heartbreak of his divorce in 'Blood On The Tracks', his faith in 'Saved', and the pure joy in playing American music in the 'Genuine Basement Tapes'."

THE 'GENUINE Basement Tapes'? Obviously one more eclectic than the eventual official release. Enter Greil Marcus's superb book *The Invisible Republic* which treks back to Big Pink. Back to the big old mansion and the sessions that became legendary. Into the world from where at least four double albums of obscure recordings have so far been bootlegged. I've seen them on my travels. I've been tempted.

The 'Tapes' delve deep into Bob and The Band's roots, dusting off the concept of 'The old free America' as first suggested by Beat poet Kenneth Rexroth and recounted in *The Invisible Republic*. They take in Bob's heritage, which is littered with snatch-

es of the roots gems that lay at the cornerstone of sepia-tinted Americana. Greil Marcus wastes no time rolling back the years, from the chance overhearing of Bob strumming 'Something's Happening Every Day' by Sister Rosetta Tharpe, which originally came from 1945, through to the less obvious image of William Burroughs "whittlin' his penis", metaphorically speaking I'm sure.

The 'Tapes' circumnavigate the history of contemporary America, with the renegade troubadours interpreting Gene Pitney's hit 'Baby Ain't That Fine' which nestles next to Pete Seeger's reading of 'The Bells Of Rhymney' and 'Bonnie Ship The Diamond' by his sister Peggy. There are cowboy tunes too. There's Johnny Cash balladeering, and a host of stuff by Ian And Sylvia Tyson. Songs by Blind Lemon Jefferson, Utah Philips, John Lee Hooker and The Carter Family. Everything that law allows... at least the law of averages.

That time under stairs obviously gave Bob and compadres enough space to work through his very reason for performing. They could revisit the heartland of American songwriting at their own pace and decipher its real position in the history of music. Surely this was the secret of Bob. This is what it's all about. I remembered when I spoke to Danny Kelly about the Great Music Experience in Japan, he declared that there were but two people who have fundamentally changed popular music.

"The first is George Gershwin, the second was Bob Dylan." He's not wrong.

Afterword

Apple Suckling Time

A COUPLE OF weeks after I thought I'd placed Bob in some kind of context, for myself at least, I was still haunted by him. Just as Bill Prince had described his recurring Dylan affliction, I realised that I too was so immersed in Bob that I had to take a breather. A rest stop. I had to somehow turn down the volume.

I was dreaming myself onto the set of *Don't Look Back*. I was enthralled by the lyrics of 'Bob Dylan's Dream'. I was wrestling with the anarchic excitement of The Rolling Thunder Revue. I was hearing Bob songs everywhere. I was wondering how his heart was holding up.

Even when I tried to unwind with a video, there he was nodding his curly mop and curling a chorus. 'Biograph' sleeve note author and budding film director Cameron Crowe had got Dylan to play on the soundtrack of his Tom Cruise blockbuster *Jerry Maguire*. Trent Reznor had edited Bob into the very fabric of his fast-splice score to Oliver Stone's *Natural Born Killers* and the Coen Brothers' stoned soul symphony (with bowling) *The Big Lebowski* had a Dylan moment. 'The Man In Me' rang through with Jeff Bridges and John Goodman looking on. Hazily.

At the same time, in the post, I got a good luck message from Jeremy Mason, along with his book *Images Of Dylan*, a series of paintings based on Bob's lyrics, which included 'She Belongs To Me' (very green and, a bit yellow, in a spherical way) and 'Visions Of Johanna' (abstract, but certainly suggesting a stolen moment captured through a curtain).

I'd also been sent a fanzine called *Bob Dylan And The Cards* by Walter Van Der Paelt. It was fascinating. From 1997, it analysed mentions of the cards (playing, Tarot or otherwise) in 'Sad-Eyed Lady Of The Lowlands', 'I Went To See The Gypsy', 'Changing Of The Guards' and 'No Time To Think'. At first I thought 'No! Nah!', but ended up thinking 'Yeah' or at least 'Maybe'. Did it explain anything? Well...

Was there to be any clarification? Anywhere? Probably not. But his music was still omnipresent. I was surrounded by it. Fine, but, after coming so far... and seeing so much, I was still puzzled about Dylan 'the man'. For instance, why did he spend all of his time on the road? Not for the money, that's for sure. Could that really be the only place he felt safe? The only place he could be secure, as some had opined.

Was it only during the live experience that he began to feel comfortable enough to really express himself? Was that the only stamping ground where he could still break the rules... change the songs and express himself fully. Or was it simply the only environment where he could gain privacy. The last place where he could maintain control. Even under the eye of an adoring, critical or just bemused mass?

MIKE PETERS *Singer/songwriter, ex-Alarm*
"We toured the States with Dylan a few years back. At the time, we were both managed by Elliot Roberts and we stayed at the same hotels. As the tour developed we'd see him every day

at the hotels. He'd always go for a swim. Bob had a fear of air-conditioning, so we weren't at top class hotels, but they were quite funky. Anyway, one day he didn't turn up to go swimming, so I asked Victor (Maimudes. legendary chess roadie) where he was. He said, 'Bob's got a cold, he's staying in his room'.

"The next day, I saw Bob and asked if he was feeling better. There was a bit of a stony silence and the next day I heard Bob had thrown Victor off the tour."

VICTOR MAIMUDES is the same chess roadie who travelled across the States with Bob on a weedathon in the early '60s? The same guy who ordered two whisky's without food when they were holed up in Crouch End. He'd gone the nine yards with Dylan. And for a moment's indiscretion, he was gone. Like that. He'd crossed the line? Spoken out of turn? For him the Bob-a-thon drew to a very abrupt halt.

Dylan gets so deep under the skin, snakes his way into your subconscious with every lasting melody, with each piece of succinctly-aimed wordplay, it's hard to shake free. You can't leave it alone. And when you hear that telling rhyme on the radio - whether it's by some obscure American punk band or, indeed, Barbara Dickson, it breaks the musical barrier and sucks you back to Planet Bob. And there Bob's in control.

Without a doubt, that's where I was. Downtown Planet Bob. I was still trawling the junk shops for epic sounds, checking things out for a direct line to Bob.

The Brothers And Sisters' Gospel covers of Bob Dylan with a suitably eclectic sleeve

I found Fiona Flannagan's soundtrack single for *Hearts Of Fire*. Hardly an epic. Not even featuring Bob, but with a tiny Dylan pic from the film on the reverse of the sleeve.

In HMV, I idly mused through the Joan Baez section - for what reason I'll never know, I don't even really like her voice - but I pulled out 'Baez Plays Dylan', a compilation of some of the covers of Bob Dylan material she's done over the years. It wasn't as beautifully packaged as her 'Don't Think Twice, It's Alright' EP of 30-plus years earlier, but the Bob legacy was intact.

As I wandered out of the store, Courtney Love's Hole was wading into 'It's All Over Now, Baby Blue', an extra track on her 'Malibu' single. I was being followed. Essence de Bob was everywhere.

Back when I started to think about putting this book together, when I began to sail towards 'Desolation Row' so to speak, I'd just been bemused by 'The Hollies Play Dylan'. It was another music coincidence. On listening it all made perfect sense. I could fully understand why in 1969, it was just about the right time for the Graham Nash-void Hollies to plug into Bob. They picked a dozen classics - including 'When The Ship Comes In', 'Wheels On Fire', 'All I Really Want To Do', 'Just Like A Woman' and 'I Shall Be Released' - and the triple harmonies of Tony Hicks, Allan Clarke and Terry Sylvester took Dylan's songs into a new dimension, kick-starting The Hollies' credibility.

But, where The Hollies had added warmth and understanding to a collection of songs that were already fundamentally familiar, my chance finding of 'Dylan's Gospel' by The Brothers And Sisters - a mere two quid in the basement of a Rare Record Shop in Notting Hill - explained far more about the depth of his writing.

I was initially enticed by the gospel set thinking it might be akin to another of my cheesy faves, a volume of cod-reggae versions of Beatles' songs called 'Yesterday'. But I was so wrong. Stripped of Bob's strumming and nasal twang, the Brothers And Sisters made a truly wondrous sound, a wall of noise that underlined the emotions of such epics as 'The Times They Are A-Changin'', 'My Back Pages' and, of course, 'I Shall Be Released'.

Their interpretation highlighted the conduit that runs from Dylan's inspiration through to a million different people, who sing his songs in the shower. To the poignancy of Tom Robinson's cover of 'I Shall Be Released' which made it a gay anthem and, indeed right to Stevie Wonder's cover of 'Blowin' In The Wind'. Stevie wasn't drumming through the song because it had a pretty tune. The lyric and the finely-paced angst in every line made it bigger than Bob and larger than Motown, an call to arms for all.

While Dylan's lack of interest in interviews and his orchestrated press conferences had just added fuel to the mystery, it also placed the onus on the excitement and the individuality of his songwriting.

While talking to Patrick Humphries, he'd recalled the startled reaction of Dylan biographer Robert Shelton when he'd asked if Bob really did just "knock off some of the songs in five minutes" as legend and ironic interview quip often had it.

"No, no." Shelton replied, "He labours over each of them for days and weeks. He takes it very seriously."

MIKE PETERS

"I remember when we were talking on tour, I just mentioned in conversation that it was amazing how he wrote so many truly moving songs. I said, 'How do you do it?' as a kind of remark and he sat down and began to explain how he did it. The basics, carefully telling me in meticulous detail."

SURE ENOUGH, Bob does take it all seriously. He's a craftsman. He isn't just casting it off

uninterested. He labours his art and the smokescreen around him blurs the mechanics, just leaving those heartstrung melody lines and those incisive insights into life and the state of it all.

In writing this book, I guess that I'd like to have put him into some neat box, professing to have reached deep within and found his personal demons or his motivational reasoning. But I can't. I couldn't. I just opened more boxes and ending up asking more questions of myself.

Trying to make sense of it, I did think back to David Hepworth's theory and observation on Bob. Now, they do hold water...

The Theory

Bob Dylan doesn't give a hoot what anybody thinks about him.

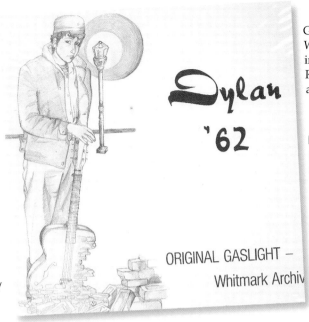

Guthrie, Big Bill Broonzy and Hank Williams. This was the starting point for me into all that, what you might call American Roots music. He pushed me into the weeds and I'm very grateful for that."

Bob Dylan is fast approaching his Sixtieth birthday. I don't know what I think of him anymore. I know I love a lot of his music. I've been moved, emotionally by his lyrics. I've seen humour in places and been fascinated by the hap hazard way he's run his life to the hilt at times. And lived through it all.

Sure, he's been low on quality control at times. He's sold himself short, followed the wrong train... but he's lived his life in public and lived it for lots of people too.

I've talked to those people, been impressed by their honesty. And my view of Bob has matured. I think of him now with the same kind

"This was the starting point for me into what you might call American Roots music. He (Dylan) pushed me into the weeds and I'm very grateful for that."

The Observation

So much of the value of music is going back, not going forward. You've got to admire Bob Dylan saying, "Go back! Listen to Jimmie Rodgers, 1929, that's interesting'."

CERTAINLY, THE observation still resonates. It's been repeated throughout. Dylan's connection to Harry Smith's truly remarkable 1952 roots, folk, country and blues six record collection 'Anthology Of American Music' is well documented. And from there the lineage of American song still flows.

In Greil Marcus's *Invisible Republic*, Harry Smith said of Dylan: "I could really believe in God when I heard Bob Dylan on the radio."

And, on the sleevenotes of the re-issued 'Anthology' Dylan revealed: "Those old songs are my lexicon and my prayer book. All my beliefs come out of those old songs, literally, anything from 'Let Me Rest On That Peaceful Mountain' to 'Keep On The

Sunny Side.' You can find all my philosophy in those old songs. I believe in a God of time and space, but if people ask me about that, my impulse is to point them back toward those songs. I believe in Hank Williams singing 'I Saw The Light'. I've seen the light, too."

ANDY KERSHAW

"Years ago, I was listening to Slade and Gary Glitter and for some reason a second hand copy of 'Highway 61 Revisited' came into my hands and from that point I veered away from the middle of the road and across the margins of folk and country music into the tangled undergrowth of blues and R&B.

"Dylan turned me on to so many other things. I then read one of the many books about him and how Bob, in the isolation of Minnesota had written to Johnny Cash and when he first came to New York and played with John Lee Hooker. Obviously Dylan spoke highly of Woody

of respect as I do someone like John Lee Hooker. Hooker is in his 80s. A legend. He is the Boogie Man. He may be ailing but he has the heart, the soul and the swagger to boot. Bob's sitting on the same bench. He's up there at Gerde's.

If you'd have told me a year ago that I'd be the owner of several Bob Dylan bootlegs I'd have been suitably amused. But, the prospect of listening to 'The Whitmark Recordings', a 12-tracker which contains eight tracks from a 1962 recording at The Gaslight in Greenwich Village, plus four songs from the Whitmark Archive fills me with the kind of goose-pimply excitement reserved for classic vinyl discoveries in unlikely quarters.

Hearing 'Cane On The Brazo', 'Hansome Molly', 'Jon Brown', 'Hollis Brown'. 'See That My Grave Is Kept Clean', 'Cocaine', 'The Cuckoo Is A Pretty Bird', 'Motherless Child', 'Bound To Win', 'Walls Of Redwing', 'Let Me Die In My Footsteps' and 'Eternal Circle' is like entering Bobland. I'm in a different place... touched by the hand of Bob. Of course.

Credit is due

Thanks for their help, contributions, anecdotes and internet intervention (or whatever): Adrian Deevoy, Al Aronowitz, Alan F. Anderson, Dr Allan Simmonds, Andrea Fallesi, Andrew Jorgensen, Andrew Motion, Andrew Collins, Andy Cowles, Andy Kershaw, Anita Rowland, Anthony Scaduto, Barry O'Brien, Ben Fisher, Bernard Doherty, Bill Prince, Blind Boy Derek, Bob Brown, Brent Hansen, Brian Mitchell, Brian Walker, Bruce Robinson, Bruce Springsteen, Carol James, Caroline Grimshaw, Cazzual, Charlie Gillet, Chris Binding, Chris Carr, Chris CP Lee, Chris Taylor, Christopher Ricks, Cliff Warnken, Craig Harris, Cynthia Marie Winkler, Danny Kelly, Dave Stewart, David Blue, David Cohen, David Fricke, David Hepworth, David Lynn, David Robinson, David Swanell, Dennis J Green, Dougie Hamnett, Elizabeth Thompson, Eoin O'Malley, Eyolf, Gary Herman, Ged Doherty, Greil Marcus, Guy Peelaert, Howard Johnson, Howe Gelb, Jacquetta Picton, Jane Graham, Jeff Kramer, Jeff Rosen, Jerry Garcia, Jim Walton, Jimmy Miller, Joan Baez, Joe Boyd, Joel Bernstein, Joey Skaggs, John Bauldie, John Berry, John Harris, John Leckie, John Lee Hooker, John Lennon, John Roberts, John Manning, John Tobler, John Wesley Harding, Johnny Black, Johnny Cash, Karen Bell, Karl Erik, Keith Altham, Keith Butler, Keith Cameron, Keith Hughes, Ken Brooks, Klas Burling, Koli Fyten, Les Crane, Luke Mulhare, Margaret Chin, Mark Ellen, Mark Lewisohn, Martin Pearson, Mat Snow, Matt Carson, Michael Eavis, Michael Fallon, Mike Kaufman, Mike Peake, Mitch Jayne, Mr Spector, Nat Hentoff, Natalie Byrd, Nick Cave, Nick Kohn, Nicola Menicacci, Nora Ephron, Pat Kahnke, Patrick Humphries, Paul Du Noyer, Paul McCartney, Paul J Robbins, Pete Smith, Peter Bennion, Phil Sutcliffe, Philip Norman, Philip Talbot, Rich Webb, Richard J. Maraia, Richard Thompson, Robert Hilburn, Robert Shelton, Robin Jatko, Rodney Dillard, Ruth Farrer, Sean Body, Sean Castell, Sid Griffin, Simon Holland, Simon John, Simon F Morgan, Steve Forbert, Steve Hunt, Steve Malins, Steve Rusk, Stuart Batsford, Stuart Maconie, Susan Edminston, Suzanne Macrae, Teri Lynn, Timothy Michael Ellmore, Tom Payne, Trevor Dann, Trevor Neal, Vic King, Wifrid Mellors, William Shatner

And thanks to my favourite magazines: The Big Untidy, Chicago Daily News, The Daily Telegraph, Le Figaro, The Listener, Mojo, Newsweek, NME, Paris Jour, Pensacola News Journal, Playboy, Q, The Scene, Select, The Sheffield University Paper, Sounds, St. Paul Evening Dispatch, The Telegraph, The Times, The Wicked Messenger

And my favourite weird websites: rec.music.dylan from where Cynthia Marie Winkler coined it for The Adventures Of Bobby Dylweed.

Then there's Ken Brooks at Agenda Limited (Units 1 and 2, Ludgershall Business Park, New Drove, Luggershall, Andover, Hampshire SP11 9RN) for the Edie Sedgwick information. Agenda have lots of neat books about cool icons too.

THE COVER SHOT is a Retna shot by Aaron Rapaport, masterfully photo-shopped by David Black

THE BACK COVER SHOT is a Chris Taylor black and white, shot at Blackbushe in 1978 and again 'shopped' by Black

THE COVER WAS designed by David Black (he did the logo too)

PHOTOGRAPHS

Phil Spector (page 10) is from the Q Archives

Bob Dylan at Blackbushe (page 66) is by Chris Taylor

Bob Dylan at Wembley (page 79) is by Chris Taylor

Bob Dylan at Earl's Court (page 81) is by Chris Taylor

Bob Dylan and Fiona Flannagan at the Hearts Of Fire press conference (page 84) is by Chris Taylor

Bob Dylan at Brixton Academy (page 102) is by Chris Taylor

Bob Dylan at The Great Music Experience (page 108) is from the the Q Archive

Bob Dylan (page 153) is by Photofest/Retna

Bob Dylan and Tom Petty (page 155) is by Aaron Rapaport (Retna)

LYRICS

John Wesley Harding's 'Phil Ochs, Bob Dylan, Steve Goodman, David Blue And Me' is copyright of John Wesley Harding.

CARTOON

God and Bob (page 25) courtesy of NME

Rock 'n Roll Zoo (page 70) by Savage Pencil from the Savlab Archives

PRESS SHOTS courtesy of Columbia Records - page 46, 60, 114, 144, 149, 156.

BOOKS

From the Henderson archives except for Tarantula (page 47), thanks to Chris Taylor.

Rock Dreams cover and clips (page 53) coutesy of Pan Publishing.

Jeremy Mason's Images Of Dylan (page 163) copyright Jeremy Mason.

Bob Dylan And The Cards by Walter Van Der Paelt, through Desolation Row Publishing.

TEAR SHEETS

Eat The Document stills tearsheet (page 50) from Q magazine

Renaldo And Clara news story (page 63) from Sounds

Earls Court queue news story (page 67) from Sounds

My Sexy Nights As A Slave To Bob Dylan (page 87) from The People

Bob Dylan at the Great Music Experience (page 107) from Q magazine

VIDEO GRABS

The Letterman Show with The Plugz (page 80)

Hearts Of Fire press conference (page 88)

Hearts Of Fire film (page 89)

Bob Dylan on the set of Hearts Of Fire (page 124) from BBC Omnibus special.

DIARY EXTRACTS

Johnny Black's exquisite penmanship (page 64)

RECORD, TAPE, CD AND MINI-DISC SLEEVES

Dylan Thomas (Forward) courtesy of Caedmon Literary

Alan Lomax (Foreward) courtesy of Melodisc Records

Pete Seeger (Foreward) courtesy of Ember Records International

'The Anthology Of American Folk Music' (Foreward) courtesy of Folkways/Smithsonain

Bob Dylan Live 1966 (page 12) courtesy of Legacy Records. Photo by Jerry Schatzberg

Woody Guthrie Dustbowl Ballds (page 17) courtesy of Camden/BMG

Bob Dylan (page 20) courtesy of Columbia Records

Carolyn Hester That's My Song (page 20) courtesy of Dot Records

Lord Buckley A Most Immaculately Hip Aristocrat (page 21) courtesy of Straight Records. Photograph by Ed Caraeff

Bob Dylan Mixed Up Confusion (page 22) courtesy of Columbia Records

The Freewheelin' Bob Dylan (page 23) courtesy of Columbia Records.

The Great March On Washington (page 24) courtesy of Gordy Records

The Dillards, Live Almost! (page 26) courtesy of Elektra Records

Bob Dylan The Times They Are A-Changin' (page 27) courtesy of Columbia Records. Photograph by Barry Feinstein

Bob Dylan Another Side Of Bob Dylan (page 28) courtesy of Columbia Records. Photograph by Sandy Speiser

Bob Dylan Bringing It All Back Home (page 32) courtesy of Columbia Records.

Bob Dylan Highway 61 Revisited (page 33) courtesy of Columbia Records. Photograph by Daniel Kramer

Bob Dylan Blonde On Blonde (page 35) courtesy of Columbia Records.

Bob Dylan John Wesley Harding (page 38) courtesy of Columbia Records. Photograph by John Berg.

Bob Dylan Leopard-skin Pillbox Hat (page 38) courtesy of Columbia Records

Manfred Mann The One In The Middle (page 38) courtesy of HMV Records.

Bob Dylan's Greatest Hits (page 38) courtesy of Columbia Records.

The Beatles' Sgt Peppers (page 40) courtesy of EMI Records.

Woody Guthrie Poor Boy (page 40) courtesy of Transatlantic Records. Photograph by Craig Wiethrop.

Bob Dylan Nashville Skyline (page 42) courtesy of Columbia Records.

Easy Rider (page 42) courtesy of Stateside Records.

The Unforgettable Hank Williams (page 44) courtesy of MGM Records.

Bob Dylan Self Portrait (page 46) courtesy of Columbia Records.

Bob Dylan New Morning (page 46) courtesy of Columbia Records.

Earl Scruggs His Family And Friends (page 47) courtesy of Columbia Records.

The Beat Generation (page 48) courtesy of Rhino Records.

More Bob Dylan Greatest Hits (page 48) courtesy of Columbia Records

Pat Garrett And Billy The Kid soundtrack (page 52) courtesy of Columbia Records.

Dylan (page 52) courtesy of Columbia Records.

Bob Dylan Planet Waves (page 55) courtesy of Asylum Records.

Bob Dylan Before The Flood (page 55)

courtesy of Asylum Records.

Bob Dylan Blood On The Tracks (page 57) courtesy of Columbia Records.

Bob Dylan The Basement Tapes (page 58) courtesy of Columbia Records. Photograph by Reid Miles.

Bob Dylan Masterpieces (page 60) courtesy of Columbia Records.

Bob Dylan Desire (page 61) courtesy of Columbia Records.

Bob Dylan Hard Rain (page 61) courtesy of Columbia Records. Photograph by Ken Regan.

Bob Dylan Stuck Inside Of Mobile (page 62) courtesy of Columbia Records.

Bob Dylan Street Legal (page 64) courtesy of Columbia Records.

Bob Dylan At Budokan (page 65) courtesy of Columbia Records.

Bob Dylan Animals single (page 69) courtesy of Columbia Records.

Bob Dylan Slow Train Coming (page 70) courtesy of Columbia Records.

Bob Dylan Shot Of Love (page 75) courtesy of Columbia Records.

Bob Dylan Heart Of Mine single (page 75) courtesy of Columbia Records.

Bob Dylan Hurricane single (page 76) courtesy of Columbia Records.

Bob Dylan Infidels (page 77) courtesy of Columbia Records.

Bob Dylan Union Sundown single (page 77) courtesy of Columbia Records.

Bob Dylan The Groom's Still Waiting (page 77) courtesy of Columbia Records.

Bob Dylan Real Live (page 81) courtesy of Columbia Records.

Bob Dylan Empire Burlesque (page 83) courtesy of Columbia Records.

Bob Dylan Tight Connection single (page 83) courtesy of Columbia Records.

Bob Dylan Biograph (page 84) courtesy of Columbia Records.

Bob Dylan When The Night Comes Falling From The Sky (page 85) courtesy of Columbia Records.

Bob Dylan Knocked Out Loaded (page 88) courtesy of Columbia Records.

Bob Dylan Down In The Groove (page 92) courtesy of Columbia Records.

Bob Dylan Dylan And The Dead (page 94) courtesy of Columbia Records.

Bob Dylan Oh Mercy (page 94) courtesy of Columbia Records.

The Specials Maggie's Farm (page 96) courtesy of Two-Tone Records.

C81 tape (page 96) courtesy of Rough Trade Records.

Bob Dylan Under The Red Sky (page 98) courtesy of Columbia Records. Photo by Camouflage.

Bob Dylan The Bootleg Series 1-3 (page 100) courtesy of Columbia Records.

The Bob Dylan 30The Anniversary Concert (page 101) courtesy of Columbia Records.

Bob Dylan As Good As I Been To You (page 102) courtesy of Columbia Records. Photograph by Jimmy Wachtel.

Bob Dylan World Gone Wrong (page 104) courtesy of Columbia Records. Photographs by Anna Maria Velez.

Bob Dylan Greatest Hits Vol 3 (page 108) courtesy of Columbia Records. Photograph by Ken Regan.

Bob Dylan Unplugged (page 111) courtesy of Columbia Records. Photograph by Frank Micelotta.

Bob Dylan Time Out Of Mind (page 114) courtesy of Columbia Records. Photograph by Daniel Lanois.

Bob Dylan The Best Of Bob Dylan (page 115) courtesy of Columbia Records.

Bob Dylan Live 1966 (page 119) courtesy of Columbia Records.

Bob Dylan Not Dark Yet (page 119) courtesy of Columbia Records.

Joan Baez Any Day Now (page 126) courtesy of Vanguard Records.

Byrds Play Dylan (page 128) courtesy of Columbia Records.

Sebastian Cabot, Actor (page 128) courtesy of Rhino Records.

Waylon Jennings The Country Side Of... (page 129) courtesy of A&M Records.

Mark Spoelestra (page 130) courtesy of Elektra Records.

Spirit Of 76 (page 130) courtesy of Mercyru Records.

Manfred Mann In The Middle Of... (page 130) courtesy of HMV Records.

Joe And Eddie Walkin' The Line (page 130) courtesy of Vogue Records.

The Flying Burrito Bros (page 130) courtesy of A&M Records.

The Rose Garden (page 131) courtesy of Atco records.

Julie Felix Flowers (page 131) courtesy of Fontana Records.

Giant Sand Ballad Of a Thin Line Man (page 132) courtesy of Zippo Records.

Rod Stewart Smiler (page 132) courtesy of Mercury Records.

Ian And Sylvia Nashville (page 133) courtesy of Phonodisc.

Glenn Yaborough Gor Emily... (page 133) courtesy of RCA Records.

Danny And Dusty The Lost Weekend (page 133) courtesy of Prima Records.

Coulson, Dean, McGuinness And Flint Lo And Behold (page 134) courtesy of Charisma Records.

Gene Clark White Light (page 134) courtesy of A&M Records.

Ian And Sylvia Full Circle (page 134) courtesy of MGM Records.

David Blue (page 138) courtesy of Elektra Records.

Nick Cave Murder Ballads (page 141) courtesy of Mute Records.

A Tribute To Jimmie Rodgers (page 142) courtesy of Bluebird/Columbia Records.

Long Ryders Looking For Lewis And Clark (page 144) courtesy of Island Records.

Bob Dylan En Roue Libre (page 147) from the Chris Taylor archive

Sister Rosetta Tharpe (page 159) courtesy of Mercury Records.

The Carter Family.(page 159)courtesy of RCA Records.

The Big Lebowski soundtrack (page 160) courtesy of Mercury Records.

Fiona Flannagan's soundtrack single for Hearts Of Fire (page 161).

Joan Baez Baez Plays Dylan (page 162) courtesy of Ace Records.

Joan Baez Don't Think Twice, It's Alright (page 162) courtesy of Vanguard

The Hollies The Hollies Play Dylan (Page 163) courtesy of Parlophone Records

The Brothers And Sisters Dylan's Gospel (page 164) courtesy of Ode Records.

Bob Dylan The Whitmark Recordings (page 167) source unknown.

PLECTRUM, TICKETS AND MISCELLANY

Courtesy of the Chris Taylor archive.

NOT TO MENTION

Emma, Maia and Lewis.

Gary, Nick and Karen.

Howard, Keith and Chris.

Blackie, Jacquetta and Claire.

Peter, Paul and Mary.

Groucho, Harpo and Chico.

the black book company

box 2030
pewsey
sn9 5qz
england

telephone
+ 44 (0)
7970 783652

fax
+ 44 (0)
1672 564433

email
dhende7730@aol.com

via the internet
www.blackbookco.com

The Black Book Mafia

regular guys
Dave Henderson
07970 783652
Howard Johnson
0976 916319

art guru
Keith Drummond

silent but deadly
Gary Perry
Nick Clode
0171 537 7144

accountingly
Karen Hansell
0171 537 7144

warehoused
Claire Thompson
@ Turnaround Publisher Services
0181 829 3009

"I just got out my little black book the minute that you said goodbye..."

(sort of abridged from Arthur Lee and Love's cover of Bacharach and David's 'My Little Red Book')

So, what's the Black Book Company all about?

Well, we're interested in music. Listening. Searching for interesting unique stuff. Hearing new things. Understanding how people consume music and quite frankly the effect it has on them.

Around the time of the "Punk Rock Wars" at the end of the '70s, the media asked "Can music really change anything?". Well, we at the Black Book Company think it can. We *know* it can. And, our books intend to look at the effect that music has on the fans and the famous.

In *Touched By The Hand Of Bob* and *Get Your Jumbo Jet Out Of My Airport*, we examine the undoubted power of, respectively, Bob Dylan and AC/DC. We reveal the obsessions of fandom and the effect that these heroes have on us, you and whoever.

Each book paints a unique caricature of its subject, by analysing real life experiences, well-researched tales and the inevitable anecdotal pub-talk. Each book looks at the effect that these idols have had on the world, complete with bibliographies, chronological biographies and, of course discographies aplenty.

"Wow! A demo version of The Buzzcocks' 'Spiral Scratch' EP autographed by Howard Devoto. Now, that's what I call sexy!"

"The Black Book Company? Why, I read virtually nothing else when I need to know about music."

This is just the start...

We'll be publishing 12 books over the next three years, cross referencing each title, but possibly not the DC and Bob, using you the readers and your music-related experineces to give a more complete picture of the next projects we undertake. So, read on, look at our publishing schedule and, er, get back to us.

And, this is the team...

DAVE HENDERSON is the Creative Director for the EMAP Metro Music Group, which includes Q, Mojo, Select, Mixmag, Kerrang! and Smash Hits. He writes regularly for Q and publishes his own music magazine called Happenstance.

HOWARD JOHNSON is Associate Editor of Football 365/Music 365. He was the Creative Director for Bizarre magazine and has written for just about everyone about music and sport.

KEITH DRUMMOND is the Art Director of Q Magazine. Formerly art editor of Select, he now rules the Letraset cupboard at the UK music market's biggest selling magazine, with a readership of 750,000-plus.

GARY PERRY and NICK CLODE fix things.

our catalogue items

Touched By The Hand Of Bob
EPIPHANAL BOB DYLAN EXPERIENCES FROM A BUICK SIX
by Dave Henderson
PUBLISHED: June 1, 1999
Paperback, heavyweight matt finish, fully illustrated
ISBN: 1-902799-00-3

Like remembering how you heard about the assassination of John Lennon, the world and their Walkman all have a story about their experience with Bob Dylan. The fans - Tim, Martin, Karl, Clare, Lambchop - and the famous - Jack Nicholson, Roger McGuinn, Billy Bragg, Paul McCartney, Bono, Jerry Garcia, Sheryl Crow, Elvis Costello, Cameron Crowe - all tell the tale of being touched by the hand of Bob.

Dave Henderson delves deep into Dylanland, discovering Fatwa-invoking fanatics, rune-juggling astrologers, hi-brow intellectuals and a bizarre circus of followers. Touched By The Hand Of Bob follows Dylan's miracle-strewn journey, meeting the people who covered his songs, copied his haircut and grabbed at the hem of his frock coat. They walk among us...

THE AUTHOR
After spending a year trying to entice Bob Dylan to attend the Q Awards, Dave Henderson saw the blind devotion which sur rounded Dylan's appearance at the Glastonbury Festival, he became enthralled by the mercurial music, then by the global effect of Dylan's very presence. While planning the 1999 Q Awards, he dived head first into the mysterious power of Bob.

THE RADIO PROGRAMME
The book has been com missioned as a BBC Radio 2 series and airs Autumn 1999.

Get Your Jumbo Jet Out Of My Airport
RANDOM NOTES FOR AC/DC OBSESSIVES
by Howard Johnson
PUBLISHED: June 1, 1999
Paperback, heavyweight matt finish, fully illustrated
ISBN: 1-902799-01-1

When AC/DC vocalist Bon Scott died in 1980 few could have envisaged that 19 years later the group would still be one of the world's most enduring hard rock acts. But what's the real AC/DC story? And why are they still so popular on the back of nothing more than a few boogie chords and a schoolboy uniform?

Get Your Jumbo Jet Out Of My Airport is the first book ever to fully document the group's massive appeal. From the obses-sive owners of 500 bootlegs to the record company execs and producers who have brought AC/DC to the world, Howard Johnson has interviewed them all. The result is a collection of the finest anecdotes and most revealing tales, revealing why AC/DC remain so special, so important and so influential. Delivering one of the most revealing pictures of the band ever, with a wealth of previously unseen pictures, this is a work of frankly lunatic devotion.

THE AUTHOR
Howard Johnson saw his first AC/DC gig in 1979 aged 15, wearing shorts and school blazer. His dress sense, however, has improved in the last 20 years and he's managed to per suade such publications as Mojo, Q, FHM, The Daily Telegraph, FourFourTwo, New Woman and Total Sport among others that he can write a bit too. Last book he authored? British Lions rugby captain Martin Johnson's diary of the incredible 1997 Tour To South Africa. This has very little to do with AC/DC, of course, but we thought you might find it interesting anyway.

coming autumn 1999

Leaving The 20th Century
LAST WORDS ON ROCK 'N' ROLL
by Dave Henderson and Howard Johnson
ISBN 1-902799-02-X
Published: October 1, 1999
Paperback, 196-pages, fully-illustrated

Tribute albums, fond memories, conventions and super fandom reach new levels when the icon of your idealism dies. In Leaving The 20th Century, Dave Henderson and Howard Johnson have collected a moving collection of rock 'n' roll obituaries, inked by the fans, the famous and the familiar. As we head for the year 2000, Leaving The 20th Century looks at the people who built modern music and the effect their spiralling from the planet has had. From Elvis Presley, Kurt Cobain, Keith Moon, Buddy Holly, Clarence White, Tim Buckley, Jerry Garcia, Tim Hardin, Brian Jones, Freddie Mercury, Pete Ham, Sterling Morrison, Marvin Gaye, Ian Curtis, Frank Sinatra, Tupac Shakur, Joe Meek, Michael Hutchence, Nico, Sam Cooke, Randy Rhoads, John Lennon, Jeff Buckley, Richard Manuel and Sid Vicious to Tiny Tim and The Singing Nun.

ROCK STAR DIES IN CRASH

CARL WILSON (1946-98)

CARL WILSON of the **THE BEACH BOYS** has died from complications from lung cancer. He was 51.

Wilson died on Friday evening (February 6) at an LA hospital attended by his wife Gina (daughter of Dean Martin) and his two sons. The group's publicist Alyson Dutch said Wilson was diagnosed with lung cancer last year but insisted on touring with the group while undergoing chemotherapy. At the time of his death, The Beach Boys had been lining up another US tour.

A private funeral is planned for this week, Dutch said.

Carl Wilson was the youngest member of The Beach Boys. When he was 14 and his brothers, 16-year-old Dennis and 19-year-old Brian, were asked to sing at their school, Hawthorne High. Legend has it that Carl didn't want to. To encourage him, Brian christened the band Carl & The Passions. The name would eventually be resurrected for a Beach Boys album 20 years later.

Carl's influence was felt in the quality of his harmonies – like Brian, he had perfect pitch – more than his songwriting which in the band's early days was the preserve of Brian.

As Brian Wilson's mental health deteriorated, however, Carl's input into the band grew. He contributed a number of songs to the 'Surf's Up' album and produced the 1972 LP 'Holland'.

Carl continued to tour on and off with the band until 1981 when he left to record an eponymous solo album. He returned to the band full-time after Dennis Wilson drowned in 1983. The Beach Boys last had a big hit in 1988 with 'Kokomo'.

Hank Williams (R.I.P.; 1923-

The usual celeb good-looking corp funny-looking lit Actually, he took finished off the the bottle finish

"I'll Never Get Out of This World Alive" Williams yowled sardonically on one of his countless hits, yet just because he knew which way he was headed, didn't mean he could stop. Country music's original bad boy was a streaking comet, who crash-landed at 29. But he's much more than a perversely picturesque disaster.

His fame has been on a slow simmer ever since. Every country singer coming up--and half the rockers--cite him as an influence for his genius in melding country, blues and pop. And he paved the way for all who followed, by writing brilliantly and from the heart on cuts like "Cold, Cold

Flung out as car is wrecked

The toll: 30 628 injured s

LAL WATERSON

Lal Waterson, folk singer and songwriter, died from cancer on September 4 aged 55. She was born on February 15, 1943.

A MEMBER of Britain's foremost family of traditional singers, Lal Waterson had a plaintive voice that was one of the great glories of English folk music. She formed the Watersons with her older siblings, Norma and Michael Waterson, her cousin John Harrison and later her brother-in-law Martin Carthy. Their rich *acappella* harmonies made them the most influential vocal group of the 1960s folk revival, and they were headline performers at festivals around the world. Lal Waterson went on to become an imaginative and unorthodox songwriter in her own right, and later sang and recorded with her adult children, Maria and Oliver Knight.

The Waterson family came from Hull, and music was always in the blood. But Elaine Waterson's first love was painting and she went to a school specialising in art at the age of 11. Always known as Lal she worked for a time as a heraldic artist, but her singing career

1964 on the New Voices an-

ing Steve Winwood, who later k the song John Barleycorn

writing original songs in a contemporary folk style, resulting

Caption: Lal Waterson with her folk singer son Oliver Knight

KURT COBAIN

No.490 APRIL 16, 1994 £1.40

PAGES 4, 6, 7, 8 & 9: GAVIN BUSH INJURED IN FRACAS WITH FANS, PENTHOUSE FACE PORN MAG WRIT, JOHNNY CASH HOSPITALISED, PEARL JAM ALBUM DETAILS

news

HUTCHENCE FOUND DEAD

MICHAEL HUTCHENCE was found dead in a hotel room in Sydney, Australia on Saturday (November 22).

A chambermaid discovered the singer and frontman member of INXS hanging from a belt attached to the self-closing mechanism behind the door in his fifth floor room at the Ritz Carlton Hotel shortly before midday. The alarm had been raised when the band's tour manager went to his room...

THE DAILY TELEGRAPH

A R T S

Reaching out for heav

When the weird get going Jerry Garcia celebrates his 50th birthday on August 1, 1992, by playing the Deadheads at Irvine

DEATH in Jerry Garcia immortally marked on his memorable *Live/Dead* album, don't have so much fun and 1995 cuts Garcia's own death still seems to me to be the saddest and most significant rock death of the year. With all

Charles Spencer mourns the death this year of Jerry Garcia, unofficial leader of the Grateful Dead and standard-bearer of the hippie generation's vision of a spaced-out world of love and peace

TRIBUTE

LAURA NYRO
1947-1997

SINGER/SONGWRITER Laura Nyro, whose original, pioneering fusion of soul, gospel, jazz, R&B and pop created a catalog of million-selling hits for artists ranging from Three Dog Night to Barbra Streisand, died at her home in Danbury, Conn., on April 8. An intensely private woman, Nyro chose not to make public her two-year battle with ovarian cancer, which ended her life at age 49.

Debuting in 1966 as a teen prodigy, Nyro was the youngest successful woman songwriter of her time. Her own records, while critically acclaimed, never drew a large audience, but her uncompromising style was not always appreciated; in fact, she was booed off the stage at the Monterey Pop Festival, in 1967.

Born Laura Nigro in the Bronx, NY, on Oct. 18, 1947, she began singing, playing piano and writing songs as a child. She was 19 when she recorded her 1966 debut, More Than a New Discovery, which included future Top 10 hits for Blood, Sweat and Tears ("And When I Die"), Barbra Streisand ("Stoney End") and the Fifth Dimension ("Wedding Bell Blues").

After becoming one of David Geffen's first clients when he was a manager, she signed with Columbia, where she recorded 1968's Eli and the Thirteenth Confession, featuring such songs as "Stoned Soul Picnic" and "Sweet

Nyro retired to the New England countryside in the early '70s. Following a divorce, in 1976, she returned to recording with the subdued, jazz-tinged Smile. After the birth Bianchini, in 1978, the music, dominating 1977 Mother's Spiritual and Dog and Light the Light views, Nyro was guardedly apolitical. In 1988, after from the concert stage, Angeles Times, "Some one success to that Angelo Zuri, said of Nyro, "I spiritual person. She live life; she didn't se the glamour."

Earlier this year, Col retrospective, The Best Stoned Soul Picnic. Set month is the tribute Love: The Music of La Place Recordings), fea Cash, Lisa Germano, Su Jill Sobule, among othe admiration age 13, wat a lot of elements in her longed for. She seemed be very free so I very poe expositions? - all chose think I could ever be," members Nyro as "a cen and even though she is as a poet of her generati really a poet for past ge tions... I am sad that a

None of this artists tribute album knew of her Fran Gallway, the d produce, and Nyro ha to the finished tracks According to her agent, earlier this year, Nyro

...and then

Young At Heart

Dave Henderson has begun work collecting people's first, second and indeed third-hand experiences through the music of Neil Young.

He's very interested to hear from fans of Neil whose life has changed through Neil's music, who experienced a pivotal breakthrough or maybe a simple epiphanal moment. Perhaps it's you.

Were you the person listening to 'After The Goldrush' who suddenly through a hazy ambience saw God? Were you one of those people who wondered whatever happened to the sleeve of 'Harvest' that was supposed to self-destruct after a certain time?

Are you puzzled why 'On The Beach' has never been released on CD and are having a life-crisis coming to terms with it? Or were you in the parking lot at Warner Brothers, in Burbank, California, when Neil's car was blocked in and he allegedly resorted to "putting the boot in" on the blocker's motor?

Or could it be, that you were thrown out of your bedsit for playing "Arc:Weld" at sleep-prohibiting volume? Whatever your story is, Dave would like to hear it. You can contact him at The Black Book Company, Box 2030, Pewsey SN9 5QZ.

Glastonbury 2000

The in-depth story of the Glastonbury Festival told by the people who've worked on the event from day one. Exclusive interviews and anecdotes already stockpiling from the people who've played there, the thousands of on-site workers, the local Pilton community, the stars who've performed, from Radiohead and the Manics to Rolf Harris and Al Green.

If you've braved the sun, the rain or anything in between, then we'd like to hear from you at The Black Book Company, Box 2030, Pewsey SN9 5QZ.

ordering information

YOU CAN order books published by the Black Book Company direct from us, or through our website at www.blackbookco.com
(details of which are on the next page).

DIRECT BY MAIL

You can order copies of our titles for £13.50 each (including post and packing in the UK and within the EC).

For overseas orders, please add £1 (outside of EC but within Europe) or £3 (USA, Canada and Australia).

If you'd like to order more than one copy, please add £1 per additional copy. Please make cheques payable to the BLACK BOOK COMPANY LTD.

If you'd like to order in bulk (over five copies), then please fax your request to us at
+44 (0) 1672 564433

Or email us on
dhende7730@aol.com

TITLES CURRENTLY AVAILABLE

TOUCHED BY THE HAND OF BOB
by Dave Henderson
GET YOUR JUMBO JET OUT OF MY AIRPORT
by Howard Johnson

WE ARE NOW ACCEPTING
ADVANCE ORDERS FOR...

LEAVING THE TWENTIETH CENTURY
by Dave Henderson and Howard Johnson
(published October 1, 1999)

IF YOU'D LIKE TO GET ON OUR MAILING LIST...

For special offers, limited edition items and news on upcoming projects, then send your address to us by fax or email, or write to us at

THE BLACK BOOK COMPANY
BOX 2030
PEWSEY
SN9 5QZ
ENGLAND

Surf right on in for Black Book news

Find out what we're doing now, what we're doing next.

Form a direct and speedy link back to us. Get involved.

www.blackbookco.com

Find out about all kinds of Black Book Paraphernalia

Buy our books, deluxe editions, postcards, limited edition stamps direct

Find out more about our books

Bow down at

The Temple Of Bob

including book extracts, sound files of interviews, audio from the bizarre world of Dylan, fan e-mails (and lighbulb information), rare photos and links to other sites.

Go deep into

JumboJetland

Including extracts, sound files, quotes, audio of the worst DC Covers, fan e-mails (discussing the intricacies of Angus' picking), rare photos and links to other DC sites.

Read extracts from upcoming projects

LEAVING THE TWENTIETH CENTURY. BECK THREW UP. YOUNG AT HEART

Then, find out who we are by entering our connected areas

Daveworld

Where things are Strange and twangy

HoJoLand

Where Things Ain't Right

Drummond Base

Where art gets brainwashed

Online from June 1, 1999

Design of great beauty by Steve Hunt

the black book company